A. J. Stewart

Falcon

ARROW BOOKS

ARROW BOOKS LTD
3 Fitzroy Square, London W1

AN IMPRINT OF THE HUTCHINSON GROUP

London Melbourne Sydney Auckland
Wellington Johannesburg Cape Town
and agencies throughout the world

First published by
Peter Davies Ltd 1970
Arrow edition 1973

*Made and printed in Great Britain
by The Anchor Press Ltd.,
Tiptree, Essex*

ISBN 0 09 907840 6

FOREWORD

THESE memories have lain in my head, either active or dormant, since my birth in March 1929. Those of which I was conscious I had to accept as being present and inexplicable, having failed to trace their origin; the dormant memories came to light more recently. I must stress that at no time was I deliberately searching for knowledge of an earlier existence, for it seemed to me that to have to pass once through this world was adequate punishment for anybody. It took me all of thirty-eight years to discover that my own problem and the Scots defeat on Branxton Moor were one and the same phenomenon. By that time I was so confused with the conflict of trying to reconcile my two identities—one of them still virtually unknown to me—that I lived with the truth apparent for quite some while before I perceived it.

All of this process of discovery will need to be the subject of a further volume. Sufficient here to say that a king's anguish for the nation he led to its slaughter finally proved stronger than all of time's effort to overlay it with the accumulating years' experience of a new lifespan. So great was that anguish, it came ejaculating out of my present subconscious in the form of a total recall of my own death five yards from the English standard upon the field that is today called Flodden. Even my screams, as I relived it, were precisely in tune with those still ringing in my head from 1513.

The actual writing of this book has been for me an endurance test, the like of which I hope I may never again encounter. The technical problems alone have been inordinate. James Stewart's memory lay fragmented within my head, like a broken strand of beads for lack of any time sense stringing them together. I have had to identify and correlate them by means as numerous and varied as the memories themselves. Where all else failed, I have had to resort to textual reference as an index—although this I have done as rarely as possible, for, quite apart from the fact that I considered it unfair to my reader, my worst problem has been trying to unlearn what others have written of me: it is disconcerting to read what posterity has to say about oneself, and I could name a few biographers whom I would not recommend to anyone anxious to have his life story set to paper accurately. At the end, beset by the problem of thinking in sixteenth-century Scots for the benefit of a reader who must know my thoughts in modern English, I have to thank an unknown lady, the publishers' editor, who in the course of her duty cut from this book much that memory had retained, but who managed to make coherence of James Stewart's original text.

The many English friends who have sustained me during the effort of setting these memories to paper, will know themselves to be included, when I say, as once I said to the mustered men at Ellem, '*Ah love ye!*'—which was the only dedication, then as now, I felt to be worthy of our Scots.

Edinburgh
12th September 1969

A. J. STEWART

I

I was born on the 17th day of March in the year 1472, at Linlithgow, first child and heir to my father, His Grace King James the 3 of Scots. I arrived inconveniently earlier than expected, and delayed the Court's removal to Stirling Castle, so all those coming at New Year to renew feu rights with my father's Grace had to squeeze uncomfortably into the smallest of the Royal Palaces. As I seemed healthy and likely to survive, my baptism was postponed until we reached Stirling where the Chapel Royal made a more suitable setting for the occasion.

My Sire's astrologer, a priest named Walter Schevez, charted the stars at my nativity, and found that Mars and Saturn were opposing forces across the sky, and that the other planets were also combined to give me no help whatever, except for the moon's presence in the sign of Capricorn to balance the wistfulness of the Sun in Pisces. When I was older, Schevez told me that I must take great care in my dealings with those born under the Crab—a useful piece of advice since his Grace my father was a Cancerian subject.

What Walter Schevez could not have told me at that time and which I discovered for myself but gradually, was that I had the 'lang ee' or the 'lang sicht', an affliction not uncommon in the Stewart family, and one even more likely to distress a King than any other individual. All my life I was to have great difficulty explaining to my Councillors why I knew certain things would happen, irrespective of whether or not logic expected them. To see the morrow before its sun has risen is a wearisome embarrassment for anybody.

My first clear recollection of Queen Margaret, my mother, is of a charming dark-haired lady in a green silk gown stitched with pearls upon its bodice, of which I had managed to detach several before her Ladies realized what I was doing and removed me from her lap. The King's Grace, my father, I remember, had the most comfortable pair of arms in which I ever travelled, but he was none the less an awesome and magnificent person who I could well believe was the most elegant prince in Christendom.

Of the world I knew little, save that a great many silken bell-shaped skirts hollowed to make a curtsey, and a good many tall, colourful columns of male legs clad in bright hose dipped at certain times, which heralded the approach of one or both of my parents. At these times I, too, was expected to make my bow; what baffled me were those occasions when I was expected not to kneel, but to present my hand to foreign-tongued gentlemen who bowed to me. Also, there were strange days upon which I ventured to the outer air, and many unknown personages smiled as though they knew me, meanwhile making a good deal of noise which sounded friendly. Thus it was, I learned eventually that I was a Prince.

To be a Prince in those years was not at all a bad occupation, except for an inordinate burden of study. I had begun to learn five languages before I realized that my Danish mother and my Scots nurse had between them already made me bilingual. At that time Celtic ('auld Scots') was the tongue spoken by the majority of Scotland's people, although not by its King. This seemed to my four-year-old mind a great omission upon his Grace my father's part, and I therefore picked up as much as I could of the Celtic tongue in order to know how my Sire's subjects thought in matters affecting all of us.

It was not a day—life being short—when it was thought necessary to have gentle preamble into matter of importance; I was told of my future responsibilities in a forthright fashion, of which I remember best my Sire's long arm dragging me through several apartments so fast that my short legs touched the floor one step in four, while the blue skirt of his long robe whipped about his feet. Outside the door of the King's Council chamber, I was dusted down and my soft loose red hair smoothed with spittle; then I was taken into a room lined with old gentlemen who bowed as His Grace and I walked past them. At the head of a large squaret able stood an elaborately carved chair, on to the seat of which I was lifted to face the eyes of the assembled Council. While my father's Grace was speaking the eyes of the kindly 'uncles' who had dandled me upon their knees, gazed at me with a look of solemn intensity which I knew as the way they looked at the Majesty of Scots, my father. Simultaneously with the end of his speech, I realized why the adult men were looking thus at somebody who was myself yet not myself: I would rule as King of Scots hereafter.

I returned to the nursery more awed by myself than by any-thing which I had so far encountered. I had already been told that I must never refer to my father unless I used one of his several titles; this meant, therefore, that I would one day be myself 'His Grace' and never again simply James. It struck me as being exceedingly sad that my friends the stable lads with whom I chatted in Celtic would one day have to dip a knee to me. What had James Stewart ever done to deserve a fate like this? I wondered.

However, there I was, and likely to be King, so I had better resign myself to it—although I would have much preferred, I felt, to grow to be a man whose business in life it was to deal with horses.

My uncle the Duke of Albany had taught me to ride upon a pony given to me by my other, favourite uncle, the Earl of Mar. I was not very old when something terrible happened to both these uncles. The Duke of Albany was imprisoned by my Sire in his castle of Edinburgh, and the Earl of Mar was confined in similar fashion in the small royal castle of Craigmillar by Edin-burgh. What they had done to deserve such treatment I never learned, but the next news was that Albany had escaped and slipped away to France. Worse followed; for the Earl of Mar was released, then took a fever which required him to be bled, and in his delirium tore off his bandages in the therapeutic bath, to die of a blood shortage. I remember the funeral mass for my Uncle John, Earl of Mar, and kneeling for hours dressed in black, wondering why it was that I knew he was dead before my mother's ladies had informed me.

Until this time, I had thought everybody knew which of us were about to die although for politeness' sake they forbore to mention it, and I was troubled to discover the facility was peculiar to myself.

It was slanderously rumoured my father's Grace had ordered the killing of the Earl of Mar, who had been imprisoned on the grounds that he had tried to secure my Sire's death by witchcraft, a charge which was never adequately substantiated. To practise magic was an amusement common in fashionable circles, but it was not likely to enchant his subjects had they ever learned His Grace was one who practised it. My Royal father and his youngest brother enjoyed few interests in common, but they were closeted together a good deal on days when His Grace wore the 'Lazarus beads', hideous grey-brown beads at his girdle, which to my child's mind looked sinister. The Earl of Mar was a dare-devil young man, and it was not at all unlikely that he had experimentally tried to summon a few devils on his own account, truly intending no harm by it; then the prank had miscarried and he found himself charged with treason. And it was not surprising that my Sire did not publish evidence incriminating to himself in order to substantiate the charge against his brother. My poor Sire always had a terrible talent for climbing out of the skillet into the fire. None of the Stewart family seemed to be lucky in this world.

King James was an extraordinarily sweet and gentle creature, who should never have been born a King, though his conscience would have haunted him forever had he admitted to himself that the Sovereign Scot was inadequate to his task. For all his tender, loving ways, however, His Grace my father had a devil in him—which would spring suddenly into sight in fits of rage, as brief as they were unexpected, and as frequently illogical; then, as suddenly, the flame would die, leaving him spent and wretched. I had a deep compassion for my Sire, and often wished that others would be as sympathetic. He had strange, silver-grey eyes which he veiled by drooping their lids, as if afraid that too many would see his soul in all its vulnerability. They were the emptiest eyes I ever saw, like twin corridors stretching to infinity, with light a long way at the end of them and a dark, small devil seeking restlessly to hide himself.

King James bore himself so regally I doubt there was ever such a Majestic presence. He was a tall man, with raven black hair and powerful shoulders uncommon for a figure so slender and spare of flesh; he carried his robes superbly. He detested riding, admitting to a fear and dislike of horses, and travelled everywhere when possible in a horse-litter. In consequence he had no use for the short, practical dress of doublet and hose worn by our more active lords, and generally favoured the long robe made either loose or close-fitting to the body. He had a marvellous sense of colour, and matched his jewellery, of which he wore a great deal, to the line and hue of whatever garments he was wearing. My Sire was a man who never purchased anything unless it were of the best quality, and his tall figure clad in the heaviest weight of gold cloth was an awesome vision, like a statue cast out of the sun's radiance constantly pouring cascades of liquid metal from its limbs.

I had always supposed that we were an exceedingly wealthy family, and it was a shock when I gradually realized that my Sire's revenues were insufficient to stand the strain of his expenditure. We enjoyed what was, by our day's standards, a graciously comfortable existence in palaces and castles which my Royal father and his building-designer, Master Cochrane, laboured constantly to improve. I can remember standing beside my father's Grace when he and Cochrane were debating how to modernize Malcolm Caen Mor's old banqueting hall in the Castle of Edinburgh. My Sire wanted to pave over the runnel across the floor meant as a urinal for the benefit of diners in more primitive days. These channels were by no means uncommon in palaces built in the twelfth century or earlier, but it offended my Royal father's sensibilities to have such an amenity beside his dining-table. The banqueting hall at Edinburgh was one of the few places which defied all their attempts to improve it—it was long, low and dark, with minute slit windows set high in the rough-cast walls, a dangerously uneven flagged floor, and a chimney too short for the windy heights of the Rock of Edinburgh, so that all the smoke and snow and whatever else the heavens rejected blew back to cover the diners. To give it light, the roof was whitewashed between the beams, but it never stayed white for more than a couple of weeks with all the filth which poured down the chimney. Master Cochrane's view was that only the removal of the kitchens from beneath the hall, and the extension of the banqueting chamber downwards would resolve the problem. We all loathed Edinburgh Castle, as the draughtiest and most primitive dwelling place the family or the Court had to endure during winter's cold, dark days and colder, darker nights, and it was the one of my Sire's extravagances which all of his lords approved, when he had the New Tower built to give more comfortable accommodation.

Otherwise, the King's preoccupation with the renewal and beautification of his palaces was not greatly appreciated by his Treasury clerks. It was said by many that my father's Grace was avaricious—a gross distortion of the truth; avarice acquires and holds tight its money, whereas my Sire's sole talent was for spending it. The truth of the matter was that he spent his money according to his own table of priorities, and his bleak soul needed the comfort of beauty about his person and his residences in a way I doubt was comprehended by his critics. His Flanders tapestries, his Venetian crystal or his silver chalices, his velvet wall mantles, and his woven silk rugs which came through Damascus from the east side of the earth, were as necessary to his survival as the air he breathed—infinitely more important to him, for instance, than the replacement white hats for the Guard halberdiers for which the Chief-at-Arms was always asking.

It was the duty of the King to supply the Realm's currency, and His Grace my father minted a mass of new coinage not of silver or gold, but of copper—and I, knowing nothing of economics, thought the pinkish-gold of these new coins was delightful. They quickly lost their glitter in all senses, however, when in the market they purchased less and less of life's necessities, and their dark patina earned them the name of 'Black plaks' or 'Cochrane's money'. (Whether or not William Cochrane truly had anything to do with their circulation, I never knew for certain, but he appeared to have great influence upon my Sire, which made most people willing to believe anything against him.) I remember the Court arriving in Edinburgh, I think from Dunfermline, and as we all rode in procession through the town and up toward the Castle, with His Grace's litter in the middle of the procession, a great crowd of angry people milled about us, shouting and trying to close in about my Sire, brandishing their fists. His courtiers and men-at-arms thrust them away, and my Royal father stared straight before him, arrogant and regal and very angry; but when the high west gate clanged behind us, shutting off the city from the Castle, and we came up the ramp through the Castle gate to safety, I looked to see how my Sire was, and saw that he was sitting with his head bent low, knotting his hands in secret misery. I doubt there ever was a king who needed love so badly or who was hurt more by the loss of his people's love.

My parents' marriage was extraordinarily happy in view of the fact that they had never met until the day Queen Margaret arrived from Denmark to be King James's bride. It was a marvellous piece of luck that a dynastic marriage should turn out also to be a love-match. It would have been exceedingly difficult for anybody not to love Her Highness my mother, for she had in her the buoyant joy of one whose faith in the goodness of everybody was inextinguishable; she somehow persuaded more people to rise to the high regard she held of them than could have been achieved by a whole Crusade dedicated to converting the Infidels. The Flemish artist commissioned to paint her portrait succeeded in making the figure of St Michael standing guard behind her look as if even he were relying on my mother's prayers to get him back to heaven. After her death His Holiness was petitioned to have her canonized, but I in my time as King did nothing to further the matter; I knew my mother well enough to know that she would have been horrified to have people pray to her as Saint Margaret. In heaven, she would have blushed scarlet, disturbing all God's angels·by trying to pretend she was not there.

She was small and slender and dark, and she wore lovely clothes as slim and unpretentious as herself. The women's fashions of my childhood were flat-chested and simple in style, and it was the Queen my mother who led the womenfolk of Scotland to abandon the towering head-dresses which had dominated European domestic politics for almost a generation and to wear instead the low, more feminine style which she had herself adopted. My mother had her crown made to her own design, of flexible small panels hinged together, so that however she wore her hair or whatever new head-dress she adopted, the metal circlet could be set to follow the contour of her head.

A fact which hardly anybody knew about my mother was that she was secretly a scholar. It was not regarded as proper, let alone necessary, to have women learned in her day, even though they be of blood royal, unless they were likely to inherit a throne— and even then it was assumed they would marry a near-royal husband to superintend their thinking for them. Her own family, and later my Sire's courtiers, left her to what were thought to be her meditations, never realizing that if a new work of philosophy came anywhere within her reach it was likely to be found tucked inside her Bible or her breviary.

Much as I loved and understood my father's Grace, there were certain aspects of his private nature which baffled me. He was devoted to my mother, yet frequently dwelled apart from her— we resided these days more frequently at Stirling than elsewhere —and his most constant companions were a group of young men, mostly of humble birth, who were all classed together by our Scots lords as 'the favourites'. The nobles detested these young men, who shared my Sire's artistic tastes and despised the sports the lords themselves enjoyed; and even my charming mother, who always sought out the best in all of us, would harden her tongue and eyes when my Sire had the favourites with him, I could never understand why it was that he would then seem as remote from my mother and me as if a glass screen had dropped between his eyes and ours; at these times my mother's mouth would tuck away its joy, and her eyes would flash intense strange fire at her loved Regal lord, leaving me with the sensation that I was witnessing a battle which took place some very great distance away, and upon another plane entirely.

In my seventh year I fell seriously ill with what the royal physicians diagnosed as a fever due to overstudying. When they had relieved me of a great deal of blood, I was so weak that I was bedridden for many weeks thereafter. On my seventh birthday my bed-chamber was filled with a great many visitors, who entered on tip-toe with the brightest and most unconvincing smiles imaginable. My mother, who was heavy with child, spent almost the entire day with me; also, there came my father's Grace, who straightened with his own royal hand my coverings. What all of this portended I may not have realized, until my young brother was born upon the 28th day of April, and they gave him the same name as myself—James—to ensure that the heir to the Crown was called by the same name as the three previous Stewart Kings. This clear expectation of my being likely to die brought me back to health immediately.

It was confusing to have two Princes of Scotland called James and distinguishable only by their titles—I was Duke of Rothesay and my brother Marquis of Ormond—and my cousin James Hamilton did not make matters of nomenclature easier on his frequent visits to Stirling. Cousin James, in the way he tormented all whom he loved, rarely failed to remind me that but for his mother's gender and the fact that my father had preceded her into the world, it would have been he and not I whose destiny it was to rule Scotland. (This family joke ceased when I succeeded to the Throne, as it had to do.) By contrast, my brother James, who truly had cause for complaint, was a stolid wee lad whose career as the king-who-never-was he bore all his life without murmur.

In my eighth year my father's younger brother, my uncle

Alexander, Duke of Albany, made a curious reappearance in Scotland—at the head of an English army under the dual command of himself and the English royal duke, Richard Plantagenet of Gloucester. He had been living in France since his flight from the Castle of Edinburgh, when the tale of how he bore his servant away on his back after the man had damaged a leg in the venture had made him a hero to the common folk, who hated his Grace my father. (Nothing was commonly said of how he burned his gaoler alive on the open fire, having stabbed him first—an incident which confirmed the instinctive fear I felt of him in spite of his Stewart charm and his vitality.) His reappearance now with the English, who had left us in peace during their own dynastic wars, was an ominous sign.

We made ready for war at Stirling Castle, my Sire coming himself to supervise the storing of food supplies against a possible siege and the increase in the garrison of men. Stirling was the safest of all our castles, and it became uncomfortably apparent to me why both of my parents were so grave and solicitous about my welfare: I was the future King, and as such likely to be the target for anybody, Scots or English, who sought to gain by my capture or destruction. As I saw my Royal father off to war I was very much aware that I might one night very soon be wakened, wrapped in a blanket, and whisked away either to find myself upon the morrow crowned as King of Scots or, as likely, stabbed to death and put down a castle drain.

What news came to Stirling was limited and confused. The English were at Berwick. His Grace my father, taking all his young men with him, had gone down to Lauder where his lords with their men-at-arms were called to muster. Thereafter there was nothing more for several days, apart from an extraordinary messenger who arrived beneath a truce flag to deliver a letter to the Queen of Scots from our invader, Richard, Duke of Gloucester. My mother's Highness, in very regal fashion, broke its seal, then smiled with sudden radiance and spoke some words of Danish which I failed to catch, but which I knew from her face meant, 'What a *good* man!' He had sent thoughtfully to ask the Scots Queen, did she lack for ought at Stirling Castle and, if so, would she name it, that he might supply it to her. My mother tore his letter into very small pieces, fed them to the fire, shook her head gravely at the enemy's messenger—then gave him a sudden vivid smile which he would doubtless bear back as her gracious thanks to Richard Plantagenet. All the rest of that day my mother's Highness was radiant in the midst of war because our enemy had shown kind thought for us.

Then there came a secret piece of news about some monstrous happening at Lauder Brig, although what had happened there none would tell me, save that my Sire was now lodged a prisoner of his own lords in the Castle of Edinburgh, with the Duke of Albany and his own uncle, the Earl of Buchan, as his gaolers. We at Stirling Castle did not know what had happened to the English invasion, but there had clearly been some major changes in the alignment of forces. The first definite development for us was the visit to Stirling of my uncle Albany—older and thickened, and browned by the French sun, which made his good teeth look even whiter. He was received by my mother's Highness, who looked grave and demure in grey silk. I was taken into their presence, and my Uncle Albany bowed very low in greeting which was strange and made me fear for a moment that my Sire had died. Then they resumed their talk about me—he seemed to be giving her advice on the proper education I should have as a king's son, which must have tried her sorely—while I stood beside my mother's chair and she absently fingered my hair to see if I were due a head-wash—a habit she had which frequently made me seethe in indignation. But I sensed upon this day that my Uncle had appeared at Stirling for reasons of his own, and that my best safeguard lay in keeping quiet. And it may have been as well I did so, for it was some months later we discovered that he had put himself and Scotland under homage to King Edward of England in return for his assistance to wrest the Crown from my father's Grace King James. We lost Berwick through this episode, and when all was discovered the Duke of Albany contrived to make his escape only just in time before the whole wrath of Scotland combined against him.

Worse to my mind, however, was the strange meeting with

my father's Grace which should have been the happiest of family reunions. Instead, my Sire was ashen and shaking, with a bleak wildness in his eyes the like I never saw before nor wished to see again. I can remember him going to my mother, to bend his head low to rest upon her shoulder, and his dreadful sobbing there, as she held his bowed majesty in her arms, her clenched knuckles white as she gripped the dark green damask swinging from his wide shoulders. I could not yet understand what had happened— and I took courage to ask my father's Grace, as nobody else would tell me, what had happened at Lauder Brig.

He sat, took me to his knee, and looked me in the eyes while he spoke, as if to say, 'This is my true self, James, come inside'. And he told me how his lords had rebelled, and taken all of his friends, including William Cochrane, whom he had created Earl of Mar at my Uncle John's death, and before my Sire's eyes had hanged them in a row along the bridge at Lauder. And all he had to say about it was, 'The fowt was my ain fowt, James. My ain fowt, ma ain fowt . . .' Then he rose, with a great sigh, and moved away. He did not tell me why they had done this monstrous act at Lauder, nor was I to discover why for several years more.

My father's Grace became a changed man after the massacre at Lauder Brig. It aged him by at least ten years, and the great shoulders, impressive in their pride of bearing, now drooped; the raven black of his hair suffered no damage, but the prince in the prime of his thirtieth year looked every day of forty. Yet I preferred this new aspect of my Royal father, for he appeared to my eye a man who had reconciled himself with the devil he carried.

My mother's Highness now had full guardianship of my brother and me, at Stirling Castle, now the permanent seat of the Queen's Household. And while formerly he had been no more punctilious in his religious observance than his duty as King required him to be, he now became the most pious among us. Incapable of hypocrisy, he must have felt he had to earn his absolution. He retired into his Castle of Edinburgh—a penance in itself, despite Cochrane's New Tower—where he devoted himself to the reclamation of his soul, comforted only by his books and music. There were no more Royal Favourites. Two of his friends who had not been present at Lauder, had now gone from his side—I suspect of their own volition—and the sole survivor of the day's gibbeting, John Ramsay, was the only one to stay constant to him. John Ramsay, a lad of nineteen, was the one whom I had always liked least, and it seemed characteristic that while the swaggering, brilliant Cochrane had gone to his death bravely (they said), Ramsay, squealing his terror, had locked his arms so tightly about the neck of His Grace that had the rebel leaders persisted in trying to wrest him away, they would certainly have strangled the King. That he should be the one who shared my Sire's seclusion made no sense whatever to me—although, surprisingly, my mother, who had formerly shared my dislike of Ramsay, looked upon it as the most proper conclusion to the tragedy. She said His Grace and Ramsay were 'haulden by their vow as twa monks ta dow penance', whatever that meant, and she bowed her head so solemnly I was too awed to ask her more.

My Sire's penance lasted a long while. Parliament and people grew restive. So did his lords. I did, as well; reared to be a King, I was now in my ninth year beginning to think as one. My Royal father's meticulous ordering of his Household had led me as a child to suppose that all of his subjects obeyed him as promptly as did our castle servitors, and the realization had come late to me that our Royal garden patch existed among weeds and briars of an encroaching wilderness. At the Castle of Stirling where I dwelled among the Queen's ladies and saw little of the world beyond my study-chamber window, my knowledge of state matters was limited to a survey of Scotland's past history. This I had to know, in order to prepare myself for the future, but I wished at times my tutors had brought to me fewer documents from the archives, and more information about the present day's affairs.

I was a precociously brilliant child, and I am afraid that like all such children I had a tendency to query what I was taught. I accepted nothing I was told until I had worked it out for myself and reached the same conclusion. We all enjoyed the debates, but a good deal of time was spent in this way which might just possibly have been more profitably used had I been kept to the task originally set before me. I was fascinated by language and could reproduce any accent that I heard; I soon mastered enough vocabulary and grammar to see me through a philosophical discussion with my French, Spanish, German, Danish, Flemish or Italian tutors, but when in later years my linguistic abilities could have helped my letter-writing so much, I had to rely upon Latin, which was the only tongue I wrote as well as I could speak it. I would have been better served had I been a shade less brilliant and my tutors a good deal more strict with me.

In my tenth year a new Royal prince arrived to bear us company—named John, which augured well for the survival of both Ormond and myself. His Grace gave the child the title Earl of Mar, which I was happy to hear restored to the family. (I had never approved my Royal father's bestowal of that title on William Cochrane.)

Had I but known how soon the sweet, calm years of my mother's company were to end, I would the more have appreciated them. As it was, I often felt stifled among so many women and longed for other masculine company than my tutors and the stable lads at Stirling Castle. In the year that I was twelve, Ormond five and wee John scarce more than a baby, the Queen our mother died—very quickly in the middle of one night, as graciously and with as little fuss as she had done everything else in her life. It all happened so suddenly that she had barely time to thank her ladies who rushed to her side, and she was dead before her confessor could be summoned to shrive her. We did not hear the ghastly news until we wakened in the morning.

The proclamation which was sent forth to all the burghs to announce the death of Scotland's Queen was received with a dumbfounded horror, the like of which I doubt the Kingdom had ever before shown at the death of a Royal Consort. It was strange that Her Highness, who had such a small visible part in the Realm's affairs, should have been so well known for her goodness. Had I known then how deep were Scotland's troubles,

I might have realized that, while their Danish Queen lived, his Grace's long-suffering subjects could always hope that she would spur him on to put his Realm's affairs in order.

Black horses caparisoned in black and gold, their black-clad riders bearing before them at staff's length the dipped flags of Denmark and Scotland, and the quartered Arms of the Danish Royal House and the Lyon Rampant; then all of our bishops and abbots walking in twos, the bishops' jewelled mitres and gleaming croziers, together with the lesser clergy's varied vestments making an island of colour between all the black; then came the coffin, black-draped, with our mother's own quartered Royal Arms upon it, its bier resting upon the shoulders of Scotland's six senior earls; after the coffin came my Sire, entirely in black, for once in his life bare-headed, with Ormond and me behind him and wee John carried by a male attendant—and Aunt Margaret with us and possibly Aunt Mary Hamilton, although I think she walked further behind with her husband among the lords; then all my mother's ladies, black-clad, followed by the lords with their ladies, the representatives of the Third Estate, and finally all who had ever served my mother's Highness or had official reason to be present. The cortège brought the coffin from St Michael's Chapel at Stirling to the Abbey of Cambuskenneth for burial, and all along the way stood a scattering line of Queen Margaret's subjects who had come, many from long distances, to see her pass.

It was a funeral procession so awesome that it made me temporarily forget that it was my mother whom we brought to burial. There was an amazing number of ordinary people there upon the road openly crying for a lady whom, so far as I knew then, they had never met. Queen Margaret had given frequent and long audiences to anybody who appeared at Stirling Castle, but it was not until later, when I found the same knack of collecting everybody's troubles, that I realized how many of Scotland's plain-folk had known my mother well. She had kept her learning secret, and she appeared to have guarded her philanthropy in the same way.

The Requiem Mass and the series of prayers delivered for the repose of Queen Margaret's soul continued throughout most of the day, and what I remember most vividly was the smell. Too many people packed together too close for too long, and all of them wearing mourning clothes so elaborate and costly that they were handed down through generations; brought from a chest made airless to keep out the moth, then dusted with fullers' clay and saffron or other spices to kill the stale body odours, they stank unbearably when the wearer's body grew warm in the confined space of the chapel. Not even the smell of incense could disguise the reek of ages-old human sweat. To add to the misery, I could smell my own sweat leaking into my new black velvet doublet as I knelt rigidly with my elbows tucked decorously into my sides and my hands pressed together—the latter for me always a painful feat because the extreme distance between my fore-finger and thumb levered my other fingers apart. I was glad when I could relieve my fingers by telling the beads of the jet mourning rosary which my father's Grace had given me, as was customary, in memory of my mother—and which later I put round my neck for safety, and wore there, tucked inside my doublet, for the rest of my life.

When the obsequies ended and state formalities were over, three motherless princes were brought from Stirling into His Grace's guardianship at his Castle of Edinburgh. To escape the attentions of a Court bent on smothering us with kindness, we were smuggled in at the postern gate above the west face of the Rock, which then was hewn into steps to form a path—now long since crumbled away. Dressed in our black, my hair as usual lank in need of washing, I can remember clambering up the path, and turning at the most dangerous bend high above the North Loch, to give young Ormond a guiding hand as he came puffing stolidly behind me. He had not cried; Ormond hardly ever was known to cry; stoic from birth, he was the most self-contained child imaginable. John was carried by one of our male attendants, and his nurse brought up the rear; it was a forlorn small party in the afternoon sun, with the main strength of our retinue gone by the cobbled lane through the city wall to distract attention from our own arrival. Several raps upon the gate, and we were admitted—to be whisked away at once to our Royal father. His Grace, white-faced and gaunt in his mourning, held out his arms to take the three of us simultaneously, whereafter we all wept together, even Ormond, watched by a sympathetic court. Even our tears were the property of the Crown.

2

AFTER twelve years of predominantly female society, the masculine company of my Sire's lords and courtiers came as the breath of life to me. Our Scots lords were at no time docile, but whatever respect my Royal father might have commanded from them had been dispelled entirely as his reign progressed. His total lack of interest in the manly pursuits of riding, hunting and hawking so dear to our rough Scots noblemen, and his understandable preference for those who shared his own intellectual tastes had caused him to have favourites, which is always damaging to a kingdom. In order to love a beggar it is not necessary to despise a duke, and my Sire's choice of low-born friends in preference to his domineering earls, who had gained the ascendancy when he had come to his throne as a child of eight, had left the latter with a genuine grievance. It was part of my Sire's tragedy, I began to discover, that his virtues as a man were those which are vices in a king. He was repelled by the need to inflict pain upon any of his subjects and he gave pardons so readily that malefactors flourished at the expense of those who should have been protected. I soon found that the court in which my brothers and I resided crackled with conspiracy like a wooden house alight with unseen flame, and I was at that time too young as yet to realize that in such an overcharged atmosphere, my presence was sufficient to bring the temperature to explosion point.

When I came upon the scene I was young, strong, masculine and adept in all the sports which our Scots lords most highly regarded. I was growing to be a handsome lad with a natural air of royalty, and I have always had the Piscean facility immediately to come to terms with all sorts and conditions of men. What was more to the point, although I did not recognize it at the time, was that I showed already an aptitude for statecraft.

What had always puzzled me about my Gracious father was the way that every mistake he made in public or in private life seemed always to call forth greater acrimony than his misdemeanour warranted. It was as though he were forever being blamed not for what he did so much as for what he was. The more I had pondered on this mystery, the more convinced I became that the key to it was to be found, if anywhere, in the affair at Lauder Brig, where men who had dined at his table suddenly united in an act of such inexplicable ferocity. I never found it difficult to talk to the Earl of Angus, who was a man more diffident and sensitive than his leading part at Lauder Brig might suggest, and I resolved to ask him about the episode which had earned him the nickname 'Bell-the-Cat'.

When Angus was next at Court and after he had put down several pots of ale, I asked him frankly why had they hanged my Sire's friends at Lauder Brig. His companions looked uneasy at my question and tried to interrupt our conversation, but Angus said, 'He wull ken, wull he noucht?' and, turning to me, said flatly, 'We hanget a laud o' feathers.' With that he swallowed his ale and went with the rest.

This left me no wiser. Obviously the word 'feather' carried greater meaning than I had supposed. Baffled, I went to consult Deughal, a stable lad, older than myself, who had been a useful source of information on earlier occasions. He explained the meaning of the term 'feather' applied to a man, and he did not mince matters. To me, aged thirteen, the revelation concerning my own father came as such a shock that it affected my attitude toward sexual matters for a long time afterwards; nor was my attitude toward my Sire ever quite the same again.

I could now understand what it was in my Royal father which

so much repelled his subjects, for sodomy has never been a Scots vice. And I understood at last why, although he had loved my mother so greatly, they had rarely resided together—also, the meaning of those looks exchanged between them which had puzzled me as a child. Yet out of it all grew a new kind of respect for the King my father to replace that which the new knowledge had stripped away: he was a man who had fought and conquered his vice; his eyes made that plain. King James the 3 left no great record as Scotland's ruler, but he lives in my memory as the most punished and least daunted human soul I ever met.

Hidden behind his books and screened by his musicians and choristers, my father's Grace could have been a ghost for the scant respect that now was paid to him. It troubled me not a little that I should be so much in the company of those who were his enemies, but I could see no good likely to accrue to the realm from my overt rejection of all who disapproved of the King my father's administration; also, they were good friends to me. Associating with these men, I grew further away from him, although, when I could, I showed my genuine interest in his music, architecture and other intellectual pursuits.

There was another danger in our situation, for I now began to deputize for him on certain ceremonial occasions, neither he nor I realizing that my aptitude for royal dignities was to be our mutual undoing. He trusted me, and it did not occur to me that I was creating about myself the aura of sovereignty.

Trained since infancy to sustain my part through hours of ritual, and being favoured like my Uncle John of Mar with natural grace of movement, I had eloquent hands, together with the erect bearing which is vital to anyone who will have to wear for many hours a diadem that is made of a material heavier than lead. I thanked God for all these features. When told by several that my head was 'ane that sall bear a crown richt (right) pertaintlie' I acknowledged it as a compliment relating to physical fact, not recognizing that the statement carried graver implication.

Much might I have forestalled had it been easier for me to approach His Grace. Such was the formality surrounding kingship that even I could not attend my Sire without first sending one of my gentlemen with a request for a private audience. The message then had to pass through one of the King's gentlemen, who would pass it in turn to Ramsay, now my Sire's constant watch-dog, who, although he could hardly refuse to deliver it to the King, would be alerted to take good care His Grace did not converse with me unless he himself were present. Of course, my Royal father could have sent Ramsay away, but I suspect that he found his presence a relief; by this time a real mutual embarrass-ment divided us. I was in agony to let my Sire know that in spite of any other rumours he might have heard, I had his interests foremost in my mind, but I could find no way of reassuring him. Treachery between father and son is not a subject easy to discuss for either party.

As a final defeating blow, I could no longer approach my father's Grace informally as one of his choristers. My voice had broken early, and although it had begun to reform itself, it did so in an extraordinary way which left me with no control over its tonal range. I warbled alarmingly.

One of the chief points of dispute within the Court at this time was the King's proposed marriage alliance. King Richard III of England, the last and to my mind the best of the Plantagenets, was now dead and his throne usurped by the Earl of Pembroke, Henry Tudor. Of him we knew little save that his uncertain hold upon his crown was likely to make him welcome the Scots alliance, which alliance might also strengthen my Sire's hand against his rebellious and powerful nobles. My father's Grace had a second reason for wanting a new consort, for his Court since my mother's death had the aspect of an all-male household, and calumny was once more gaining hold. That he should take a new wife would have been an excellent idea had he sought her else-where than England. We had an old saying that 'noucht ane guid cam furth of England' . . . no good thing ever came up from England: it was the profound voice of all our Scots experience.

To make matters worse, my Sire, who never did anything by half-measures, had the idea of importing not merely one English wife for himself, but two more—one for me and one for my brother Ormond. One English bride our Scots lords might possibly have tolerated, but three, each of whom would be accompanied by her retinue and native customs, savoured too much of a large-scale English invasion. Amongst the many who spoke out against it was the Earl of Hume, head of the most powerful of the rebellious great houses and my Sire's enemy of a lifetime. This so infuriated the King's Grace that he finally roused himself from his languor to take up the challenge of his lords. True to his birth sign, the Crab, he set out toward his objective sideways, and the fact that he wished to supplement his choir made him cast his eyes upon the revenues of Coldingham Priory. . . . That this would bring him into a clash with the Earl of Hume was inevitable.

The Humes were a Border family whose influence now stretched from the Tweed almost to the Solway Firth. Those of the family who took Holy Orders usually secured benefices at the nearby Priory of Coldingham which they had now come to regard as 'their' Priory. For generations a Hume had sat in the Prior's chair, and Lord Hume himself was hereditary bailiff.

My gentle Sire never lacked cunning and I believe had he used the same means to tackle the problem fourteen years earlier, he might have won the day against the Humes and others of their kind. He petitioned His Holiness Innocent VIII to close Coldingham Priory and allocate its revenues to the Chapel Royal at Stirling in order that His Grace might have the service of a second choir to glorify God's name. At the same time, he applied for the right to select for himself candidates for ecclesiastic benefices on the justifiable grounds that Scotland was remote from Rome and the Rota: there would be no more Humes or other noble families bribing their way independently to ecclesiastical authority. In all of these matters he had the support of his Parliament whose members, particularly of the Third Estate, were greatly heartened to see him at last bestir himself to set the Kingdom in order. An Act passed as a safeguard measure against possible Hume interference with my Sire's plan made it a treasonable offence for any to challenge His Grace regarding the sequestration of Coldingham Priory. My Royal father meant to call his enemy to heel and this time took no half-measures about it.

His Holiness granted the petition, and out of the revenues annexed to Stirling's Chapel Royal, the King's Grace financed a supplementary choir to attend him everywhere, contributing to our lives a constant supply of magnificent music. Neither Lord Hume nor his kinsmen, however, were men likely to accept quietly the loss of their family revenues by the closure of Coldingham, and when both the displaced Prior and his brother, the Earl, vanished from the Court, it was reasonable to suppose they had locked themselves in their border fortress to plot rebellion. Another kinsman of the Humes, Patrick, Lord Hailes, vanished from our sight simultaneously.

When the King's Herald took to Hume Castle a strongly worded message telling them to return immediately to appear before Parliament on a charge of contempt, they stripped him of his cloak, boxed his ears and tore up the Royal Warrant. They were at war: and so, by this time, was my Royal father.

I was desperately anxious to prevent open warfare, for I knew well enough what the rebellious lords had in mind for me, and the last thing I wished was to be used to depose my father's Grace. I chose the latest possible moment in the day, and went without sending any preliminary messages straight to the King's apartments. My long stride and purposeful mien daunted any who would have stopped me in the presence chamber, and at the bedchamber door I halted.

Through the half-open door I could see the great scarlet and gold canopy of the bed, and from beyond the bed I could hear voices, several of them murmuring together in the area screened from me by the bed-hangings and the angle of the door. I sensed an urgency to the discourse and I had a moment's hesitation: ought I to continue upon my mission, or fall back and wait in case the matter in the chamber was of greater urgency than my own? But could any problem exist that was of greater urgency than the one which had brought me? I put out my hand, watching it take the door ring with firm competence, and my hesitation left me. I knocked moderately upon the door, then pushed it open.

I saw a curious collection of people gathered upon the far side of my Sire's bedchamber, among them a guard in his steel cuirass with headpiece and halberd gleaming, and (surprisingly) a servitor in a white linen apron. Ay, and there, sure enough was Ramsay, Earl of Bothwell—clad in striped black and yellow which marvellously matched his waspish nature. There were others whom I would have known had I paid heed to it, but my eyes were on His Grace and they all seemed to melt away—including for a moment, Bothwell—as I met my Sire's eyes and bowed to him.

His Grace was seated in his great chair, one sandalled foot upon the stool before him. His hands were outstretched upon the rests of the chair, which hollowed his chest and bent forward his head. He did not seem at all surprised to see me. I asked if I could have speech with him, and he nodded. Then I saw him glance toward the door behind me, and the slightest of frowns appear on his brow. I knew the only one to remain would be Ramsay—and so he had, moving forward into my line of vision with the mincing arrogance which took it for granted that in all the King's affairs his own presence would be natural. For once, however, he was wrong, for His Grace bade him leave us—pleasantly, but meaning it.

'James . . . quhuit brangs ye a' sic hour?'

I did my best to explain . . . that it was fear for the Kingdom. I offered myself as moderator between the King's Grace and the Earl of Hume, but as soon as I mentioned the name of Hume, my Royal father's face blackened in a way that I knew presaged a hurricane.

I knew it was no use to pursue the matter further. If my father's Grace felt so strongly against the Earl of Hume, there was nothing more that anyone could do about it. My hopes of becoming Scotland's peacemaker had been few from the beginning, but there was—I had reckoned—a faint chance that fear for his own desperate situation might prevail upon my Sire to heed me. I could hardly speak openly of my fear that his nobles sooner or later would rise to depose him in my favour, for between King and Heir to a Throne, such conversation is impossible.

Yet it was the King's Grace himself who came closest to mentioning the banned subject, for he closed our conversation by telling me to prepare myself for departure upon the morrow to Stirling. *Stirling* . . .? I knew that no plans had been made for the Court to progress to Stirling Castle. There could be two explanations: either that he suspected me of conspiring with the nobles, and was sending me to Stirling as a Royal prisoner, or else . . . he had wind of a plot to enthrone me, of which I was myself as yet in ignorance. He told me it was the safest place for me to be, which could have meant anything. And it was not for me to ask the Majesty of Scots for further explanation.

He came with me to the door, and opened it for me with his own hand. I dipped my knee to kiss his fingers—and as I rose, I saw His Grace my father silhouetted against the door, as if he were a cut-out of a painting of himself . . . All motion gone, all sense of time leaving me, I seemed to stand for ever noting every detail of my Sire's presence. His black hair, prematurely greying, was receding slightly from the temples (he wore no cap at this hour, being retired for bed). He presented a figure of great beauty, standing in the shadow of the doorway. And this would be the way I would remember him. . . .

I had made my mental keepsake picture of my father's Grace, and I turned away to leave him, regardless of the terrible discourtesy in leaving the King's presence showing him my back. I had no choice. I could not for all the world have turned back to look at him again, for it was still my superstition that if I did not admit to myself that I had seen him for the last time, I could divert the fate that threatened.

I did in fact see once more the Majesty of Scots—in battle array, before me, his vizor down. I saw the King across the field, but I never again saw my father.

I went the next day alone to Stirling, with an escort of armed cavalry. That my brothers James and John did not accompany me was significant: my internment at Stirling was connected with my position as the King's heir, not with my safety as a member of the reigning family.

It was a wearisome time. I could not ride out for I was impounded within the gates of the Castle, and while I understood the necessity for it, it was hard to forgo my favourite exercise— which further increased my inability to sleep at night. I found enough to occupy my quiet hours in playing the lute, or practising my Celtic speech in conversation with the small daughter of one of the men of the garrison.

My formal studies too progressed during this time spent free from outward distractions. Three of my tutors had been brought to Stirling, doubling their duties as gentlemen in attendance, and my falconer had brought my best birds—which could be flown from the Castle ramparts to give my soul its share of freedom, if not my body. All was happy enough, so long as I closed my mind to events taking place elsewhere.

It was January. I braved the cold to take what exercise I could upon the battlements—and it was there I was standing when the look-out signalled the approach of a body of horsemen riding from the South. I knew that at some time or another an effort would be made by the rebels to prise me out of my stronghold. The Governor of the Castle, Master Shaw, had been instructed by His Grace that on no account were any to be admitted other than those who might come under the insignia of the Royal Household. Master Shaw had known me all my life and could be relied upon to protect me. Stirling, I knew, could withstand a siege almost indefinitely.

The approaching company of men-at-arms, who carried Hume or Hepburn pennants, numbered so far as I could judge between two or three hundred. A tidy-sized body of men. At their head rode the Earl of Hume, together with Lord Hailes and the Lords Lyle and Grey: the forces had been mustering.

To understand what happened next, you must know something of the character of those concerned. The Earl of Hume was a man of great integrity, for which I admired him, even if it frequently brought the two of us clashing together, heads down, like stags in the rutting season. He was as bold as he was honest, to the point of impudence or imprudence; he went at life like a lion, charging his way through opposition as it were brushwood, never dreaming that a man in full possession of his faculties could disagree with him. A natural leader, he had shown at first surprise and later exasperation, when, as a thirteen-year-old boy, I refused to conform to his way of thinking unless it matched with mine. As it happened, our opinions coincided upon most subjects, but agreement was never reached without a tooth and nail fight. Above all—and this is vital to my tale—the man had charm, enough to tempt the devil to honesty, and where he used it he could win well nigh any man.

The four leaders left their company at a distance of about a hundred yards from the Castle walls and themselves approached abreast up the castle ramp to the gate, where they stayed their horses. Hume was in the middle, magnificent in a scarlet cloak which billowed out behind him—he looked a leader; which is why he wore it, if I were any judge, for it was a long-cloak, not easy to manage on horseback across Stirling plain on a windy January day. Like the other three, he was part-armoured, in cuirass and cuisses. I drew out from behind the battlement to get a closer look at them—just as Hume glanced up and saw me. Even at that distance, there would be no mistaking who I was. In a flash, he had doffed his cap and waved. The impudence of the gesture, and the merry smile I saw outlined by his short-cropped black beard, so much amused me that I was taken off my guard. Before I thought what I was doing, I lifted my hand to return his greeting.

It was a masterly piece of strategy, and I had walked straight into a trap. From the battlements I could see and be seen by all within a radius of miles—Prince James, heir to his father's Kingdom, exchanging warm greetings with the rebels. I cursed Hume; I cursed my own stupidity. I could have cried my vexation—and my dismay, for I am quite certain that my greeting paved the way for all that followed.

Leaving the battlements at once, I ran down the turret stair, and through into the great hall to find someone I could send to summon Master Shaw to me. I found nobody—all were much too interested in the events taking place outside. I fumed with impatience—for I dared not show myself outside again—waiting for Master Shaw to come himself with news of what was happening. He never came. Word was brought to me, eventually, that Master John Shaw had actually gone to the gate to parley with the rebels.

The sequel was inevitable. I could have predicted what would happen when the Earl of Hume, lord to a vast Borderland estate, talked with humble Master Shaw of Sauchie. . . . Shaw was a stout hearted fellow, but he was no match for Hume's ability to charm and brow-beat simultaneously. It had to end the way it did—with Master Shaw opening the gate to admit my 'rescuers'. . . .

I received them in the great hall. Hume's vast red cloak splashed flamboyantly around him as he gave me a very low bow, and he would have kissed my hand, I suspect, had I not prevented it by holding my two hands clasped firmly together.

There was not a great deal to be discussed. They had come to bear me away as claimant to the Throne held by my father, and there was not much that I could do to stop them, outnumbered as I was. But I meant to show that I was not a mere tool in their operation: I told them to wait while I considered the matter. The Earl of Hume, I could see, was infuriated by the delay, but he could not gainsay me for I was, after all, son to the King's Majesty.

I went to my study chamber. There was the chest filled with my juvenile treasures, and the long broad oak table marked with the spilled ink splashes of my schooldays, now turned brown. I had so often in the past stood at the high window looking out over the windswept plain of moorland starred with tufts of bog-cotton, and the ridge of hump-backed firs crouched against the nor'-easterlies, considering my destiny and the problems that faced a King of Scots. Now the time for action had come.

My Royal father had neglected his kingdom in disastrous fashion, and while it was possible that a new Queen Consort might stir my Sire to activity, he had loved my mother's Highness and she had not been able to influence him; from what I had heard of King Edward's widow, Queen Elizabeth (Woodville), she seemed to be a lady who would bestow more privilege upon her relations than attention upon my Sire. Of one thing I was certain, that my father's Grace, in the present condition of spiritually exhausted lethargy, was in no state to hold his own against an invasion by English courtiers pressing King England's demands.

The Earl of Hume was right, and all were right who felt, as I did, that my Sire's choice of alliance with the English monarch was the worst possible way to mend Scotland's troubles. We had suffered all through our history from King England's arrogant challenge, 'Ye are my vassal!', while his subjects took every opportunity to raid and plunder us across the Border. We had no illusions about the English: they never meant us well.

There was no choice left to me. If His Grace my father had not a king's head upon his shoulders, he had at least sired a son who had.

From the study chamber I went to my bedchamber closet and gave orders for my clothing chests to be taken to Linlithgow— for I meant to go nowhere else the rebels might suggest. Upon our own Royal territory, I would be master. Then I made them dress me in my scarlet doublet—only a shade different from Hume's cloak—with red hose, and the red cloak with the satin lining that flashed in the sunlight when it blew open. Today I meant to have it blowing open, no matter how bitter the cold. I had them find my gold shoulder-chain, which I rarely wore, and set it upon the doublet so that it showed across my chest beneath the cloak. I had turned the tables on the Earl of Hume who would now look as if he wore my livery. . . .

Then I descended to the great hall, where I told them I would go in their company, *of my own free will*, on condition that we took Linlithgow Palace to be our headquarters. And on condition I received their assurance that they intended no harm to the person of the King's Majesty, James the 3 of Scots. This assurance they gave readily—almost too readily for my liking. I searched each face in turn, and each of the four seemed honest enough. . . . I had to take them at their word.

We went out into the stable yard, where a groom held ready my horse. Several people had gathered there, including Master Shaw of Sauchie, now I think a shade anxious that by admitting the rebels he had committed me—and himself—to more than he had recognized at the time.

Master Shaw took the bridle while I mounted. It was my custom to vault into the saddle, disregarding stirrups—a minor acrobatic feat of no great difficulty, but requiring perfect co-ordination of wits and muscles, otherwise it irritated the horse and made the rider look foolish. Today I had other things pre-occupying my mind. I mounted decorously, from the stirrup held for me by the groom. I took the reins in my gloved hands —I had kept them waiting while I put on my gloves in my customary careful fashion—and spoke down to Master Shaw from the saddle.

I thanked him for his good custody of me during my residence in the Castle. If this implied a reproach for surrendering me to the rebels, it was not deliberate. Master Shaw's problem of explaining to the King's Grace my father why, against his ex-pressed instruction, he had opened the gates, was his own affair. His kindness to me had been, as always, considerable.

The lords were mounted now, preparing to leave. I turned to give a last look, with a wave, to the small girl who had befriended me and helped to improve my Celtic speech. She stood unsmiling, behind a barred low window of the corner block by the stable gate, watching me. Her mother, beside her, spoke to her, urging her to wave—she then called to me a blessing which shocked me to the bone—'*Beannachd Dhia leibh—a righ!*' *A righ!*—what right had anyone to address me as *King*? I saw the woman put her hand to her mouth, no doubt as shocked as I was—but I had no time to wonder whether she had used the word in error, or whether her Celtic vision had sent it surging to her lips before she could contain it. A light touch of spurs set us cantering away.

Hume moved in beside me, Hailes upon my other side, Grey and Lyle followed after. And thus we came to the gate. But as we turned in the narrow curving neck by the battery, I nudged my mount secretly with my knees, and we had shot a half-head length beyond the pack of them before they realized. Thus I came first through the gate, where they had to fall behind me. And here it was that the Castle's Guard rang out a cheer for me, spontaneous and ragged, which echoed in the vaulted roof of the arch, with the clank of pike-butts and the sound of hoofs on cobbles.

It was my scarlet the mustered men-at-arms saw first upon the ramp, not Hume's; I came as their Prince not their prisoner. What I did would be no help to His Grace my father, but I had struck a blow for the authority of the Crown.

I was nigh fifteen years of age*, and I rode out smiling. *Ah waz nau' born James o' Scots fur nought!*

---

* PUBLISHER'S NOTE: The Julian calendar being at this time in use, the year ends on 20th March. Prince James will be fifteen at his next birthday on 17th March 1487, just before the new year.

3

WE pronounced it in my day Li'lithg*ow* – and very uninviting Linlithgow Palace looked, as we came in sight of it that raw, late-January afternoon, as twilight deepened in the hollows of the low surrounding hills; not a light was to be seen anywhere except in the town, which we had skirted cautiously to avoid sounding the alarm.

The old Palace had a single main frontal block; behind it, to the south, was a huge black barbican gate with small corner towers, the side walls of the barbican abutting the main block to form a square courtyard. An archway entrance at the front was reached by a drawbridge usually left down upon its buttresses. The water in the moat was taken from the loch to the north-west, and on the evening I arrived with the rebels the moat surface was frozen, with tipped-out garbage scattered across the ice. It looked dreadful.

There was no warmth in me of any sort as I sat, frozen to my saddle, looking bleakly upon the shuttered windows and the desolate mounds of rubbish waiting for the ice to thaw and let it through to its watery grave. Not a soul appeared, to give sign either of welcome or of hostility. Linlithgow Palace had gone into hibernation.

Hume reached for his horn and sounded a note which shivered the domestic close of winter twilight. A casement opened quickly above the gate, and a light appeared, followed by the silhouette of a guarded head, and a voice I recognized demanding to know who we were and what brought us. Hume shouted up to the window that he was attendant on the Duke of Rothesay—at which name, the Keeper, for it was himself, leaned out to take a closer look at our company. The scarlet attire and the gold chain served yet another useful purpose on that day to identify me, for within a moment I heard the startled cry of welcome, followed by rapid signs of activity. Our company of five rode down to cross the bridge as the gates scraped open over the stone cobbles.

As we came in through the archway we met the characteristic Linlithgow smells: the Keeper's men had quickly hung horn lanterns upon hooks in the wall of the archway and the stink of their mutton-fat candles was mixed with the stale air which belched out when the door within the arch was opened. Due to a trick of air circulation, all the cooking smells collected behind this door, together with the odour of damp stonework characteristic of a castle left untenanted for long periods. The foul odours in the entrance passage were one of the reasons why my Royal father did not like this Palace, but I found them familiar and cheering in the present circumstances.

The Keeper, whose name I forget, was waiting for us in the courtyard with a puzzled but welcoming smile upon his face. I felt grateful for his warm greeting for I was chilled to the bone after our long ride—I had meant to look royal if it killed me, and almost it had. I must have shown my distress, for the Keeper remarked upon it and bade me take shelter quickly in his own apartment up the stair where there was a fire. But I was having none of that. My role was to grin and bear it until such time as we had brought the men-at-arms into shelter, and I was not intending to have the Earl of Hume organize this or any other operation while I sought shelter. I had to show these men unknown to me that I cared more about their welfare than any man alive in Scotland; I must—for that was how I meant to win my Kingdom, through love of it.

This led me to suggest, not altogether I suspect to the good Earl's liking, that the men-at-arms be brought into the Palace to be temporarily quartered in the apartments normally occupied by courtiers. As these were empty, and the men could not possibly dig themselves into the frozen ground at this hour of night, the suggestion was an obvious one which could have come from Hume himself had I allowed him time for it, but I had to show from this, my first day, that when I became King, I intended to exercise my Sovereign right to have the first and final say in any matter affecting the welfare of my subjects.

I stood now in the archway, hiding my shivers, exchanging a word or a grin with as many of the men as I could, as they filed past me bearing their cooking pots and bedding rolls up the stairs to the court apartments. 'Yane es a guid lad', they would say—I hoped—as they settled themselves for the night, and would bear back this report of me to their families in the Borders. I was not made to be a tyrant; smile by smile, man by man, I would win back a Kingdom lost to gods of chaos.

Hume and I stood together, red cloak to red cloak, in the smoking yellow light of the archway, our breath streaming white as two plumes upon the frosty air. We spoke nothing to each other, which was the nearest we ever came to expressing our agreement.

The following day the men set about constructing their camp overlooking the main approach to the Palace. They dug into the hard earth rectangular pits to accommodate two, three or four men sleeping horizontally, over which they stretched frames made out of osiers from the loch, which they covered with stitched-together hides or jute canvas.

To my relief, my retinue arrived from Stirling the same day, bringing furniture and baggage with them. I had never before been separated from a bevy of attendants who washed, undressed and put me to bed with a carefulness which I had many times cursed inwardly but which I would appreciate more in future. I badly needed my bath-tub after a night spent unwashed and fully clad in my day-attire. Like most who are subject to the rule of Pisces, I have a natural affinity with water, and my three or four weekly bathings were due more to spiritual necessity than an avid addiction to cleanliness—although, in fact, I did find the odour of stale sweat offensive, and in later years it was well known among my courtiers that a petitioner's best hope to please me began by washing his neck and paring his nails. After a hot bath and a change of clothes I felt a great deal warmer and readier to face the future.

In the weeks that followed, however, my spirits sank inexorably. No one came near us, although the Earls of Angus and Argyll sent secret messages of support. We heard that his Grace my father had gone north to Aberdeen to confirm the allegiance of his northern lords—Crawfurd, Buchan, Errol, Glamis, Marischal Earl, a couple of Lindsays, and such knights and gentlemen as Innermeath, Inderby and others.

We had snow in early February, followed by a sudden thaw which left the countryside around Linlithgow constantly a-drain with water. Everywhere I looked showed darkening patches in the drifts where snow was melting, and there was not a cornice of the building to be seen which did not add its constant drip of tears to my depression. Worse yet, to my mind, were the wood shavings. . . . The sole defensive strategy we could employ at Linlithgow relied on a low earth dyke wall which surrounded the Palace at a distance. Into this were set spikes of timber, thrusting outwards at an angle of something like fifty degrees, supported at the apex of two joined staves each of which crossed at its base the supporting stave of the next spike in line. This was an old form of defence against cavalry—it ripped the belly from a horse if he tried to jump it—and was now used mainly to prevent the mounting of siege guns within range.

In the process of sharpening the two ends of these timber stakes, a great quantity of wood chippings was produced, which were borne away by the sharp easterly winds to fall wherever the eye could see. They blew about the inner courtyard, invading every doorway, and scattered the royal park to its farthest perimeter. They were trampled deep into the mud where the men had worn paths between their dug-outs—everywhere, there was no escaping them. They troubled no one else, but they drove me nearly insane with an inexplicable depression. It was to be another twenty-five years before I knew—or thought I knew— the explanation of that unbearable melancholy captured at

Linlithgow: on Flodden Edge we fortified the east escarpment in that same fashion, the only other time in my life that I saw it used.

I became ill for a while, to my lords' very great concern. I had the constitution of an ox when my spirits were high, but when my spirits fell my whole physique bore them company. I was accustomed to this state of affairs, but those with me began to reckon up their own chances of survival if the Heir they had captured failed to live out their expectations.

March brought shreds of a clear washed blue in a sky long overcast by the greyish murk of snow. I had always taken vigour in the month of my nativity, and my fifteenth birthday we celebrated with as much ceremonial as if it had been my first— a fact not surprising in view of the fact that my lords had had the fright of their lives so recently. What added greatly to the occasion was the arrival of Angus 'Bell-the-Cat' to join forces with us, his great 'Yeh-heuw!' ringing forth across the perimeter defences to reach our ears where we sat at meat in the main hall of the Palace. The old hunting cry has a ring of native Scots exuberance which no other sound, to my ears, can equal, and the upsurge of my heart and spirits was immediate. When 'Bell-the-Cat' brought his towering presence into the company, I knew that action of some kind would soon terminate the weeks of inconsolate waiting and apprehension.

Soon afterwards, indeed, the Earl of Argyll came to our banner. The Palace of Linlithgow was now thronged with people, as if we held court there, for each of the six noble lords had been joined by a considerable number of his kinsmen and greater tenantry. We seven held aloof from the general throng, for we were those who would pay the penalty if our schemes went awry, but to be all together now, combined upon a common project, bred a degree of mutual sufferance impossible at other times. Our small, closed community, propagating its own family jokes, created its own reality in terms which bore no connection with life outside Linlithgow. So far as I was concerned, these next weeks could have gone on forever; I had not enjoyed any great measure of true fun in my life, and this barrack style of living brought me real boyish happiness.

They were also profitable weeks in that our varied company gave me useful practice in the art of balancing incompatible personalities—which, as that would be the business of my life thereafter, was an experience I greatly welcomed. The one of the company who most noticeably differed from the rest was the Earl of Angus. Behind the ringing voice and hearty laugh of 'Bell-the-Cat' there was a great humility, an almost total lack of human vanity, which impeded him dreadfully in competition with the thrusting lords who were his contemporaries. Where his practical eye saw the need for action, he acted—drawing with him those who had been wasting their time competing for leadership. When his aim had been achieved, however, he would stand aside, while his followers squabbled over the spoil. He had no interest on his own behalf, until he had been cheated—and then he would feel hurt. Even in these early days at Linlithgow I could see that there was one among us who required to be defended more than the rest.

We received messages from the Kings of England and of France which annoyed us greatly. They reprimanded us for uniting in rebellion against the King's Majesty of Scots—although I could not see what right they had to interfere in our domestic affairs, even at my Sire's instigation. It was my hope that we could persuade His Grace to abdicate in my favour, if not the regal title, at least responsibility for all the work which he found irksome, while he could lead a far happier and more useful life among the books and music that he loved so well. But I could not blame him for his dogged dedication to the duty for which he had proved himself so unfitted; like myself, he had been born James of Scots, and it was in the marrow of his bones.

We were now threatened with real civil war. King James had mustered sufficient of the Northern lords to his banner to have taken Linlithgow long ago, and I could only suppose he had not done so because he was uncertain of my position. He came, however, to the Point of Blackness, some five miles north-east of the Palace, where he and his Council took up residence in the Castle beside the Forth, while his army encamped close by upon the headland to guard the approach road. Our noble lords and their men were delighted that at last, after our wintry confinement, an opportunity had arrived to come to grips with the King's men, and after a minor engagement in which I was not involved (Hume was furious that he had had to stay behind to guard me while Angus led our force), we negotiated with His Grace the truce we had already set in writing during the dismal days of February against the time when it might be required.

The agreement, signed by four witnesses upon either side, obliged King James to surrender full power to me as Regent as soon as I was considered old enough to administer the affairs of the Realm. When my father's Grace agreed, albeit reluctantly, to the terms of the truce, I felt the weight lift from my mind and heart for the first time in weeks.

I had been made deeply uneasy by a report which suggested that during the affray at Blackness an attempt had been made upon my Royal father's life. I was told that His Grace had turned a ferocious attack upon Lord Grey, who had been obliged to defend himself in natural fashion, whereupon the Earl of Crawfurd had come to His Grace's support in demonic style. I was assured that the incident had occurred in the heat of an engagement ill-managed upon both sides. I reminded them all of their promise to ensure the safety of the King's Grace, and I could only reflect gratefully that as His Grace had yielded to the terms of the agreement he would now be in a position of less peril.

King James no sooner returned to his Castle of Edinburgh than to my horror he repudiated the treaty and made it known that he would carry on the fight. Perhaps I should not have been surprised, for my Great-Uncle James of Buchan, who was one of His Grace's advisory council, was notorious for his belief that in war or in love chivalry should yield to expediency; but I had looked for better of His Grace my father. I felt very deeply and bitterly against such a flagrant betrayal of the integrity of the Crown.

We heard that Errol, Huntly, Marischal Earl and Glamis had turned their armies homeward in protest, abandoning His Grace's cause. My Royal father now had few reliable advisers: Bothwell and Buchan were not likely to be conciliatory toward us, while

Bishop William Elphinstone would play for time; only the Earl of Crawfurd—created Duke of Montrose for his gallantry at Blackness—was powerful enough to give the King good advice that would be heeded. It looked a thoroughly unpromising situation.

We decided to proclaim to all the burghs that we made war upon an unjust King. I made the lords soften the language of the proclamation a good deal from the original draft, but its meaning had to be precise or we should not achieve the deposition of the King in circumstances which upheld the authority of the Crown, nor could we expect recognition from other princes.

A party of our force besieged King James in Edinburgh Castle; he made a bid to escape by ship from Leith toward—as we thought—the Continent. No effort was made to detain him, for it would have been the happiest solution to all our difficulties had he chosen exile at the court of one of his brother princes. But he was next heard of in Fife, trying to remuster his forces—and apparently with some success, for it was an army of fair strength that he took to Stirling Castle, where Master Shaw refused to open its gates.

Now determined to force the issue one way or the other, we decided to go in force to Stirling and compel His Grace to give battle. We were now in the month of June, and our men-at-arms would soon be needed back at home for the harvest. Scotland had problems enough without a deficiency of corn for the winter.

On the eve of the day we set out for Stirling, my new Lyon Rampant banner, stitched for me by Hume's lady, was brought out and set in its place in the great hall, apart from the rest. At night, on the point of retiring, I felt a sudden need to go again to look at it where it hung in shadow between the chimney breast and the wall. Always I had known this crimson-and-gold presence lay in wait for me at some point upon my life's road. The fire had died down in its basket when I stood alone in the minstrels' gallery looking down into the hall. The last few flickering flames struck a glint from the gold cloth, although the shadow in which the banner hung forward heavily changed the crimson of the Lion almost to black. It was an awesome confrontation between myself and my destiny, in the quiet of the hall where the banners and emblems of our followers dipped among the shadows between four towering walls of stone. The sight of my banner did not excite me; I was dreadfully aware that its presence carried the injunction to submit my own human vanity to the needs of the Crown—and my battle against James Stewart's mortal vanity would have been my life's greatest war, even without the Regal obligation to subdue it. I felt rather sick, lonely, and frightened, as I stood in the gallery; I know that I cried a little, because I felt too young to deal with it all, and upon the morrow there would be nobody in Scotland to take away my responsibility for *me*. I crept back, weeping, to my bed.

We avoided Stirling Castle, not wishing to be ensieged there by my Royal father's forces. Our intention was to draw His Grace into the open. We sent our challenge to him in the town of Stirling by Hume's herald. He replied that he would meet us upon our chosen ground—a place slightly to the south-west of the site called Bannockburn where King Robert the Bruce had smashed the evil Edward Plantagenet. It was a level piece of ground with a firm soil beneath the grass, a good place to give battle; it never had a name to my mind, just 'the field by Stirling'.

It was a scorching hot day with a cloudless blue sky, and the short wiry grass of Stirling plain was already whitened at the tip; it was not the kind of weather anybody would have chosen willingly to fight a battle. My position was in the centre of our formation, surrounded by the Hume and Hepburn cavalry. My Lyon Rampant banner was borne by a Hepburn—I think it was Lord Hailes's younger brother, placed to my left and slightly behind me. It looked very fine, the gold glittering in the sunlight, but it made me uneasy. In the great hall of Linlithgow it had seemed to be mine by right, but now I felt a traitor and a usurper, about to face my Kingly father fighting beneath a standard to which I was not entitled. All my life I had been instilled with the idea that the Crown would pass to me upon my Sire's decease, and only at his decease.

Upon this 11th day of June, my head prickled with perspiration inside the close-fitting helm and gorget. My hair had been scraped back and tied over the crown with a leather thong to keep it clear of my eyes, and the tightness of the band was an added irritation. My body armour was not so hot and uncomfortable, for the polished metal surface gave back a good deal of the sun's heat. It was only the headpiece and the gauntlets that I detested, and the helmet was the worst affliction, for it muffled one's hearing and limited vision. Even with the vizor open, it was almost impossible to turn the head to see what lay behind; with vizor lowered, the most that could be seen was a pattern of movement beyond the grill, so framed that it was impossible to see immediate or large objects in their entirety. Constant attempts were made to discover a vizor design which gave greater visibility, but it always came at the end to a choice between horizontal or vertical slats, or a pattern of squares, of which I preferred the vertical.

For this reason, my knowledge of what happened upon the field that day—or, indeed, during any other battle—is limited. I saw the King's force enter the field with himself riding at the head, superbly accoutred, upon a giant grey battle charger. It was quite the biggest warhorse I had ever seen; it must have stood close upon nineteen hands. My heart lurched at the sight of my father's Grace astride it. What on earth were those upon his own side thinking of, who knew his miserable inability to handle anything bigger than a palfrey, to let him even mount such a brute, let alone take the field with it? I watched closely, and could see already the twitching head that showed he had it on too short a rein: man and mount were as wretchedly ill-matched as it was possible to be. I sensed disaster.

I had made my lords and gentlemen give me yet again their promise, before we set out for battle, that none would allow my Royal father's life to be endangered—otherwise I would myself have no part in any of it. This they had done. I had not foreseen that danger might come from the other side, where there were doubtless those who were as weary and exasperated as we were by His Grace's vacillations. I had no cause to suspect a conspiracy, but I was worried by that horse.

So engrossed was I in my terrible reflections that the trumpet alarm to start the battle went unheeded, and a shower of arrows arrived upon us before I had put down my vizor—which I did hurriedly, scowling behind the grill which obstructed my view of my father. I was not interested in much else, although I watched a man within my field of vision go down convulsing as he tore at the arrow shaft through his cheek, with its barb protruding beneath his jaw-bone. I had fought until now only in the lists and this was my first experience of an engagement in which men died.

It was an ill fought match, with no marked sense of strategy or enthusiasm. We met to resolve the Kingship, and any sort of intensity of feeling between the opposing factions was visibly lacking. We made a short cavalry charge upon the enemy's position, which they held for a while, then fell back. I lost sight of my father's Grace during the charge and when I looked back to where I thought he had been, both the grey horse and its rider were missing. I turned my constricted eye-line upon every part of the field I could reach, but saw no sign of him. Nor did I see the grey horse standing riderless, which relieved me. It was reasonable to assume that he had retired from the field but for all that, I was uneasy. My instinct told me more than I wanted to know.

Back at Linlithgow, I waited for news of my father, hoping that he had been in hiding or had taken ship to the Continent. A search had to be made, for until we knew where he was my position either as Regent or as King remained undecided. Upon the evening of the fourth day word was brought to us at Linlithgow that the body of the late King's Majesty had been found beside the millstream of Bannockburn, where the riderless grey horse had been seen cropping grass close by; they had borne the body back to Stirling Castle and it was thither I rode at once with the Earl of Hume, Lord Angus, and Patrick Hailes. I was now the King of Scots.

All the way I was aware of Hailes trying to gain the others' attention. I almost asked him what they were hiding from me, but my instinct already knew the discovery that awaited me.

The late King's body lay upon a catafalque in the Chapel Royal of Stirling Castle—Master Shaw having admitted him now it was too late for it to benefit him. A coffin was being prepared, but meanwhile the corpse lay covered by a purple velvet pall and his royal standard. Candles had been lighted in the four sconces set around the bier, but otherwise the chapel was dim in the dusk of the June evening. I bade my three companions leave me.

When I had heard the clank of the door behind them, I approached the catafalque and drew back the cover from my dead father's face. It was clean of blood or dirt, but the bruises and torn skin showed that he had taken a fall and had doubtless been dragged by the horse. The expression of his features told me nothing. I rolled back the pall to inspect the rest of the body. I counted five stab wounds to the abdomen and chest, of which any one of three would have been fatal. Also, my eye fell now upon the three long incisions, no deeper than scratches, which ran from his head down to his neck, ending where his cuirass began. These were sword scratches, received in an exchange with others while he had been riding helmetless. It looked to me as if he had escaped the first attack, and then as he tried to get away, the grey charger had thrown and dragged him. Tangled in the harness he would be helpless against any who made to stab him to death, with or without removing his cuirass.

They had murdered him. Filial grief might prompt me to make an effort to discover his murderers, but kingly common sense knew that the discovery would not promote my work for Scotland's unity. I remembered what my father had said upon the affair at Lauder Brig, to blame not the perpetrators of the act, but to put the blame upon himself. This seemed such truly royal advice that almost it cheered me now to recollect it; no other words spoken by my father in all his life so plainly conveyed that however else he had failed to serve the interests of the Crown, he comprehended truly the reason why he wore it.

The door groaned upon its hinge as I went out to where my three lords were waiting for me. The lords looked at me; I looked at my lords; all were aware of the subject left unmentioned. I found I had no words in me to say, and they were waiting until I spoke of it. A gesture resolved my difficulty. I held out my right hand of Scotland's Majesty, for each of them in turn to kiss it.

Then I turned on my heel as they bowed behind me, and left the Chapel. It was not until I had the seclusion of my old study chamber that I broke down and wept. All night I kneeled upon the floor beneath the window, alone with my grief, weeping and praying until I had exhausted myself—and the sun rose upon me thus, the first day I knew myself as Scotland's Ruler.

My brothers were brought to join me at Stirling immediately. I could not run the risk of having King James's now leaderless forces adopt my eight-year-old brother James, who had been created Duke of Ross before my father's death, as their candidate. Also, I was troubled about him: he seemed to bear me no ill-will, but appearances could be deceptive with James and I was anxious to know how he would feel about my part in our father's death, for he was a dour, uncommunicative child. He shed few tears at our father's funeral and interment beside our mother at Cambuskenneth; and although for a week after that he accepted his privilege as the mourning younger brother to the monarch to share my bed, he did not confide in me.

There was no time to lose, or England's monarch would claim that Scotland needed his protection, having no true and rightful King. I was brought to my coronation at Scone Palace by Perth, upon the 25th day of June, 1488. I was clad in black, like all of my lords, and would have had no colour visible had not my confessor asked, did I mean to punish all my subjects as well as myself. In compliance, I wore a red mantle which to me resembled blood as much as revelry. I wore it short so that I required no bearers. My brother James wore blue—and my cousin James Hamilton caused an unwanted furore because he had the notion to wear green upon his black, which I would not allow.

It was not only James Hamilton who threw a tantrum that day. I have never known Scotland's lords behave so badly. Even without their temperamental displays, it was a sorry enough occasion in the gloom of Scone's musty, neglected Palace (which, although Perth was still nominally Scotland's capital, was rarely used by my family, having as it did the memory of my great-grandfather's murder to make both Perth and Scone unloved places). Nothing had been prepared; even the gold cloth canopy above my head was an old one found in a store room—I think it had been my grandfather's. There was a third of Scotland's lords absent, and, if I remember, the list of bishops lacked several, including Elphinstone. Nobody came to his crowning with less enthusiasm of his lords than I.

The worst trouble was that there had been yet no chance for a convocation of Parliament to appoint office holders, with the result that we had no established order of precedence, and my lords fought for places like a herd of schoolboys. Angus 'Bell-the-Cat' who had acted as Regent these past two weeks since the battle by Stirling, for which I blessed him, was insulted by Hume's peremptory manner, and went away to sulk—therefore needing to be sought, found and comforted by myself. Hume had a quarrel with his brother the Prior of Coldingham, Argyll was not on speaking terms with Lord Grey, and there was some Bishop, whose See I forget, standing in the courtyard delivering his opinion that the woe of the deed had brought upon us the woe of the day. The only two people who tried to help me were my eight-year-old brother the Duke of Ross, who took his role as my supporter literally, and Bishop Robert Blacader of Glasgow, who seemed to grasp the fact that the one worst afflicted by all the recent happenings was myself. I never forgot the kindness of these two, in my hour of need.

For my Anointing, which to my mind was the most important part of that day's ceremony, I had all banished from the chapel save my brothers James and John, and the higher clergy. The lords thereafter jostled in the doorway, making such a noise with their competitive whispering that I could hear it where I knelt at the altar.

I cannot remember whether it was our Scots custom, or my own choice, that had me crowned upon my knees before the altar—but I did not sit until I had walked to the stall with its carved wooden canopy that I see yet above my head which was made steady by the diadem. The diadem gave me great troubles that day. It was made for King Robert the 1 (the Bruce) who must have had a larger skull than his descendants. It was customary to pack the circlet discreetly with padding, and in my case, as in my father's, a lid of velvet to match the hair was added within the diadem, to take the weight from the crown of the head so that the circlet would not slip forward on the brow. A fitting before the day of coronation was a necessity—but I had shied from this, suddenly sickened by the thing of yellow gold and jewels which had cost my father his life. I could not bear to touch it, nor to let any put it upon my head. In consequence, the packing and the lid of velvet had been measured from one of my caps, so that when we came to the Rite of Fealty I was aware all the time of the diadem swinging loose from my brow as I leaned forward.

All went well as I scooped up my robe in my left arm to sit within the stall. And I can remember watching my hands as I took the sceptre—as I always watched my hands; thin hands, almost skeletal, they seemed to me to be an entity that was myself existing apart from myself. Strange hands, with their palm lines almost invisible, like ancient writing upon a tablet, worn away by time; to me, my hands seemed always older than myself; it surprised me ever when I watched them that they should be *my* hands, controlled by me, James Stewart. Taking the Sceptre this day, I seemed to see a dead man's hands.

Otherwise, my crowning was as anti-climatic as would be all the other 'great days' of my life. My luck ran true to Stewart family form. I had loved my father by whose death this awesome event had been purchased, and this knowledge had taken away all the excitement which my mind had visualized when, as a child, my crowning as King had seemed to offer the sole recompense for all the years of study I had contributed while other children set out upon their ponies across the courtyard below my turret window.

The one great hour that I do remember, was the Rite of Fealty, when Scotland's lords took their oath of allegiance to the Sovereign. In the great hall of Scone, with the family banners of all those present hanging from the walls, I sat feeling very small and still beneath my gold canopy as they came in a long line to set their hands between mine and swear into my service their lives, their goods, and the lives and goods of their families and their liegemen. I remember the slender pointed sheath of my boy's hands closing over their gnarled fists—many lacking a top finger joint in my father's or my grandfather's service—and wondering, why *me*, James Stewart? And the Lyon Rampant swinging from the canopy gave the answer.

The Scots are a proud race of men who do not give their allegiance unconditionally, and their oath of Fealty to their King has been as often honoured by the breach as by the observance; but on that day at Scone Palace, as I listened to their vow, I did truly feel that both sides meant it. And if you will look at the list of our Scots lords who died with me on Branxton Moor in 1513—which is all but four of them—you will have proof, if proof were needed, that we stayed true to the vows we exchanged at Scone upon my otherwise sad, and disorganized, coronation day.

4

IT was the year 1488. I had put aside my books, and I set forth
to learn at first hand my Kingdom's requirements. Fortunately,
I was young and filled with energy and enthusiasm to be a
good King, otherwise I think the lack of hope which I saw
everywhere might have been contagious. A dispirited acceptance
of all life's miseries characterized the entire population; nor was
I myself at first too popular, on account of the manner in which
my father had died.

I loved my Kingdom and its people; I would not have changed
my rough, poor, knowing, small country for all the empires
earth had known chained together to make an Eden. I required
no crown to be a king, with a falcon or hawk to my wrist, a
proud spirited horse, and the endless expanse of springy moorland
turf to ride from sky's rim to sky's rim, with no obstruction.

Lashed with wind and rain, blanketed with snow in winter,
or busy with bees visiting the heather's bell for its summer crop,
the terrain of Scotland made few concessions to the gregarious.
It was in truth a wilderness, where the only landmark would be
the occasional tall tower-dwelling set gauntly upon its crag, or
isolated upon a loch's island. These strongholds were forbidding
places, with their narrow unglazed windows shuttered in part,
or entirely, by wooden casements. They rarely showed sign of
life; as dark fell the merest chink of light between the shutters
signalled their presence to the stranger. Unless the traveller was

known to be a friend, he was assumed to be foe—which, at that time, most usually he was. In summer there would be herds of shaggy, short-legged cattle with their great spread of horn, grazing the nearby pasture, together with nimble thin sheep whose load of wool made them seem bigger than they were; and there would be figures of men peacefully at work, shepherds and herdsmen, upon the distant slopes; but behind the tower's battlements there was a look-out posted, to give the alarm should there appear between the distant hills a company of horsemen. Then the women and children would flee to the castle, while the menfolk, armed to the teeth, set forth to give battle.

Scotland's population always seemed four-fold greater in the summer than in the winter months. A hamlet of half-a-dozen turf cottages with brown earth walls and green-growing roofs was almost invisible to the approaching traveller in winter. Only the smell of peat-smoke brought on the wind told of the hearthfires beside which the cottagers were busy converting their small crop of wool and leather hide into clothing and shoes. The greater part of their communal herd was slaughtered to make salt-meat, and the frost-bound earth yielding no encouragement to cultivation, the peasant folk and their livestock seemed to hibernate like bees upon the stored food and warmth that their summer's industry had won them.

We had few roads in 1488, except where packhorse trails had worn away the turf to make a mud surface, scattered with stones by the travellers themselves upon the steep gradients. Wheeled carts, or sledges in winter, were used to carry property, but nearly everybody could ride after a fashion, and horseback was a great deal more comfortable than the lurches, bumps and perils of the horse-litter. The best roads ran between the burghs, some of which—Edinburgh, Dunfermline and Perth, for instance—were still contained within their walls. To limit a town's boundary, however, gives no scope for graceful expansion, and as the population of the burghs had grown, all manner of ugly excrescences had appeared beyond their walls.

Few as yet, anywhere, were the houses built of stone. Such an atmosphere of impermanence, distrust and insecurity imbued the land that few men would afford the great expense. Except within the walled burghs, most of the burgesses lived in tall wooden houses, their timbers pitch-coated to preserve them against the weather—which, with their shutters half or fully closed against the wind and rain, gave them a dark and sinister aspect. Their only gracious feature—and this was frequently hidden from the passer-by—was their enclosed courtyard and garden at the back, surrounded by a high wall built of stone. Entrance to the house would be at first-floor level, either from the courtyard, when a heavy timbered door, close-fastened night and day, would seal the entrance passage, or from the street, by a ladder—it could scarcely be called a stair—which, as like as not, would be up-drawn at night, and in times of emergency during the day as well. There was nobody in Scotland gave a welcome to any in 1488.

The only possible exception to this rule was Glasgow. Although it was not yet a burgh in the full sense—it could engage in local but not in foreign trade—it had a Bishop (my distant cousin, Robert Blacader) and two monastic foundations of sufficient standing to make it second only to St Andrews in ecclesiastical importance. Whether its monastic hospitality was an influence, or whether it was due to its soft, sweet western air—or whether, in fact, it was simply that Glasgow was so beautiful that its people wanted to share its pleasure with strangers, I cannot say; but Glasgow gave more promise that our Realm of Scotland truly had a future than any town I knew. There were no walls, save those surrounding the monasteries; but almost all the houses were built of stone—grey granite houses, owning stately gardens with flourishing fruit trees. There was a quayside along the Clyde, where burgesses moored their small fishing boats at their gardens' edge, and the river was second to none in Scotland, broad and fair and smooth and crystal clear. I reckoned that if all our towns could be made as charming as Glasgow, the Realm of Scotland would have a great deal for foreign guests to admire.

But before we could build prosperity within the Realm the first necessity was to restore some semblance of law and order. The four main criminal offences—murder, arson, rape and robbery—were 'Pleas to the Crown' and at that time were judged by the King personally. The King my father had believed that Christian forgiveness would show even the worst of men the error of their ways; his judgements had caused very great bitterness, however, among those who tried to live honestly, and even as a young boy I had seen that mercy randomly administered breeds greater discontent within the Realm than does severity justly and consistently applied.

My lords and I restored the lapsed Justice Ayres to those burghs and towns where they had existed previously, and codified the Law—which my father had neglected—but our greatest problem was, and remained for many years, a lack of trained men to administer the law. This was due largely to the fact that far too many of our rural gentry considered that while the younger sons needed education to equip them for the Church, the eldest son, who followed in the steps of his father, needed no more than the ability to write his name on vital documents and the eye to read the good points of a horse. Later, in 1496, we took the serious step of making education compulsory for the sons of knights and gentlemen—and the de'il of a job it was to put such an Act through Parliament. Those of us who supported the measure were accused of taking away man's basic right to decide for himself whether or not his own children were to become scholars.

Meanwhile I was anxious to show my people that innocence would be protected, and that to bring their grievance to a law court was their obligation and their privilege. For too long the kinsman of a local landowner could escape all consequence of his crimes by intimidation of the law's officers—and indeed it was probable that the interested lord was the law's officer in judgement on the case. I meant to have no more of this mockery of justice. The clan feuds were not a way of life, they were an evil; and an evil which spread through every level of our Scots society. I would eradicate them, even if it meant hanging one of those lords dearest to me.

And this it finally did. Lord Drummond of Perth became my very close friend in the first two years of my reign, when he helped me put down the fires of rebellion which flared throughout the Kingdom. He had five children but only one son, George

Drummond, a young man not a great deal older than I, of great gaiety and charm, whom I liked well for his enthusiasm and impulsiveness. George Drummond had for some while been engaged in a feud with the Murray clan, which ended with sixty members of the clan burned to death in the kirk where they had taken refuge. At the trial, I could believe George Drummond when he said that he had only meant to singe their beards and truly believed that most, if not all, would escape. The prank, however, had cost the death of almost the entire family of Murray, who were my subjects; and George Drummond knew as well as any that we had decreed the end of clan warfare. George Drummond was hanged at Stirling. I witnessed his hanging, as did his father. The lesson served us all: Scotland's law bound all of us, myself and my friends included.

There were happier aspects of my efforts to secure order within my Realm. At first, when I went in person to judge the court plaints I had been received with sullenness. But it was not long before I received a warmer welcome, as the news travelled of my efforts to deliver fair judgements to all. It was heartening to see this sign of returning hope among my people. One of my clearest and dearest memories is of leaving the tolbooth of a market town, where the court had been held. As I passed between the ranks of people, with one of my retinue or a court officer preceding me with the shout, 'Make way—make way!', an old woman suddenly broke out of the crowd on my left and seized me in her arms, weeping for joy and gratitude. I think I had found her son not guilty of a felony of which he had been accused. Before they pulled her away, quite gently—which had to be done, else it would have set a dangerous precedent—I remember that I gave her a hug in return, as warm as her own. Then I went for my dinner to a house nearby and had great trouble afterwards to make my way out of its door owing to the throng which had gathered there. I know that as I rode out of that town the shutters of the wooden houses lining its street were flung wide for the folk to wave and cheer, and, riding almost abreast of its windows, I shook many of the hands held out to me.

It was not everywhere so easy. I had hoped to be able to

reconcile to the Crown without force those who had given it service through my father. I had never regarded those opposing us upon the Field by Stirling as being 'enemies', and I had supposed—ingenuously, I daresay—that reconciliation would be achieved by persuading Montrose, Buchan and the rest that all which mattered now was the common good of Scotland. Unfortunately, I had not reckoned with the foreign princes who knew nothing and cared nothing about Scotland's internal problems, except where these could be exploited to their own advantage. Only England might attack us, but she could plead a good cause if other princes disapproved of my path to the throne.

It was quickly made plain to me by Hume, Argyll and others that our best defence against accusations of regicide was to arraign as 'traitors' those who had been loyal to the late King. It was a disgustingly hypocritical business and I was not the only one to express my dislike of it—'Bell-the-Cat' denounced the idea in heated terms. We were not vengeful—we had no moral right to be so—and we finally agreed that a formal examination by our Parliament in the Edinburgh Tolbooth would be enough to show that we were the true rulers of Scotland. I had to put my Kingdom's interests before my private principles, at least on this occasion, for I knew that Ramsay had fled across the Border and would do all he could to encourage King Henry to intervene in our affairs. (I had stripped Ramsay of his title, Earl of Bothwell, after my coronation and conferred it upon Patrick Hailes, who had earned it; it was also a good way to balance the domineering tendency of Hume, by making his close colleague in the Borders equal in rank to himself.)

The list of those arraigned for 'treason' was proclaimed, but of all summoned to appear for examination by the Lords of Council in Edinburgh, the only one who did so was my late Sire's uncle, the Earl of Buchan. The sight of his portly small figure doubled up on its knees before me, head bowed to touch the ground, was so ludicrous I was not sure whether to blush for shame or to burst out laughing—added to which, my uncle 'Hearty James' was no longer young enough, or sufficiently slender, to adopt such a posture without serious discomfort. I quickly gave him my hand to help him rise, and told him that he was forgiven for having taken the field against me—although I reprimanded him in private for having encouraged my father to break the Truce of Blackness.

Although the senior earls failed to present themselves, there was a fair gathering of the lesser lords, knights and gentlemen who had been upon the Field by Stirling. The object of the Council was to prune the list of as many as possible before the remainder were brought formally to trial before Parliament. I also hoped privately through some careful questioning to discover who upon either side had reason to be suspected of complicity in my father's death. I wanted to settle the matter in my own mind once and forever, for I did not like to think I might be working in collaboration with any who had had to do with his murder.

The Edinburgh Tolbooth, built by the city's burgesses to house their Council meetings and other administrative business, had been enlarged during my grandfather's reign to accommodate assemblies of our national Parliament when he moved his principal residence from Perth to Edinburgh. It was now a fine stone hall, with a vaulted roof, and lancet windows lengthened in my father's time and glazed with many coloured fragments set in lead panes. A fore-gallery or 'long room' gave entrance from the street, up a street stair, for like all our buildings, it was used at first-floor level, the space below being storage area. A single doorway on the left side of the hall, facing my chair at the head of the hall, joined the 'long room' to the assembly chamber. The wall facing me had not only a stone sedilia—as went round every wall—but it was also decorated with a high stone relief of arcading. My Bishops and all clergy representative of the First Estate sat in front of this wall, those who were fortunate enough to have seats against the wall being accommodated in niches—I have many recollections of having to quell my rising amusement when I looked across at my mitred bishops seated in a row like a windowful of glass saints on the point of elevation. My lords of the Second Estate sat upon my right, looking awesomely impressive with the long spears of coloured glass window rising behind them. The commoners sat on my left, where they had to suffer in the draught from the door—on very cold days I would be the worst sufferer of them all, for while they could be muffled from the toe to the eyeball, I had to show a royal disregard for cold, unblanketed.

Upon this day, however, only the Lords of Council were present, and I was watching closely to see who among the examiners, as much as the accused, showed any reluctance to speak about the late King my father. I knew from my uncle, the Earl of Buchan, that one of those present was he who had given my father that giant grey war-charger—and this man I tried to examine closely. I may have pressed him too severely upon the matter, for he had a brother present who took fright on his behalf, and begged me to let him act as his brother's advocate, which was in fact his profession. Whereafter followed an entertainment greatly to the delight of all present save myself, for I had not known that these two worthies were a pair of nature's clowns—although he who was the advocate had nothing clownish to his wits, when he called for me to leave the chamber as an interested party to the case being tried and therefore disqualified from acting in any judiciary capacity. The devil of the matter was that he was perfectly correct, and I had to leave the chamber and go into the 'long room' where I stood at the far end, fuming to the point of bitter tears, for this intervention had cost me the chance ever to learn more about that great grey horse and those stab wounds left by my father's murderers.

It was the sole time in my life, when I could not take a joke against myself with humour. I am afraid I let down all my ideals about true justice, by causing the advocate to be sentenced to a term of imprisonment for too well defending his client. As soon as I had spoken, I could have bitten out my tongue—but it was too late to gainsay it: my father had lost his crown, by speaking first hard and then soft so that none came to rely upon his word. Right or wrong, my sentence on the man Lindsay had to stand; and it may not have been a bad way to demonstrate that I was not to be trifled with, however cleverly.

It was not easy for me to go on working with these men, still knowing that some of them might have conspired to slay my father. I blamed myself the more since I had no one else to blame to such an extent, that it took a severe toll upon my health, which was neither good for me nor of help to my Realm. If I had some way to do real, true, great penance for it. . . .

The idea came to me while watching a smith by the forge, shoeing a horse. I thought, if only a shoe of iron could be nailed to *my* foot, to take the weight from my soul and put it upon the body . . . And I knew then the solution—to have made a girdle of raw iron chain, to put about my waist, for so long as it was necessary.

The man I chose to make it for me was one of the Court smiths—a youngish man, about thirty, with yellow leonine hair, and the marvellous gift of silence. This man was to become over the years one of my few close intimates. I had meant to wear the chain for but two or three years, but as my life progressed there seemed always something else in the Kingdom adding to my burden of guilt. I thus began the practice of putting extra links upon the chain, for my soul's salvation; and always the same man forged each new piece for me. None other handled it save he and I, and there was so much of myself, James Stewart, built into that chain that I grew jealous to have it out of my sight—and would go down to the smiddy to watch Tam at work as he fitted the new link to it. I would talk, and he would listen; he knew my private matters, although never state business. Occasionally, when I wanted Scots reaction to what was a known measure I proposed, I would get it from Tam—by God, I would, all irons clanging! To be taciturn is not to be void of opinion.

Tam became known as 'the King's Smith' and it was the greatest triumph of our relationship that the words were never spoken as if to mean 'King's favourite'. All that Tam ever had of me was the gift at New Year's tide which he received in common with all my household. Beyond this, he had one present of a small jewelled knife which he had seen me wear and once admired. I took it off and gave it to him, but this was my habit on many occasions when somebody shared my appreciation of one of my possessions.

My train of siege guns, pulled by oxen teams over the rough ground, their crews labouring with pick and shovel to ease their way, had become by the end of two years an accepted feature of Scotland's landscape. More often than not, they arrived to find their work already done for them by Lord Drummond's men-at-arms and my own, but they were sometimes necessary to force an entrance into a stronghold of insurrection.

It was not only against supporters of the late king my father that I had to lead my forces. Some of my own allies also turned against us, and most notably the stalwart Angus. Angus had acted as unofficial Regent after the battle by Stirling (in which capacity he was invaluable) until we could call a Council meeting to settle the administrative appointments. Hume and the rest had immediately made known at the meeting which positions they wanted, but Angus in his usual fashion had said nothing, assuming that the reward for his services would reach him of its own accord. In no time whatever, an argument developed between the Earl of Hume and his brother, at the end of which Angus, who had grown restive, suddenly rounded upon everybody with the accusation they served only to forward their own ends. Before I could speak, I myself had been included in the general remonstrance, and with the word 'ingratitude' and a mighty doorslam thundering upon the air, 'Bell-the-Cat' had left us.

There was nothing I could do. A King newly come to an insecure throne in an unstable kingdom cannot go running after a contumacious Earl who had—unpardonably—slammed the door in the face of his Sovereign; it would have cost me my crown. I had no alternative but to share out the offices which I had intended for Angus between the rest. Thus Patrick Hailes, the new Earl of Bothwell, became Scotland's High Admiral, who turned out to be the worst sailor imaginable—not that it greatly mattered, with our meagre sea-force in the hands of Sir Andrew Wood, whose ability was already a legend.

The Earl of Angus went away to brood in his great Border fortress, Hermitage, taking his son from court with him to show his displeasure. It was not long before King Henry approached 'Bell-the-Cat' with invitations to London and persuasions to change his allegiance. Angus havered, although he did not yield, but there was one point when my siege guns had to make it plain to 'Bell-the-Cat' that I could not tolerate such behaviour. Altogether, it took four full years to persuade Big Angus that King Henry would never love him half so dearly as I did. And it was to be another fifteen before I was sufficiently confident of my own place in Scotland's affections to be able to take him by the arm in moments of emotional crisis and assure him in the presence of the rest that if I did have a favourite, it would be Angus 'Bell-the-Cat'.

Angus was not the only old ally who showed a fit of temperament. We had made Lord Lyle Lord Judiciar and given him no other office, for the law of the land was in such a state it would take all of one man's time to reorganize it. He expressed himself content with the appointment, and gave fine service to the Kingdom for the first twelve months. Then suddenly he joined Huntley and Lennox in rebellion, parading my late father's bloodstained shirt upon a flag-pole through the Kingdom, and calling upon King England to help them avenge Scotland's late Majesty. The only happy thing this proved to me was that Lord Lyle had not been a party to my father's death, for we were a superstitious generation and he would not have dared to take part in such a gesture had the bloodstains been of his causing. Otherwise, it was more work for my siege guns.

For all my boyish exuberance when I saw my siege guns bring tumbling down a piece of masonry, I had made the vow that out of all this rubble I would build a community so peaceful within a land so prosperous, that in future times our descendants in their hours of crisis could look back to my reign and reassure themselves that what had been done before could be achieved again. The scattered fires of rebellion, each quenched as it flared, began to tax my patience for I was anxious to show my mettle in a more creative fashion. Having quelled a rebellion, I was prepared to pardon the rebels, but Henry Tudor, who encouraged them, was another matter.

We had of recent years enjoyed a respite from England's efforts to subjugate us, due to her preoccupation with her own dynastic wars, and since Henry Tudor had come to the throne, he had for a while been more concerned to hold on to his own crown than to covet mine; but this happy state of affairs could not long continue. It never did.

I held few illusions about King Henry when I came to my throne, but at least he was a Welshman, and he had given some assurance to my father that he bore goodwill toward the Scots. At fifteen, trying to learn my job as quickly as possible upon an unstable throne in a disunited kingdom, I did have a secret juvenile hope that my princely neighbour would show me a kindness such as I would have offered him had our situations been reversed. Had he done so, he would have bound me by gratitude for my lifetime to safeguard his Kingdom's interests as I cherished my own. Instead, King Henry chose to poison my subject's loyalty with bribes, send supplies to the rebel strongholds, and attack my shipping within my own coastal waters. When I sent envoys southward to seek a Truce of friendship, he accorded it all smiling—and while it was being signed at Coldstream, he made use of the proximity to solicit treachery amongst my nobles. When I learned of this, I reduced its original term of five years to a mere eight months. It was the longest time we could hope to get honesty out of King England.

While Mars thus engaged my attention, Venus was not entirely neglected. There was immediately a scheme afoot to find me a suitable wife. Within the dynastic pattern of our times, I had done well to remain unwed at fifteen, and I could not complain even if to my mind a lot of better things could have been done with all the useful money collected from my subjects to buy me a bride. Parliament had levied a tax called Matrimonial to finance the costly exercise of sending ambassadors to search for a suitable lady. Their first visit, to the court of Charles VII of France, helped to restore the good will between us, broken at the death of my father, but while this was necessary and useful diplomacy, there was no French princess available. The Emperor of Austria, Maximilian, had a daughter Margaret, and his court was next upon the list for my ambassador's visitation.

Meanwhile, we needed a lady at my court to invite and supervise the noble young Scotswomen who customarily joined the royal household in search of eligible husbands. The predicament was considerable, for a bachelor King could not help them sustain the polite excuse that they came to attend my bath or to make themselves useful beside my tapestry frame. The only solution was to call in the Princess Margaret, my late father's sister, to act as the Realm's Royal Lady, until my much sought-after consort arrived to take care of my female subjects' matrimonial requirements.

Aunt Margaret was a lady of great character, of whom I had been terrified all my life. She was then in her mid-thirties, and therefore immeasurably ancient to my eyes. Tall and gaunt—she was the same height as my father—she had the unmistakeable Stewart long, straight nose and a mouth inclined to irony as much as tenderness. We were said to look a great deal alike, but this I could never see—although, in later life, I found that I had developed the same tilt to my head when walking: her chin was thrust forward to take life's punishment squarely while her eyes focussed upon some high and distant objective.

The Princess had been educated in a convent, although it was hard to believe the nuns would have approved of some of the ideas she expressed. She showed no inclination to marry and might well have spent her whole life in bookish seclusion had not my father, who thought the world of her, decided to bring her to Court in the hope of marrying her to one of his lords before her youthful charms had faded. She had, however, proved so unmanageable that he thankfully acceded to her request for privacy and independence, and he instated her in a house upon the Castle Hill in Edinburgh, where he visited her frequently. They shared a taste for music and astrology, and it says a great deal for her intellectual accomplishments that my meticulous parent could bear to enter the house he had given her, for she was incorrigibly untidy and it was always cluttered with innumerable books and impedimenta.

When I requested her return to Court, she came apparently quite willingly—leaving her house shuttered against her return—and arrived at Linlithgow Palace with her belongings stowed in shameless disorder upon a train of oxen carts. A rabble of untidy servants accompanied her, while she herself sat high upon one of the carts, totally oblivious of its lurching, as she read what may have been her breviary but was as likely to be a book which my Bishops would condemn as heretical. She looked like a tinker matriarch leading her tribe in from the wilderness.

The Princess proved, however, to have an unexpected talent for her task, and her female charges had their morals uplifted and their minds widened in a way they could not have enjoyed elsewhere. What manner of duties she gave them to do of a more feminine kind, I cannot imagine, for she herself could not bear to use a sewing needle. However, if their talent as embroideresses languished for lack of employment, they would go to their new households well equipped to keep their husbands entertained with anecdotes about Aunt Margaret.

I had at this time a deeply personal problem which could not be resolved so easily as that of my young female subjects. I had not yet known a woman. I was intensely shy about all sexual matters—I had been reared until puberty in a female household, and the discovery of my father's trait had been no help to me. I knew very well that my subjects would be delighted to have me prove my masculinity by siring a bastard—the more so, in view of my father's own sad reputation. It did not help that the only girls available to me were the daughters of the nobility, whose fathers, uncles and brothers all hoped to benefit by their daughters' elevation to the position of Royal Mistress. I did not intend to repeat my father's mistake in making favourites of either sex, and I had determined that no lady should ever share my bed to counsel me there upon State business; my personal and public life would remain separate.

The young noblewoman who most attracted me was my cousin Isobel, daughter of the Earl of Buchan, but that was the last connection which I wished to make more deeply personal at this time. It was unfortunate that my physical passions were not aroused until I had formed a deep emotional attachment, and that I liked only fine-boned, thinly-padded women whose bodies made the eye aware of their mortality.

Even if I had succumbed to one of these many invitations, the impossibility of having any sort of privacy in the matter would have dissuaded me from active collaboration. The formality required to put the King to bed was such that often I postponed retirement in dread of the interminable ritual that awaited me. Young noblemen who hoped to gain administrative appointments began their careers as Attendants to the Bedchamber, and it was in fact an exceedingly useful way to discover a man's personality and capabilities while he stretched my stockings upon my legs, or brushed my hair, or held the cup into which I dipped my finger to polish my teeth. Thus occupied, we talked of many matters. But it was a wearisome ordeal for a man wanting simply to go to bed after a hard day's riding and a formidable amount of work. The idea of bringing a woman to share the ceremony was more than I could face. To arrive when I was safely abed, she would still have to submit to the scrutiny of my bodyguard in the outer room; there was no place to hide her in advance within my chamber, and if there had been a closet, it would have been thoroughly searched for assassins. Even less promising was the prospect of visiting her by stealth in her own chamber, for it would be noticed within minutes if the King's bed were left untenanted, and the ensuing hue and cry to find my abductors would bring the entire Court to share our love-nest. Perhaps none of these problems would matter if one had a zestful approach to amours, but without this attitude I managed to reach the age of eighteen without ever having kissed a girl or squeezed her hand. I found I had quite a talent for bestowing flirtatious gallantries upon ladies contemporary with my aunt, but I had not one soft word to whisper in the ear of a blushing bedmate of my own age.

I was so desperate that I took my problem to Aunt Margaret. On closer acquaintance she had proved much less terrifying than I expected, and although unwed, she had been the recipient of my father's confidences and it was reasonable to suppose that if she could understand his difficulties, she was capable of dealing with my own. The dear woman rose to the occasion with such forthright common sense that I wished I had had the courage to consult her years before. I had decided on the girl I wanted—a lovely dark lass, Margot Boyd, who had given me several inviting glances when I visited Lord Lyle at Duchal Castle, in such a manner that I felt I could rely on it that her interests corresponded with my own. She was now at Court and it was only a matter of finding a way to bring her to my bed. This my aunt organized with a military precision so remarkable, I would willingly have entrusted her with the command of my army had my lords welcomed rule by Amazons. Her plan was that I should ride to Linlithgow for a day and a night, while she held back the Court at Falkland. I was to take with me but two gentlemen, leaving all the rest behind. The simultaneous arrival of Margot Boyd at Linlithgow would be organized by the Princess.

The whole scheme worked beautifully, and the loss of my virginity was an experience I would not have missed for worlds. Margot was two or three years older than me, which was a considerable help, and she was 'all but' a virgin, whatever that meant, with a sweet sympathy and understanding of my predicament which yet did not make her warm enthusiasm for my kisses maternal. I proved to our satisfaction that there had been nothing wrong with me at all.

It was wonderful to have somebody to love, for the Sovereignty is a lonely way of life. When Margot became with child, I took her firmly into my custody as my mistress, in full face of the world's approval or otherwise. The first child miscarried, but she later brought me upon my own birth date the magnificent present of my first-born son, whom I called by the royal family name of Alexander. He was a princely baby, and my subjects gave him as great a welcome as if he had truly been a prince.

My domestic happiness could not continue. My bishops were as pleased as any by the arrival of my son, but they were not by their profession allowed to look with approval upon the woman who bore him. Also, as they were obliged to dwell celibate—at least in theory—they doubtless saw no reason why their unwed monarch should not do the same. When Margot was again with child, the stern glances we received began gradually to diminish our happiness. I refused to part from her, however, until she had been safely delivered of our daughter, Catherine, whereafter I gave her a dowry and a husband of her own choosing, for she had no lack of suitors. When they were past infancy, I took my children into my own custody. I reckoned that in a society which decided inheritance through the male line, it was more important that a child should have knowledge of its father than of its mother. Also, Alexander was the son of a King and his place was in my household.

I was saddened when Blacader's embassy brought back the news that the Emperor Maximilian's daughter was already bespoken by the heir to Spain. There was an exceedingly warm message of regret from Maximilian and I replied in the same tone. Although I never met the man, through the next twenty years' infrequent correspondence, his heavy missives full of woe and harassment were to arrive upon my table like old friends plumping down to tell me all his troubles. He would have made a lovely father-in-law.

5

IT was typical of my Stewart luck that I should come upon the marriage market just at the time when there was a dearth of suitable princesses. Henry Tudor of England had offered me his niece; but I was determined that if dynastic policy had to dictate my domestic life, I would have no other but a true princess. I wanted none of the one-time Earl of Pembroke's Tudor relations. I told him I would have his daughter Margaret, who was barely four years of age at this time, and to my relief he refused me.

I was beginning to feel that I had had enough of Henry Tudor. He had made three unprovoked attacks on shipping within my own coastal waters; two were real sea-fights, and the English lost both of them to Sir Andrew Wood. Their ships were brought in as prizes, and their crews I released after a stern lecture to their masters. On the second occasion I sent King Henry's captain home with the message that I had twice pardoned his men, but I could not guarantee my good humour if it happened upon a third occasion: we had quiet at sea for some while. Although we were supposed to be bound by the terms of a truce, I had begun to feel that the auld enemy was less dangerous to our Scots Realm when not masquerading as anything else. And I had a good plan for dealing with the menace south of our Border.

The Plantagenet Dowager Duchess of Burgundy had written asking me to lend my support to a Yorkist Pretender to the English throne, her nephew, the younger of King Edward IV's two sons. One knew to be suspicious of pretenders, but there was no reason to suppose that Richard, Duke of York, was other than he claimed to be, or to expect that Margaret of Burgundy would claim an impostor as her nephew. Since Henry Tudor had strengthened his claim to his crown by marrying the boys' elder sister, now England's Queen Elizabeth, there had been no word out of England concerning the fate of either of the two lads who had greater claims to the crown than Pembroke's Earl (though one of the scullions in England's royal kitchens had once claimed to be the elder brother, Edward) but that was now adequately explained by the Duchess of Burgundy's account of the Duke of York's exile in Flanders. I was aware that Margaret Plantagenet had a strong reason for wanting to see the Tudor usurper displaced and her own dynasty restored; but that to my Stewart mind increased rather than lessened the likelihood that this man was her nephew, for the sense of clanship does not as a general rule substitute an outsider for the true heir when trying to restore a claim to a title.

Whoever he might be, I had reasons of my own to take an interest in the Yorkist Pretender. I could never know how many of our Scots lords had been in league with Henry Tudor in spirit if not in deed—I could, had I so chosen, have taken my uncle 'Hearty James' of Buchan, Huntley, Lennox and Lyle, even 'Bell-the-Cat', and gibbeted the lot of them along the Border as a warning to King England to leave my lords alone—but I had no mind to hang my own subjects to atone for Tudor mischief, and if I could find a way to embarrass King England in my lords' eyes, they would be less likely to pay attention to his blandishments. At this particular time—the year was 1494—Henry Tudor was not popular with his subjects. His lords and commoners resented his lack of royal birth, and he was reputed to be exceedingly avaricious. Also, now that the Plantagenet dynasty had ended, people were more inclined to remember its virtues than its vices. If the Yorkists had any chance of restoring a Plantagenet Pretender to the throne, this was the time. Whether I gave my active support or not, nothing would be lost by inviting the Duke of York to my Court, and a great deal would be gained by the embarrassment of Henry Tudor. In shaping my plans, I was unaware that Venus meant to take a hand in them. . . .

The Earl of Huntley, who was my father's second cousin, had two exceedingly beautiful daughters. I had never greatly liked the elder, Katherine Gordon, though I could respect her for her strong will. Her beauty was unquestionable: a white complexion and magnificent red-gold hair, combined with a pair of great dreaming eyes; I might have known she would find a dispossessed prince irresistibly romantic, expecially when that prince was a raven-haired, handsome young man with a sensitive face, an apt turn of courtly phrase, and a great appeal for the ladies. It was love at first sight.

I was not a cold-hearted dynastic schemer by preference, but Katherine's great beauty and her Stewart ancestry might one day make her useful to cement an alliance with a foreign dukedom. That would have been sufficient reason for forbidding the match, but I had personal grounds at this time for being sympathetic toward lovers caught in circumstances similar to my own; my real problem was—did Scotland gain or lose by having its King related, albeit distantly, to the Pretender to the throne of England? It would certainly secure the allegiance of the one-time rebel Earl of Huntley: with his daughter married to Henry Tudor's rival, Huntley would be in no position to pay heed to King Henry's overtures. And if my kinswoman married the Yorkist Pretender, it would be an added barb in Henry Tudor's flesh.

The Earl of Huntley viewed the prospective match with mixed feelings; while he would be greatly delighted to see his daughter become Queen of England, he was also exceedingly fond of his bonny Katherine, and the Pretender's success was by no means certain. His Countess besought me privately not to give her daughter to the Duke. I had sympathy with all sides in the matter. I warned Katherine that if the Duke were the true heir to England's throne, his prospects of securing it were balanced by the unwholesome future which awaited him if he failed; and I did not leave her in any doubt that my active support of his cause could not be counted upon simply because she was my kinswoman.

The authenticity of the young man's claim to be Richard,

Duke of York, was something which I never resolved entirely to my satisfaction. Certainly, those in Scotland who could claim to know believed he had strong Plantagenet facial characteristics. (It was unfortunate that there was in existence no portrait of my great-grandmother Queen Joan so that I might have checked for myself.) His own story, when I questioned him, was not lacking in detail as to how his elder brother had died of consumption and how he himself had been smuggled out of England some while prior to Henry Tudor's invasion. In Flanders he had lived in the house of a family called Warbeck, and it was as Perkin Warbeck that he was known until the Yorkist exiles reminded him of his duty to his late father's English subjects and his true right to the Crown. It was all as likely to be true as any other tale one heard.

Katherine married her Pretender amidst scenes of public rejoicing. My subjects had so far been deprived of my own nuptial festivities, so that I felt I owed them a spectacle. The bakers sold special small biscuits made of oatmeal, honey and ginger, stamped with a rough likeness of a crowned head representing the 'trew King of England', which the commoners called 'Perkins'. I derived much secret satisfaction from the thought that a report of it would reach King Henry from his spies based on Berwick. Even the Earl and Countess of Huntley looked more favourably upon the match when they saw that I meant to treat their new son-in-law as my Royal equal.

It was a heavy cost on my treasury to keep a 'trew king' in the state to which he was all too readily growing accustomed. The lad had no funds of his own, so I had been paying him a pension since his first arrival. Katherine had brought him a substantial dowry, to which I had contributed, but I now had to face the prospect of supporting what was virtually a second Court within my own, in order to demonstrate my faith in the 'trew king's' pretentions. Scotland would need to have real value for my money.

It was gratifying, then, to learn that Henry Tudor was disconcerted by the recent developments. Letters from his allies, Their Majesties of Spain, arrived at my Court in advance of the Spanish ambassadors who were travelling to Edinburgh from

London. I naturally opened the letters, and discovered that one of them was a covering letter for the ambassadors' eyes only, instructing them how to deceive me. (This chicanery was typical of Ferdinand and Isabella, and they thoroughly deserved the diplomatic embarrassment.) I was therefore on my guard when the ambassadors finally arrived at Linlithgow with the offer of a Spanish Infanta (whom I now knew to be betrothed elsewhere) and requests that I should abandon the Pretender's cause. They were exceedingly crestfallen when I handed over their letter, and there was not therefore a great deal to negotiate.

I have to confess, however, that I gave a warmer welcome to their gift of a sword and dagger, forged and tempered in Toledo of Damascus steel—the *espadon*, a double-handed battle-sword, was so marvellously balanced that I could use it single-handed with ease. These Toledo swords were highly valued, even among princes, and its cutting edge was so keen that I could slice through the low-hanging twigs of foliage in Linlithgow's park scarcely feeling their touch upon my blade.

While the Spanish ambassadors were at my Court, together with the Duke of York, a situation had arisen in my personal life as agonizing as it was ecstatic. On progress to the Palace of Falkland, I had met a party of our guests riding toward me; having arrived early they had set out to meet us upon the road. Even at a distance, the girl riding beside Lord Drummond immediately took my eye; I cannot say why, except that as soon as she appeared a strange kind of stillness had come upon me. I wanted to dismount where I was, and curl up on the grassy bank—a new feeling, as though all of James Stewart's private pilgrimage had ended safely.

The girl was clad in palest pink, trimmed with the copper hue of squirrel fur, and she wore not the hood now commonly the fashion, but the older type of head-dress such as my mother's generation favoured, shaped like an almond, with two loose veils of pleated lawn floating from its side points, and a gorget of muslin to hold it securely beneath the chin. This girl dressed to please herself, not to attract the eye, and with a pleasingly modest independence. As all women, she rode side-saddle, but I knew few who would have chanced their seat upon such a mettlesome roan gelding; I watched her with approval, admiring the magnificent control she had of the horse and the easy way she sat the saddle.

Our chance meeting was not the occasion for formal presentations, and when we arrived at the Palace I had many duties to attend before I could meet my guests. The first day of our arrival anywhere my tenants would always bring me news of the joys and disasters which had overtaken them since last I was among them; it pleased me that they treated me as their friend and would save up their grievances to present to my ear, and mine alone. It was not until the supping hour, therefore, between five and six hours after noon, that I had time to look about me and see who were my guests, and it was not, in fact, until after the meal that I could discover the identity of the young lady in pink.

I had no great love of food; one main dish usually sufficed me, and of that I took but little; I preferred ease of movement to a great, well-fed, bulky body and I managed to keep the same weight of flesh to my bones through all of my life. However, knowing that my austerity did not suit everybody, I would leave the table when I had finished eating so that those who preferred to continue might do so. I used to go into my own hall and there conduct what business I had until the great hall was cleared for the evening's entertainment. So it was upon this particular evening when I adjourned and later returned to my guests and courtiers, mingling informally as they awaited my return. As I entered, a scene took my eye upon the far side of the room, where the girl of the afternoon was determinedly resisting a kiss from the gentleman upon whose arm her hand had been resting. Her behaviour startled the rest of the company, while it amused and pleased me greatly. I was enchanted by the way she drew back like a deeply offended young mare, arching her neck with brittle hauteur and an avowed determination not to accept bit and bridle. I laughed aloud at the discomfiture of those who were with her—not one of whom had the least idea how to handle this girl.

I had, though. I knew it by the fire which had taken hold of my loins and heart and brain: this was *my woman*. And I walked straight across the hall to take her, causing a hush by my total disregard for all the accepted rules of social procedure. Others with her dipped their knee, or curtsied—but not she: her eye held mine as taut and steady as the fishing line is drawn between hunter and captive. She did not curtsey until I had reached her, when she bowed her head very low. I raised her by giving her my hand open, palm upward, for this girl's kiss I wanted upon James Stewart's mouth, not upon Scotland's hand. She laid her hand into mine; then she smiled . . . and I saw the flawless white teeth glistening with tiny effervescent bubbles between their edges, framed within firm and shapely lips. I had known this smile forever, and the dark eyes which shone above it with a mixture of amusement, fear, consternation and sheer helplessness.

I heard Lord Drummond present his daughter: it seemed to me, with the girl's eyes holding mine, curiously presumptuous of him to claim parentage of a girl who for all the time which mattered had been mine. I wished that all of them would go away and leave us together. But they could not, for I was the King and this girl was no Queen, but simply my guest and subject, and thus I had to treat her. I had her sit beside my chair, however, after my other guests had been presented, while we watched a company of jugglers and listened to the minstrels playing from the gallery. I was exquisitely contented just to have her sit beside me; I felt so close to the girl in spirit that physical communication between us seemed unnecessary.

She came out into the garden with me, later, and we walked together in the April darkness, her small firm hand resting confidently upon my arm. That we had left behind us a buzz of gossip was a certainty, but I did not care—nor, apparently, did she. Of what we talked I cannot remember—our calm together was more important than the words. It may have been then that she recalled to my memory—for she did recall it at some time— how our eyes had met, at Scone Palace, upon the day I was crowned King.

After my coronation I had been conversing with my lords in the hall when I had caught sight of a child of eleven or twelve, who came in from the antechamber through the crowd of women screening the door. Her buoyant yet modest air set her apart from the adults surrounding her and, as I watched her, she turned her head suddenly to encounter my eye. For a second we held each other's gaze as if the great hall had been emptied of everyone save ourselves. Then, realizing whose eye she held, she had curtsied in confusion and disappeared among the throng. I had never discovered who she was, but inexplicably that moment had remained my most vivid memory of that day. I knew now where I had seen before the glistening teeth and the eyes, and the independent set of the head—as I had known this great solace of spirit once before, although but momentarily.

I had not meant to kiss her yet . . . but it was in a moment when she was laughing, and her white teeth flashed against the twilight and the bloom of spring and the depth of the sky. The soft white folds of her wimple fluttered out like a halo of lawn about her pale oval face . . . she was the loveliest thing I had ever seen. I took her face between my hands . . . watching my hands and seeing them for the first time not as ghosts but as *my* hands, living and real, James Stewart's hands framing Margaret Drummond's face. We stayed thus a long time, with no word spoken. Then my fingers strayed into the hollow at the back of her neck, and I felt a small escaped curl of her hair coil round my finger, beneath the floating veil of white lawn . . . And that is the last I can remember until we broke apart because clothing became a reminder that we had in fact two separate bodies.

It could not have been many days before I took her to my bed; what brought us there was not passion alone, but chiefly that we could not bear to part after an evening in each other's company. It appalled me that so many others had to intrude for the nocturnal ritual of putting me to bed, but when I whispered as much to Meg, she replied, 'Can Yur Grace noucht dismiss yur ain attendants?'—which caused me to marvel at the absolute simplicity of life if one happened to be born other than a prince. It had never yet occurred to me that even I might have a right to privacy. What a blessing to me was this sweet girl's common sense.

I banned them all too eagerly, however—totally forgetting that my napkins and washing basin had not yet been brought, and my beard was untrimmed. I was horrified to think that this delicate creature would have to suffer my unwashed body and my chin in no condition to spare her gentle flesh, but she smiled and said she did not mind. One other thing I had forgotten—and this you will not understand unless you remember that all my life I had been dressed and undressed by others: I did not know what to do with my clothes when I took them off. There was nothing in the room to give me any indication; all I knew was that when I lifted my arms above my head, my doublet disappeared as if by magic.

I began with my surcoat, which I laid upon the bed. Then followed a jewelled gold shoulder chain I had worn that night, which I laid down beside the surcoat. I had pulled my doublet half over my head, when I realized that at this point it should have vanished, and here was the wretched thing, still there. With my head muffled, I was stopped by the realization that my clothes would either have to lie upon the bed, which I required for other purposes, or be laid upon the chair which I had given to Meg. I was baffled. What did happen to clothes once they had left the human body?

I felt kindly hands come to my assistance and draw the offending doublet over my head. I stood in my shirt, looking at her helplessly as she folded it up and laid it on the chair. She turned, and she was laughing—gorgeous laughter, her teeth flashing, her eyes running with tears, and her delicate skin flushed with merriment. I could not for a moment understand why she was so much amused—and then I realized that if one were allowed to attend to the basic human needs oneself—and I say 'allowed' for it is far different from being merely able—it would seem hilariously funny that a grown intelligent man of twenty-three years could not undress himself. I joined her in great gales of laughter at the ridiculous plight to which my royalty had brought me, until we rolled helplessly together to support each other. . . .

I could not have Meg call me 'Sire' as we lay together. Nor could I have her call me James, for this too was now my regal self. I suggested she call me by a name of her own choosing, and she called me 'Jamie'—without the contemporary aspiration which made 'Hiamie' or 'Hiemmie' the diminutive of James. As she said it with quick embarrassment the first time, her 'a' sounded more like an 'i'—'Jimmie'. It was a new name to me, quite enchanting because Meg spoke it thus; and thus we kept it, unchanged.

In those first days of April at Falkland, it was almost possible to believe that if I played my cards carefully, others would realize that James Stewart would be a better King if he had Meg Drummond to his side. Some may have seen it; but there was none prepared to let me forget that the price of my marriage bed was a treaty with some other of Christendom's princes. Everybody adored Margaret Drummond, and it was obvious to all that she had every quality required in a Queen of Scots—except for that one fatal blemish, that the Crown of Scots had nothing to gain from a union with Perthshire.

I took Bishop Blacader into my confidence. A handsome man, now in his thirties, he had an impeccable mien which made others seem ill-kempt by comparison. This crispness of person was reflected in his mental processes, which were quick to the point of abruptness. I knew he was a man I could trust; his shrewd, grave eyes would never leave my face until I had finished speaking, and no word or flicker of expression went unnoticed. I told him that I knew there was no woman upon earth for me but Meg; she was the only woman who could harness those emotions in me which would otherwise flail in all directions like the chains of a winnowing machine. I was not being selfish to the exclusion of my Regal responsibilities, for I knew my own strength and weaknesses, and I had known for a very long while that I could as easily destroy Scotland as I could make her great. If I had Meg to calm my torments, I could employ my energy and my brain constructively.

France had no bride to offer me; the Austrian Princess was already betrothed to Spain; England's daughter had been refused, and I had in any case grave doubts about the wisdom of any marriage alliance with England. The only hope offered, by Spain, was deeply suspect, even if—as Blacader pointed out—one could not predict whether the shifting tides of Their Most Catholic

Majesties' diplomacy might later leave one of their daughters high, dry and available.

He listened to me with his eyes narrowed, enigmatic, his jaw set. At the end of my recital he said little. Ours was a hard relationship, no quarter asked, none given. He reminded me that he had been away seven years on the quest for a princess; I remembered that his expedition had been financed by a Matrimonial tax upon my subjects. We agreed it would be necessary to seek Papal sanction for a marriage with Margaret Drummond, as her family was distantly related to my own; and there would be an immediate outcry from almost the entire Scots nobility—particularly from those who themselves had marriageable daughters. A dynastic alliance was their chief concern, not the settlement of my emotional problems.

I was born a loser. I had talked myself out of what small hope there had been almost as soon as I had raised the subject. My only course would be to wed her secretly and then to present her to my Kingdom as its Queen, but it was not my way to cheat the Scots. I instructed Blacader to go again as my ambassador to Their Majesties of Spain (he had been at their Court when their ambassadors had arrived in Scotland, negotiating for an Infanta), to secure a firm answer to the question of whether one of their daughters was available.

My brief dream shattered, I now realized that the only way to protect my bonny Meg from the jealousies of the nobles was to instate her formally as my mistress, as I had previously established my liaison with Marion Boyd. The King's Mistress had a recognized position, whereas James Stewart's lass had not. I sensed a great relief at Court as soon as I made it thus apparent that we meant to bide by the rules. I resented having to treat Meg in this way, and it gave proof of the depth of her love for me that she resigned herself to the unwanted prominence of her position in my Household as the unwedded lady of my affections. Once she was instated, I discovered to my joy and pride that she was extraordinarily well-qualified to lead Scotland's court society, and I delighted in showering upon her the honours and gifts that I would have given my Queen.

6

ISHOP BLACADER soon returned, having had no success whatever in his attempt to procure a straight answer from King Ferdinand. Their Spanish Majesties sent yet another of their ambassadors in his company, the further to waste my time with meaningless diplomacy.

The new Spanish representative I had intended to treat coldly, but I was disconcerted to discover that Don Pedro de Ayala was a man impossible to dislike. He reminded me greatly of my own Island chieftains in the lithe, graceful way he moved and the pride of bearing which is native to the Spaniard as it is to the Celt. His flashing black eyes were Spanish, and the aquiline nose suggested a trace of Moorish ancestry—but the engaging quirk of the eyebrows and mouth were a feature all his own. Here was a man who found humanity comic and endearing; he was amused by his mission, and I had the feeling he meant me to know he was not expecting me to take it seriously either. He was the oddest emissary I had ever received. What was most startling about the fellow was his patent honesty—a less likely qualification King Ferdinand would require in an ambassador I could not imagine, unless his chicanery had by now so confused His Most Catholic Majesty that he required one who could untangle it for him.

Within an incredibly short space of time de Ayala had become one of my chosen companions. He merely sighed gently when I told him that if he had come with the purpose of persuading me to abandon the English Pretender, he was wasting his own time as well as mine. The Yorkist sympathizers exiled in many kingdoms had been hard pressing me, as had their Duke, to invade England in their support, assuring me that King Henry's subjects needed but my encouragement whereafter they would rise for their Duke to a man. I was not altogether convinced by these arguments, but the fact remained that word out of England suggested that King Henry's popularity had reached what must surely be its lowest ebb since he usurped the Throne, and there seemed to be a reasonable chance that the venture might succeed.

I had formulated my plans carefully during the months the Pretender had been sharing my Court. I could see a great deal of use for this young man. Although he was not a strong personality, he gave me the impression that his people's welfare would be more important to him than his own glory as a prince: it was only latterly I had begun to learn that this royal quality was a uniquely Scots tradition. The main flaw in him as a potential king, was a sentimental regard for small issues at the cost of greater; this, however, could be mended by experience (perhaps), and with a strong woman behind him, the likes of Katherine Gordon, he might well make a wise and a fair ruler, whatever the secret of his birth.

We signed together a Treaty, he in the name of King Richard IV of England, by which I gave him my active support in exchange for the restoration of the town and fortress of Berwick and the indemnity of all cost to myself and my subjects of any campaign waged on his behalf. Somewhat to my annoyance he quibbled over the sum, which seemed to me exceedingly premature in view of the fact that restitution could not be made at all unless we were successful in our mission, and that meanwhile all the cost of sustaining our invasion (and himself and his followers) was risked by me. However, I was never prepared to argue about money. What chiefly concerned me was the restoration of Berwick, which King Henry had used too long as a spying base deep within my territory.

It was chiefly the commoners who supported me in any planned attack upon England. I noted all through my reign that the Scots commoner understood the ways of King England a good deal better than did our lords. Our lords England could use to his own advantage, and he was therefore more inclined to bribe them than to slaughter. For the Scots peasant he had no use at all, seeing him merely as an encumbrance upon land which he himself would have preferred to see a wilderness. The Scots peasant and the Scots King alone shared the uncomfortable privilege of being superfluous to King England's plans for Scotland.

News of my warlike preparation had reached King Henry, who made a sudden effort to mollify me by offering me the hand of his daughter Margaret, now aged six. I remarked to Blacader that if the child kept on growing and I stayed long enough unwed, we might yet have an English consort for sheer lack of any other mate. I spoke in jest; yet I was uneasy. I cannot say why—unless it was the 'lang ee' warning me; but I began to have a secret dread of that wee girl down in England.

We were to attack England in the early autumn, when the harvest was gathered. King Henry's fleet had been anchored off our coast for some months, but Sir Andrew Wood, whose experience made him an authority on the matter, told me cheerfully to dismiss from my mind whatever fears I had about the English fleet—it was in poor fighting trim to attack the mainland. I was inclined to dismiss its presence as a piece of bluff to deter me from invasion; and I further shared Sir Andrew's view that it would scuttle home with the first of the equinoctial gales. The English ships tended to be top-heavy, old-fashioned vessels, too close to the floating castles of mediaeval times to be either battle- or sea-worthy in our fierce northern waters. Our navy, small as it yet was despite my industrious efforts to increase it, could disperse any English raiders whose captains were intrepid or foolhardy enough to linger through into the gales of autumn, and the rocks of Scotland were enough to do the rest.

The success of our venture depended upon the amount of support given to the Duke's cause by the English once he crossed the Border. I made it quite plain that I was not prepared to do more than help him raise the English in his favour. Privately, I felt that it was no business of mine to impose a new monarch upon the English. In order therefore to discover how much support we could reckon upon, I sent down a force of cavalry mustered by the Border earls to stir the English northern counties. They reported back that they had met neither opposition nor a welcome. The Yorkists assured me that it would be another matter entirely when the 'trew King' showed himself in England —and it was possible they were right; at best of times, Northumbrian folk would be suspicious of the Scots, as were my Berwickshire men unlikely to linger for words with invading Englishmen.

Don Pedro de Ayala, as was customary when travelling, had brought armour with him to wear in the lists or for use in an emergency. His mission was, however, to repair the rift between Scotland and England, in whatever way that might be accomplished, and I was therefore surprised to be informed by my friend Tam the smith that among the suits of plate now being repaired, there was an elegant set much admired belonging to the Spanish ambassador. I thought it wise to enquire of de Ayala upon whose side he would be fighting. At this he gave a great laugh, although he apologized for not having yet asked my permission to accompany us. It was not unusual for allied or neutral ambassadors to be present as spectators during a war, but as de Ayala's express purpose had been to prevent this particular campaign from taking place, the glee with which he received my invitation to participate would not, I was sure, so well have pleased King Ferdinand.

We set out in September, having sent ahead the siege guns for use upon the English Border fortresses. We mustered on the Burgh Muir of Edinburgh, and all the townsfolk assembled to cheer us on our way, while the autumn sun shone brightly on the yellow and russet leaves of beech and oak which clustered thickly in a great swathe across the hillside. We had arranged to meet our Bordersmen at Ellem, and from there we sent out heralds to proclaim in the English Northern counties that King Richard IV was upon his way to London to reclaim the crown of the Plantagenets. To Ellem came secretly several messengers from the English minor gentry to offer their support—which, as I pointed out to King Richard, would have been a great deal more reassuring had they promised their assistance openly. I could not blame them for their caution, for I knew enough to suppose they were waiting to see what the Scots achieved, but I did not set much reliance upon volunteers too canny to give overt support. The heralds reported that their proclamations had been greeted with apathy in the English countryside, which was more disheartening, but King Richard assured me that once he had shown himself and our army below the Border, his new subjects would come flocking out to meet us. He might possibly be right, but I greeted his words with caution, reminding him that an army merely one and a half thousand strong was no use against King Henry except as the backbone of a considerable rising.

Once below the Tweed, we found a landscape barren of people, of herds, and of welcome. Across the straw stubble left by the harvesters, crows and ravens picked their fill of fallen grain, no living thing to disturb them save occasionally a stray hen, or a goat, which had escaped the fleeing herdsmen. We knew by these signs that all peasant life in the area would now be huddled away into the squat, black stone towers which their feudal lords were preparing to defend against us. Unless they chose to join us, there was nothing to be done except to raze them to the ground, for we dare not leave them behind us. We gave them the chance to surrender and to join our cause, but at each we met no welcome but a rain of arrows.

Against the reivers' raids, the black stone towers held their ground; against my cannonade they were inadequate. Hans of Nürnberg, my master gunner, brought up falcons and culverines, and blasted the wooden gates to splinters. Even the guns were barely audible above the din of lowing cattle, shouting men, and screaming women from the enclosure where they huddled amongst their piles of household pots, bedding, bags of grain, and sheep and hens and cattle and children. When my guns had gouged out the huge gates on either side, the cavalry and the infantry charged through, and the noise within died to a silence which could be felt as much as heard. Some while after, out would come our men driving before them the sheep and goats and cattle; then barns and ricks were fired, and a few more cannonballs would demolish what of the walls the flames had left standing.

It was atrocity of the kind that all of us, except King Richard, had seen before. De Ayala and I stood together watching at the third or fourth of these small sieges, as our heralds' trumpeters gave the inhabitants their alternative to destruction—as usual meeting only with defiant arrows spurting into the air from the fortress. We lifted our shields as protection against the arrows which sped our way, and Don Pedro observed that life nowhere afforded much joy to the peasant dwelling in frontier territory. He sighed, saying the iniquitousness of it depressed him whenever he contrasted the pleasures of his own life with the toil of his peasant tenantry.

King Richard irritated all who had experience of the Border raids, by taking no part in the assaults, appearing only afterwards to lament the innocent folk slaughtered by our soldiery. I told him there were no innocent folk upon the Border—thanks to the hate bred there by the Plantagenet 'Hammer of the Scots', which had lasted ever since his time. From the cradle, these folk were reared to hate and kill, and such as we slew now would have put to the sword my Scots with equal ferocity. I said that he should bear in mind the killing when he was himself 'King England'; if Henry Tudor had ever seen a typical Border raid, we might have had less hypocrisy when he talked of a Border Treaty.

Our alliance ended suddenly. In the presence of my Border Earls and the Spanish Ambassador, the Pretender struck an impassioned pose and demanded that I cease at once from further slaughter of 'his subjects'. At this I told him bluntly that in calling them 'his' subjects he presumed too much, for I could see none who showed willing to fight in his cause. At this he strode out of our company, and next was seen horsed and waiting for his followers' servants to bring out the baggage for their return home to Scotland. I was furious to be obliged to see him riding away into Scotland, back home to his wife at my Court, leaving me with a war upon my hands bereft both of purpose and of justification. To put a friendly monarch upon England's Throne had been worth a gamble; whereas to slaughter and burn in what was merely another Border raid, giving England reason for reprisal, left me disgusted—and bitter. The war had been undertaken to end the Border raids, not to perpetuate them.

To get the best possible Truce terms from Henry Tudor after this disaster, we should have pressed further into England, but we were hampered by the innate vice of Bordersmen of either side, who cannot separate their lifelong domestic business from their service to the Crown; my men had taken their chance to plunder, and herds of animals, together with bales of hay and whatever else the men had chosen to take home with them, were now in temporary pens surrounding our camp or else straying through our tents, while Hans and his gunners furiously repelled parties of curious cows interested in the siege operations. It was pandemonium. Had they been given time to take home their plunder, the men would doubtless have returned as loyal Scots to continue their King's war upon the English; but with the possibility that an English army might well be on its way to meet us, it was no time to let half my army slip away home on these compassionate grounds. I knew when I was beaten. It was impossible to continue the invasion hampered by this travelling menagerie. I gave the order to retire. The Scots army which should have set a friendly monarch upon the Throne of England, turned about and crept ingloriously homeward, like a nomadic tribe shepherding its flocks and herds before it.

We were back in Edinburgh within three days of the Pretender's arrival—and there, as the last bitter drop to my cup, I had to listen to Katherine Gordon, with wifely pride, extolling the compassion of her beloved lord who had been willing to renounce his crown rather than to expend the life of one more of 'his' subjects. That we now had open war with England did not appear greatly to alarm the Pretender, who, reunited with his wife, was settling down to winter comfortably in my palaces. I continued to pay his pension, for I felt it my duty to maintain him until fresh plans had been made for his future—he had, after all, served my purpose no less than I had served his. However I felt it only fair to suggest that we might providently reduce Household expenses by shipping home his retinue to Flanders. He was rather haughty about this, and his wife truly reproachful that I should lower the status and dignity of England's rightful King by denying him a Household sufficient to his rank. I marvelled greatly, wondering at what point gratitude changed to contempt for good nature.

I spent the months of October and November in the Borders with Hans of Nürnberg and Pedro de Ayala, preparing our fortresses for the attack by England. We received news of King Henry's preparations to invade Scotland; all he had needed was the excuse, which now we had given him. Pedro de Ayala did not accompany me only for my personal preference; I knew he would report on my Border defences to King Ferdinand, which might prove useful if ever Aragon's Majesty should encourage an English King to make war on France after reducing the Scots Border fortresses.

England's threatened invasion did not materialize. King Henry too had his troubles, not unlike my own. I heard later that his Cornishmen took great exception to being taxed to pay for a war upon England's northern frontier and came in force to London, whereupon Henry Tudor was obliged to turn and give battle to his own subjects. On hearing the news, I offered prayers of gratitude to God and St Ninian for those good men of Cornwall, whose purely selfish interest had spared Scotland great miseries.

King Henry showed eager to arrange a truce. He proposed, however, that I should surrender to him the Pretender. This, naturally, I refused; I would be happier without my guest, but I was certainly not going to deliver him to the uncertain mercy of the King of England. King Henry next suggested that I should myself negotiate with him in London. I knew full well, however, that sooner or later any courtesy visit of mine would be recalled as 'an act of homage', and the wearisome cry, 'Ye are my vassal!' would once more trumpet forth across the Border. No King of Scots could afford to go to London except on terms of war; and I had resolved from the beginning that I would never agree to meet any English King except at our common Border.

I had no alternative but to continue the war. I remustered my army, and we crossed the Border for a second time. Sparing the lesser forts, we laid siege to Norham Castle, the stoutest of the English border fortresses. Before we could reduce it, the Earl of Surrey came up with a formidable army and, knowing our own force to be too small to beat the English in pitched battle, we had to retreat before Surrey's army could come between ourselves and the Border. Thereafter Surrey based himself at Berwick, raiding our East Border March. The war had fallen into the usual, vicious pattern of all Border warfare. We remustered to march south, but we faced the same problem: we were outnumbered by an enemy whose population was ten times greater than our own. I and my Scots had to stand by helplessly while Surrey's men razed Ayton Castle.

I was weary to my soul of this brutal pattern of hostility between Kings, in which our Border subjects suffered every time. As I watched the burning of Ayton, there came to me an idea: I would end this war by engaging the English commander in single combat, the winner to take Berwick. I sent my herald to the Earl of Surrey, who, I was delighted to hear, accepted my challenge. True, I was risking my life, but I was a young man and a ferocious fighter, and—what was more vital—my instinct told me that upon this day my luck was running fair and that I would not die in battle.

My earls and lords thought otherwise. For half a day we argued. They asked, who could lead the country if I died? I told them that I would not die upon that day. They asked me how I knew. I was obliged to tell them, feeling foolish, that *I knew*. As ever, they would not accept this as an answer. Then they used the argument to which I had been trained in obedience since the cradle, that my life was Scotland's most precious possession. Considering my subjects' willingness to die in my service, it was extraordinarily difficult to persuade any of them that I had a man's right to return the compliment. Finally, in despair, they called in the Spaniard, de Ayala, to reason with me; although they might resent it, they knew his influence upon me was strong. Don Pedro reminded me of all our conversations, when we had discussed how we could best improve the world. He had, he said, seen no land other than Scotland wherein the rights of the humble man were so properly safeguarded; and it would be a tragedy for the poor people if a Prince who had the opportunity and the will to cherish and build on this tradition should be slain before his time. I should not rely on my instinct to see me safely through the battle, for my responsibilities were too great.

It was a powerful argument. I yielded to it. To my shame and chagrin, I had to withdraw my challenge. With my army I went northward, sending the Earl a message to say that for a Scots King to engage an English Earl was unequal combat; for while an Earl could die and leave his master's realm yet provided with a monarch, the death of a King would be catastrophic to his Kingdom. I apologized for my lack of chivalry in repudiating a challenge which he had honourably accepted, and I promised him that upon a day in later years, when I had sired an heir to succeed me, I would if he were agreeable renew my challenge. For a man of honour, it was truly the most humiliating day of my life. It was also one of the most depressing; my repudiated challenge seemed to hang over me like Damocles' sword all the way back to Edinburgh. I should have gripped it on this day when I knew my luck held; next time, I knew it, I should have to reckon with the Earl of Surrey on a day when my luck was out. And so it was to prove seventeen years later.

The English army came no farther. Defeated by winter and their own commanders' bad provisioning, Surrey's men deserted. Nor could I blame them. English leaders were notorious for their indifference to their soldiers' welfare, and it was a stock army joke that 'y'ane eatet like an English prisoner' when a man bolted his food.

We made a Truce with the English at Ayton Castle, to last for the next seven years. I did not secure Berwick, as I had earlier hoped, but we ensured that the treaty listed in meticulous detail all the functions of the Wardens' Court for the Border Marches and included strict rules concerning the surrender of criminals by each side to the other. We would never have peace at the Border until we had established the rule of law so firmly that two Kings could mend their difference at the Wardens' Court—whereafter we might hope that one day even our subjects might take their plaints to court instead of continuing their feuds.

The English Pretender was still at my Court. I agreed in the Truce to make no further active effort on his behalf, nor to style him King Richard IV of England; further than that I would not go, neither to surrender him to King Henry nor to deny him his title Duke of York if he chose thus still to call himself. I did not know what to do with him. If he would only renounce his claim to the throne of England—which did not mean confessing to an imposture—and submit himself to me as my subject, he could become a useful member of my Household, and in time I would confer on him a lapsed Scots title. To be a Scots Earl with a real homeland, where he could live out his years with his adored wife, seemed to me the best opportunity life could afford to the wandering Pretender.

He turned down my offer. Instead he went, with his wife, by sea to England where, after a vain attempt to raise a rebellion in Cornwall, he surrendered to the mercy of King Henry—who hanged him.

It was his end which finally decided me that there must have been some validity in the Pretender's claim. To my own Royal mind there was but one reason why a man would go to his almost certain destruction in his claim to a crown, which was birthright. Yon lad was a Plantagenet, sure as my own name was James Stewart. King Henry as good as admitted it by hanging him. An impostor he would have ridiculed—and me as well, for giving my support to the fellow; King Henry could have made far better use of Warbeck alive, had his name truly been Perkin Warbeck. But I do not know whether he was really Richard, Duke of York. Possibly he may have been a Royal bastard. The only person still alive who was likely to know the answer was Margaret, Dowager Duchess of Burgundy; her letter to me at the beginning had described him as being '*on de nostre sang*', which she avowed in terms that would have been blasphemous were the statement inaccurate. Many months after his execution I received a secretly delivered letter out of Burgundy from the last of the

Plantagenet Royal line; in it, she thanked me for my *'tendresse paternelle'* of which she had heard from his Yorkist supporters whom I had shipped home to Flanders. Of one thing you may be sure, he had somewhere English Royal blood in him: I would not have given 'trew king's state' within my court to a mummer fellow.

My war with England now ended, I was once more back at Linlithgow continuing the improvements to my favourite residence. I had started to rebuild this Palace in 1492, retaining the main tower and replacing the old bailiwick walls with a series of new structures built round a square green lawn, which was to have a fountain in the middle of it. On the south side, we had erected a new chapel dedicated to St Michael, with its fine tall lancet windows filled by panes of a new yellow-tinted glass that came, I think, from the Low Countries. This glass gave a constant sense of sunlight, and we used it a great deal at Linlithgow, so that all my memories are of apartments into which the sun appears always to be shining. All our efforts, however, failed to cure the odours in the east entrance passage—no longer used as the main entrance—and the removal of the stairway there to create a draught merely funneled the smell to make it worse than ever. In a way, I was not sorry; that familiar reek in the passageway held for me nostalgic reminder of my childhood and my youth.

My happiest memories are all associated with Linlithgow. It was there, through my bachelor years, that Bishop Elphinstone and I talked long into the night, discussing our great plans for law reforms; for educational facilities to include his new University at Aberdeen—Scotland's third such foundation—and the medical faculty to be established there. They were great, exciting days to be alive in a thriving, prosperous country such as Scotland was rapidly becoming. It was at Linlithgow that were spent the happiest weeks of my life with my lass from Perth, Meg Drummond—for it was at Linlithgow she bore our daughter in the gales and daffodils of March, just before the New Year 1497; Meg herself was of the March-born, indeed, she shared my birthday.

Meg was delivered of child in the bachelor King's bedchamber, the only woman save my consort to be thus distinguished. Later, with the babe in her arms—raven-tressed like her mother, but with a nose plainly showing Stewart potential—she was transferred to a bed erected for the occasion in the King's audience hall, so that all who wished might bring thither their congratulation. My chair of state I had placed in a position facing them, and all of that day I worked there, feeling no fatigue, as counsellors, courtiers and plain-folk mixed in a throng to have audience with their King or to compliment us as parents of the bairn. On the wall behind my chair hung a great Gobelins tapestry inherited from my father, depicting Our Lady with the Child Jesus upon her lap, and the thought occurred to me that a link between the tapestry and my own happiness served as a reminder of many things left forgotten by dynasts going in search of Royal brides. I felt that day as though I held all of Scotland in my arms as Meg held her baby, and I do not know whether our visitors too felt this sense of great love, but their share in our joy cast a radiance about the hall like the light from the yellow window glass. I wished they who came thus to honour Margaret Drummond had recognized how much Scotland needed her to be its Queen. My heart goes back to it yet, a golden room containing all of Scotland's happiness, glimpsed down a long corridor of time, before the door of duty closed upon it.

Our life together had been blissful while my courtiers indulged a pair of lovers so engrossed, yet with a love expanding to contain the rest of the world. Now another kind of atmosphere was building up around us; I began to feel that our enthusiasm had outstayed its welcome. There had been times, I confess, when I had secretly considered abdicating the Throne in my brother James's favour, rather than renounce Meg Drummond. My counsellors and courtiers were pressing me with ill-concealed anxiety to renew my search for a foreign bride. It was brought to my notice that King Henry's daughter Margaret was now quite a young woman, being all of seven years. I knew it; but instinct made stronger by my deep, passionate love for Margaret Drummond, knew that my Kingdom's survival depended upon

88

my not marrying the Tudor Princess. If the 'lang sicht' had only given me to know *why* that particular marriage would be death to Scotland, I could the more easily have argued against my lords in Council—who, after the Peace of Ayton, were prepared to welcome a marriage between the Crowns.

In panic, I asked de Ayala, was there hope at all of a Spanish bride? I was amazed, however, not to say furious, to discover that King Ferdinand and Queen Isabella had a poor regard for my personal morals. Poor Don Pedro put it to me as tactfully as possible, but he said that I would need to mend my ways if I wanted to wed an Infanta. Fornication was not uncommon among Christendom's princes, and there were doubtless some who let their ladies run their Kingdoms for them: my mistakes were my honesty of purpose and the fact I was supposed to be a bachelor. Don Pedro said Their Majesties of Spain set great value on discretion—and although I would not have accused the man of irony, his mouth noticeably tucked inward at the corners.

The trouble with King Ferdinand and Queen Isabella was that they personally were perfectly matched. Prudish, pious and fanatically ambitious, they would have mated by choice even had they not each been born heir to one of the two neighbouring Spanish Kingdoms. There was no breath of scandal ever touched the Spanish Royal House. Spain's King and Queen were sufficient to each other, and like most people whom fortune favours in this way, they were stern in judgement of those whose luck was less. What it came to at the end, was that if I wanted the privilege of becoming Their Most Catholic Majesties' son-in-law, I would have to renounce Margaret Drummond and let it be seen for some while that my ways were celibate and truly penitent.

It was, even then, a gamble which might never come off. It would not have merited consideration but for the fact that I could see no other way to escape King Henry Tudor's child.

I had always known that unless I could wed her I should one day have to sacrifice Meg. She would never take second place in my life to any woman. On that score I had made up my mind long ago. But to give up Meg while there was as yet no definite circumstance requiring it, was yet another matter; the bare thought of parting from her drove me almost to frenzy. Not de Ayala, not all my Bishops, could prevail in their disapproval to make me end my liaison with Margaret Drummond. It was only Meg herself, and my own cross-patterned sense of obligation, that could in the end bring me to terms with the need for our parting.

I discussed it with her as we lay together, unsleeping, her dark head to my shoulder and cheek, and her long hairs finding their way into my mouth as usual—it was a joke we shared, that I was always pulling Meg's long hairs from my tongue. As we shared in everything, we shared my duty to the Crown. And above all else, we valued each other's integrity. This kind of love cannot compromise, for if it did, it would die. What we had now to decide did not concern the outward appearance of our liaison: the matter was simply, did I care more for Margaret Drummond than I did for Scotland? And I had to answer: yes—which answer, I knew, would cost me Margaret.

Our last night together was both our happiest and our most wretched. It was the wretchedness which came uppermost as daylight broke, and the handbell was rung to stir me. Every morning of my life for twenty-five years I awoke to the celestial-sweet chime of this bell, but this morning Margaret and I lay unneedful to be wakened. It was our last moment together. I drew her toward me for a last, all too short embrace. Then my four closest personal attendants opened and secured back the bed-curtains, bidding us good day. Meg had always chosen to return to her own chamber to be dressed, leaving me to the attentions of my gentlemen; upon this day, however, the formalities were changed. Meg stood waiting—she would not sit—all of the while that I was washed and clad.

It was my custom every morning to take the heavy iron chain from where I had hung it the night before about the bed foot-post, and hook it about my waist. Nobody in the world, other than Tam the smith, was allowed to handle the chain but myself. Today Meg Drummond broke that rule for the only time. Quietly, when I was ready, she came from the corner where she had been standing close by the fire new-kindled with blazing logs, and took the chain before I myself could reach it. Without a word, her head bowed low, she came toward me holding the chain between her small hands; she put it about my waist and fastened the S-shaped hook into one of its links. Then, without a word or a glance, she bowed, turned, and left the chamber. At mid-morning, news was brought to me that she was gone— it was the best she could do for Jamie's Kingdom, whether it broke her heart or not.

I lived celibate with no difficulty. My clergy approved my new ways, but I doubt my counsellors would have been pleased to know that I was keeping faith with Meg: pain of separation was the last experience we had left to share together.

7

IN the New Year, March 1498, I left behind me the Palaces echoing with Margaret's absence, and set out upon my third visit to the Islands of the North West. Due to the Border wars and other commitments in central and north eastern Scotland, it had been four years since I last showed myself among the Islesmen—a lapse too long in view of the fact that I was now their feudal overlord since the forfeiture of the Lordship of the Isles to the Crown.

The Act of Forfeiture had been the only way that I could see to make this region become an integral part of Scotland. The legacy of the centuries when the Western Isles had been a fiefdom of Norway was such that it carried not only in fact but in its thinking the independence of a semi-autonomous community, which aired its grievances against the mainland as though Scotland had been a foreign nation. The natives had terrain to their advantage whenever they came into conflict with my Law's officers, of whom, in any case, we had a severe shortage in that area, and as their nearest Justice Ayre was at Inverness they could not too much be blamed for taking the law into their own hands when local clans offended their neighbours.

King England was never slow to exploit the situation in our north-western territory, and the last Lord of the Isles to succumb to English persuasion had been old John Macdonald, who, in my father's time, had gone so far as to swear an oath of fealty to King Edward IV of England. Old John was a wily, charming gentleman who had long been a good friend of mine, his misdeeds forgiven and forgotten; it was his nephew who had been the cause of the Forfeiture—once more raising the flag of rebellion, and plundering his way across the mainland to Inverness, where he had the impudence to breach the walls of my own castle there, and would have done more damage had not the Clan MacKenzie put him to flight. What most I needed in the North-West was a vassal to act upon his own initiative in keeping the peace there, and on these terms either Old John's nephew or his grandson in bastard line could have inherited the Lordship with my blessing; but when a claim to the Lordship served merely as an excuse to go rampaging across my mainland territory, the time had come for the Crown to put the Islemen's house in order. By Act of Parliament in 1493, the Clan Macdonald forfeited the Lordship to the King and the King's heirs thereafter.

As their new Lord I had gone to the Isles at the age of seventeen, with the legendary Stewart charm and my own spontaneous warmth to win them over. Also, I had the great advantage that I spoke their tongue—the first Stewart King to do so in four generations, for which I blame my great-grandfather's (James the Lion) eighteen-year-long imprisonment in England which had cut him off from what chance he might have had in youth to learn the language of his northern subjects.

The word *gael* means simply 'a highlander' and in my day there was no particular name for the old tongue spoken in our rural areas and among the Islesmen. Some called it Irish, but I myself knew it simply as 'auld Scots'—for it had been the auld Scots tongue until the eleventh century, when Malcolm Caen Mor's Queen, who was Hungarian born, had found the Celtic language difficult to master and therefore had cultivated Saxon as the tongue most used at Court. This rejection had led to the denigration of the Celtic language and culture, and the schism between our urban and our rural populace. It was common in my time for the southern burgesses to describe their kinsmen of the North-West as the 'wild Scots'—a disparaging term which enraged me. Our dainty folk of Edinburgh and St Andrews claimed not to speak a word of 'Irish' but I noticed many times they could when heated curse a Celtic-speaking traveller in his own tongue with marvellous fluency. I soon found a way to attack this urban superiority upon its own ground: whenever I heard anyone speak the contemptuous phrase 'wild Scots' I would find some reason to draw him close and amiably present him to others as one of my tamed or 'breckit' Scots; and it was astonishing how deeply this gave offence to a man, far more than if I had accused him of being wild. After a while I noticed that the term 'wild Scot' was no more used in my hearing.

I have in my head an isolated memory of a ceremony that I can but conclude must have taken place upon my second visit to the Isles, when my reasons for being there were to further my acquaintance with my clans' lieges. It is in the clear, chill early morning of a summer day, with the sun not yet risen sufficiently to dry the heavy dew from the grass. A castle wall is behind me, and I am walking out toward a rough stone set in the field, which is surrounded at a distance by a semi-circle of mounted clansmen dressed in the long coats of chain-mail then worn by our Island chieftains. I never used a train-bearer, even at my crowning, for I preferred always to manage my own robes—and on this occasion I am wishing that I had thought to pick up my furred velvet mantle, and take it over my arm, for it drags upon the wet grass behind me. Also, I am more than usually conscious of the diadem upon my head, for my stately processional glide—setting first the balls of my feet in order to slow the pace—is uncertain upon the rough moorland turf, so that I am tempted to glance downward instead of looking straight ahead of me, and the Bruce's large crown makes its presence felt by its weight. It is a very long way across the grass to that rock; and everywhere there is silence. Deep silence, not only of the hills, but of the intent, motionless clansmen upon their close-reined horses. When I reach the stone, I find the covering square of blue-purple cloth is made of four strips, like a frame, so that when I sit down the uncovered middle of the stone is chill to my buttocks. There I take my oath in the Auld Scots tongue, and a great clamour breaks out among the clansmen who are answering it, as though taking part in a liturgy. I am vowing to guard their interests, as Lord of the Isles.

I meant that oath. There was work to be done, bringing the culture of the Islands forward in time to combine its great spiritual wealth with the material development of the southern Scots urban areas. My new castle at Kilkerran, in Argyll, was more than just a fortress: to me it was the beginning of a city. Peaceful folk, drawn to dwell in its shelter, would establish there a hamlet. The hamlet would grow to be a town, and subsequently a burgh with its charter to engage in foreign trade. Kilkerran was but the first of what I hope would be a chain of such castles linking the mainland to the Islands.

Meanwhile, I was building up a fleet of fast galleys—which were more reliable in these rock and gale infested waters than any sailing vessels. The galleys would patrol the seas between the islands, ensuring peace and safety for the law-abiding; and my chain of fortresses would become their provisioning stations. In course of time, a small stone jetty will grow to be a harbour; a harbour used not only by the local fishermen, but by the trading vessels plying between the Islands and the mainland—and one day, so went this great dream of mine, the ships of Venice, of Iceland and of Middleburg in Flanders would think it worth their while to chance rough seas in order to secure the Islands' salt fish, wool and hides, and the exquisite Celtic patterns wrought in tapestry and silverware. Within my lifetime (pray God) we would end the division between the Islands of the North-West, and the mainland, and all would become one Kingdom with its every corner linked with the outside world.

In 1498 the barriers between the two parts of my Realm were not merely historical and lingual, but also physical. The chain of Great Lochs which lie in a line from Inverness to Lochaber were joined at the southernmost end by the Forest of Mamur, while the more northerly land bridges were wild moorland, perilous to winter travellers. The best route was a track upon the edge of the Forest, but even there the wolves and wild boar made travelling become a hunting expedition more safely than a solitary enterprise. Mamur (or Mamore) was true forest, of the kind elsewhere now gone from Scotland; ancient trees, many tumbled and rotting, woven into a dense mass with creeper and briar, all tangling with thorn undergrowth and whatever else chanced survival in the battle for light and growing space. Whatever happened there was left to happen, be it animal or vegetable, and some extraordinary varieties of plants grew there, all ogres of their species. Travellers kept to the narrow track between the loch edge and the darkness of the forest, guarded yet by an old round tower buried in the trees which had belonged to men of ancient times.

This geographical feature of the land split my Kingdom in such a way that one third of it, the North-West might well have been a foreign land to the burgesses dwelling in central and southern Scotland. Equally, the clansmen of the Islands had little interest in laws made by a Parliament in Edinburgh, away at the other end of the world. My problem was to administer all these territories fairly, so that none of my Scots should feel neglected. I often wished there had been a plurality of James Stewarts to keep an eye on all parts of my Kingdom simultaneously; wherever I went personally, we contrived some way to have peace, yet no sooner had I turned my back than all the sparks flew up again which I thought that I had dampened. I never doubted that they all, as they claimed, loved me; I just wished they were as eager, for my sake, to love each other. I travelled widely, and I dare claim that I knew more of my subjects by name and more of Scotland's towns to call my home than any King before or after me; but I needed to have deputies, for even I could not be everywhere at once.

I had Old John of the Isles in residence at my Court for a long while (until finally he retired into a monastery) and during that time I had talked with him extensively about the administration of the North-West. We had agreed that the Isles required an administrator locally based—and, indeed, Old John himself could usefully have served me in that capacity, had I not known that sooner or later his clansmen would have risen to reclaim for him the Lordship even without his own encouragement. This was my worst of all problems, to find one man who could gain the trust of the Islanders without forfeiting mine. The only leader they would accept from their own kind was the hereditary leader—

birth being nature's lottery, and therefore acceptable to a people like the Scots who have no innate sense of inequality. But anyone remotely in line of succession to Old John, would have been thrust into the middle of a rebellion against the Crown before he had been many hours its deputy. The best solution would have been to appoint several people to act in council, but I could not do that until I was certain which of the clan chieftains could be relied upon to serve my interests, and which were unreliable: any premature mixing of loyalties, and the clan wars would begin again in earnest.

I therefore devised a plan, an interim measure, to bridge our changing times when tribal loyalties had to become national loyalties without loss of character. To feu my lands—for it was still a time when authority was tied to land investiture—I would appoint as deputy the Earl of Argyll. Now, the choice of Argyll was part to my plan; not only did he hold lands in the North-West, therefore dwelling close by the clansmen, and have fluency in the Celtic tongue—he was also the grandfather (and his son later the uncle) of the hereditary 'heir' to the Lordship of the Isles. Argyll's daughter had wed Wild Angus, bastard son of Old John Macdonald, and the issue of this match was Donald Owre, *Donoul Dubh*.

I had known 'Black Donald' since my boyhood at Stirling Castle, a blue-jowled, melancholy-visaged lad with the pallid white Celtic complexion. He was a rare mixture of pride and humility, torn by the conflict of his birthright when he had to confess to me that he had almost no knowledge of his native tongue, having been forbidden to speak it by his grandfather, Argyll, who had reared him. He had now grown up with the elemental sophistication of the highlander set down in urban society, who yet can tell the difference between what is good and what is fashionable, but who will not accept himself upon his own terms for fear he be thought a rural primitive. All the tragedy of Scotland was in Donald Owre: together with all its virtues. Like myself, he was the 'interim man' which is thrown up by a clash between two cultures, or between two epochs. I had a use for Donald Owre.

I put Donald to be my Keeper of Tarbert Castle. My Lords of Council criticized me for the risk that I was taking, and prophesied that within a year the lineal 'heir' (he was not the heir at all, according to my Parliament in Edinburgh) to the Lords of the Isles would be the leader of a new rebellion. I myself did not think so; I knew Donald; and I was willing to take the risk, while he learned to know the needs of his kinsmen—and their tongue. And I was proved right; Donald made an excellent Governor at Tarbert.

Meanwhile, I used his uncle—his grandfather now being dead —to appoint as my deputy in the North-West under the formidable title of Governor-General. He could feu my lands to suitable holders, as an *administrator*. This word I underline because it denotes a new way of thinking, gaining hold on our times, that land and authority could eventually be separated (those young men we had put to school to become the morrow's lawyers were of that ilk who would transfer this same custom painlessly)—but as in all times of change, language does not keep pace with men's thinking. This became apparent when I talked with Argyll about his duties.

Argyll was an intelligent man who could recognize the changing times and thought he saw ahead of them. All over Christendom small land units were amalgamating beneath a centralized administration, and he saw this as the very proper way that government must be conducted in the future. He complimented me upon my statesmanlike initiative in recognizing that the Island of Barra must be ruled from Edinburgh. I was aghast, for that was not what I had meant at all. I said that what I meant was that Barra should take responsibility for itself as a region of *Scotland*. I was trying to explain the difference between self-control and submission: Argyll was making the definition between tyranny and neglect. We were both in the right: simply, we could not understand each other's interpretation of the words we used. The fact that we argued in the tongue of our day does not alter the meaning of the words I use now to explain our difference of opinion.

We both had to do the best we could within our understanding; I had my Parliament appoint Argyll as Governor-General of the

North-West, to include the Isles—this combination of the Islands and the mainland to suggest to all its inhabitants that they were Scots, irrespective of geographical and historic differences. He would set my lands, and discover for me those chieftains I could trust to become Donald Owre's advisers when the time was ripe to make the latter my Governor General. Argyll did not know the plans I had to use Donald Owre to rule his once-hereditary fiefdom; nor did Donald Owre. I knew that I was thinking ten, twenty—a hundred years ahead of my time; I thought always ahead of my time, and I had learned to cau' canny when elaborating upon my plans to others. If it were known that a decade later I would put in Donald Owre as the Islands' administrator, some of his kinsmen would leap too fast to turn the whole process backwards by acclaiming him their feudal chieftain in opposition to the Crown. We needed a spell of strangeness to break the link between the old and the new way of thinking: Argyll's administration was to be the spell of strangeness. All I could hope was that he understood modern times in the same way as I did.

Ironically, it was in the 'auld Scots' tongue that I made the most progress toward the future. Talking with the Island chieftains gathered at Kilkerran, there were no temporal barriers to obscure our thinking. Celtic time is all time; and in a language which defines love in nine different ways, yet has never invented a word to mean 'no', it is possible to get to the heart of matters.

It was not alone my interest in language which caused me to take great concern for my Celtic-speaking people; they used a wiser tongue than our Scots amalgam of Saxon, Norman French and Celtic. And it was this ancient wise tongue that would be lost to us unless now, while there was yet time, it was garnered carefully. The most urgent problem was that there was no written form of the Celtic language except in Irish characters— which was known to a few, but could not be promoted for lack of teachers. What few were scholars in the highlands were great scholars imbued with a precious love of their cultural heritage; the rest were illiterate. And while the Celtic spoken tongue could safely be relied upon to carry forward its culture, there was no insurance against death of men unless it were the new invention of *imprinting* down in England which had opened up a way for books to be written that would perpetuate the vocal culture of urban life. We had to move fast if the Celtic speech were to be retained in our working life of Scotland—and it had to be retained, for I did not want men like Donald Owre to be humiliated by the term 'wild Scots'. All my Scots were precious to me.

I talked with these men at Kilkerran, seeking their advice and giving mine. It was more than talk of smoking and salting fish, of tanning hides and shearing wool—our three foremost exports (we had the potentiality of one of the richest nations in Christendom at this time): we spoke of the continuance of human life in the islands called 'the Hebrides'. What we needed was a Celtic university, where the remaining Celtic scholars could gather to adapt their language in its written form to match our moving times—its spoken form would take care of itself. There would need to be grammar schools established on the Islands (in these new burghs of mine that would rise around my fortresses) and from these local grammar schools would pass the sons of clansmen to become students of our Celtic university. Proud young men, they would take their Celtic learning back to their Islands as advocates and physicians; or they would go on for further study at the foreign universities of Padua and Würtenburg. My long vision held the day when lads from Italy and Germany would pay a visit to the thriving cities upon Uist and Lewis where lived their former classmates now in practice as professional men. It was yet a very long way ahead of us, but I had laid the first stage of this glorious Scots future already: why else do you think I had petitioned the Rota to upgrade the Abbey of Iona to cathedral status? Where would we put a Celtic university except upon Iona, blessed by the foot of St Columba—that ancient Isle, so old that even its stone has been green forever?

It was sometime during these talks with the Islesmen, in their tongue, and with the timeless embers falling in the fire, that I dared to ask—what would they say to having as their Queen a woman who was but a commoner? (I meant Margaret Drummond; there could be no other.) At which, an old man, clutching his harp of the small Celtic kind—he was uncle to one of the chieftains—leapt to his feet, and directing upon me the opaque stare of the *faidh*, cried, '*Tha beatha 'na do chridh, ch'an'eil 'na do cheann!*' And there I had the truth of it, as I had always known: life and wisdom, for me, truly were of the heart and not the head. When I let my head take precedence I made mistakes: my heart's instinct never failed me. There I vowed to myself I would have Meg to be my Queen. . . .

Alas, to find it was another climate of thinking to which I returned, when I came back to Edinburgh. It was more than a change of climate and of language: it was the difference between a living people and a dead one.

The pestilence had struck my fair city of Edinburgh during my absence. The worst was past when I arrived; the sealed gates were opened, and the pale face of its surviving population was peeking from the shutters to smell the acrid smoke of paper burnt to clear the air of contagion, too benumbed as yet to feel the absence from its family circle of those whom the death cart had carried away. There is no way to write of my beloved city of Edinburgh in that summer of 1498; one had to see the dazed folk counting up their number who had lived through it all, while I had been away. There is no way to describe the impact of the plague: all I can do is weep for it, as I write, all of these centuries later.

At the age of twenty-five the Scots King came formally of age. Scotland's sad history of too many minor rulers had brought about the custom of giving its King a chance then to undo grants and laws made during the years of his minority. Every item of Parliamentary business passed during his reign was automatically repealed and then reviewed, either to be enacted again or disqualified. It caused a tremendous amount of work for everybody, and quite a number of old quarrels were once more taken out and shaken vigorously, but it was the best way to give Government a thorough spring-clean that any nation had ever thought of. It was also true that not only the King but a good many of Parliament's members welcomed the chance to improve upon a decision which they had made in earlier years. I seem to remember a great deal of laughter during the several days' assembly to deal with all this business, so I think we must have cleared up our past mistakes with brisk good spirits. It was an excellent way to make sure that neither the Kingdom nor we ourselves stagnated: trust the Scots to make a virtue of necessity.

I commissioned a new portrait appropriate to the occasion from a French limner called Jacques le Boucq. Le Boucq was a small, dark slip of a man, harassed and nervous in his intense passion for his art. In making his preliminary sketch he was insistent that it should include my hands—with which I at once agreed, for I had always felt that they were my most important feature. There was already a portrait of me, supposedly of myself as a child, kneeling behind my Royal father, in which the artist had captured perfectly the pose of my hands in prayer: I could never put them flat together for the width between my finger and thumb levered apart my third and fourth finger.

The face he drew superbly. It was the best likeness yet made. I faulted it only for the left eye, which I said he had made to look odd. He gave me a strange glance and asked, would I have my attendant bring me a looking-glass? Surprised, I compared my reflection with his portrait, and realized that my mother had been right when, long ago, she warned me that if I continued to raise my left eyebrow independently of its partner, one side of my face would ultimately fail to match the other. It was true, and in the portrait, my left eye had greater depth of lid than my right, having been stretched by my upward-shooting eyebrow. I apologized to le Boucq and complimented him upon his honest artistry.

It was a tragedy that a portrait which began so magnificently did not complete its own intention. It was the hands which defeated him. He failed to catch their skeletal quality, which had made him so much want to draw them. He had not listened when I told him he must begin drawing my thumbs at the wrist. Poor fellow, he was bitterly disappointed.

It had comforted me greatly for the expense of my recent war with England, to know that while I was attending to matters upon the North-West Coast of my Realm, there were three Scots and three English Wardens keeping a trained eye upon potential trouble-makers in the Border Marches. I was therefore not at all pleased, shortly after my return, to have news brought to me of an incident involving the Governor of Norham Castle, which was an English fortress owned by the Bishop of Durham.

Three lads came to me with their tale of woe, outraged and indignant over the fate of their comrades slain by the Governor's men. They were all about sixteen; one had a finger shorn of its two top joints, and another had a bandaged head with so much fresh blood seeping through the linen I suspected he had given it a daub of goat's or sheep's blood in order to impress me, for otherwise he would have died at my feet of blood shortage. (I was learning by the age of twenty-five to take what my subjects told me with a pinch of salt when it had to do with the wickedness of Englishmen, or a clan fight with their neighbours.) It was a terrible story, how the Governor of Norham Castle, unprovoked, had sent out his men to make an attack upon their small company. I asked, what were they doing in the first place so close by Norham Castle? They were shocked by my question, assuring me that they went there innocently, merely to show a friendly regard for Englishmen dwelling so close by our Border. Eventually, however, the tale came out. They had not *done* anything; merely they had stood, a long line of horsemen, upon a hillslope, silently contemplating the English fortress. Then a few had ridden closer to take a look at its outer defences, and made a show of reporting back to their comrades. They had spent an entire afternoon engaged in this fashion. The next day they had returned to repeat the performance. I was not surprised that the Governor's strained nerves, after two days of these antics, had caused him to send out a party of his men to enquire what they were up to. The Englishmen, and this I could well believe, had hardly been polite about it; whereafter had followed an exchange of insults, after which, blows—and both sides were soon fighting for their lives, of which my Scots lost several, being outnumbered.

There was a court joke about the feuding clansman alleged to have pleaded with his judges to hang him rather than submit him to His Grace's eloquence—and it was true, I did have a streak of the schoolmaster. I admonished them now, these lads whose silly prank could easily renew the war upon our Border. They were good lads, just a wee bit young and irresponsible: I, who had been ruling my Kingdom at sixteen, knew what irresponsibility could cost upon the Border. So did they by now, with their friends and cousins dead. We parted good friends, and I told them I would see to it that the kinsfolk of those slain had reparation.

I was angry, though, against Norham's Governor, a highly officious gentleman whose bustling reputation may have been the reason why these young rapscallions had gone out there to annoy him. Their behaviour must have been unnerving, but he could have known that a dozen lads openly displaying themselves on horseback were more likely to be there for devilment rather than as trained scouts for an approaching army. A welcome to the castle would have shamed and tamed them better than my lecture. It required so little to make Scots and English friends on equal terms, but such as Norham's Governor were not helping us.

Lord Hume and Lord Darcy, the paired East Wardens, would arrange matters through the Wardens' Court; meanwhile I wrote a strong but courteous letter to King Henry advising him of the incident—to receive, in return, an equally pleasant letter telling me that my news was grievous to his ears, and that he would instruct the Bishop of Durham to attend me to discuss reparations. This extremely civilized exchange brightened considerably my view of England as a potential friend and, possibly, a future ally.

My Lords in Council were most impressed by the new spirit of co-operation, and began nibbling again the idea that Henry Tudor's daughter might be the means of consolidating this happy atmosphere. She was now eight (I was sure she was growing up more quickly than was natural). I protested once more, but the only alternatives were daughters of Dukes and minor Kings who were of neither dynastic nor geographical value to Scotland. A marriage to England's daughter could promote peace along the Border, but there was nothing to be gained from—say—Ferrara or Savoy. I saw the net closing in upon me.

I went to the Abbey of Melrose to receive the Bishop of

Durham. When we had discussed the matter of reparation to the kin of my slain subjects, I raised the subject of King Henry's daughter, Margaret. I was so reluctant, I had been speaking for several minutes before the good Bishop comprehended the question I was trying not to put to him. I was also slightly embarrassed to have to admit that I had been trailing my eligibility round Europe for ten whole years, without a single purchaser: I was starting to wonder what was the matter with me. The Bishop could not himself advise me about the availability of the Princess, but he gravely undertook to carry my enquiry to his master.

I rode home with a heavy heart; but I believed even yet a miracle would happen to save myself and Scotland.

8

NEGOTIATIONS for the marriage alliance with England pressed inexorably forward during the following year. It was typically a case of my saying 'Y . . . e . . . e . . . s', meaning, 'I will give thought to the matter', and then finding out too late that everyone had taken my assent as final. I suspect that many another bridegroom has found himself trapped in the same way.

The child now was in her tenth year, well nigh a woman by Royal standards. I tried to discourage King Henry by pressing him hard for a larger dowry, hoping this would offend him as a father or as a miser: it did neither. I think he approved my effort to drive a hard bargain for his daughter's hand and therefore enjoyed the more beating down my price. Henry Tudor, while he may not have been princely, was a formidable statesman, and I felt strong forebodings when the English, during our negotiations, seemed unnaturally warm toward the marriage. They held out as an enticement the promise that as Margaret's husband I should be third in line presumptive to England's throne. I reminded our Lords of Council of the ancient caution 'Noucht ane guid cam furth of England'—and was asked, did I mean to teach our old Scots proverbs to my English bride when she arrived? It was as near as anyone dared go to being impertinent. At times I felt that only my inherited Royal distrust of King England stood between Scotland and our hidden, fearful future. We were walking blind into a trap—I *knew* it: King England gave nothing ever to the Scots which was not a bait with a hook inside it.

I had abandoned my fidelity to Margaret Drummond. Abandoned it for Scotland's sake, not for my own. Nor for hers. She had wed no other. I knew she waited yet in her father's castle of Stobshaw, hoping, as I did, for a miracle. There was not a day or a night after we parted but the longing for her would come upon me suddenly, so intense that I felt it as a physical blow to the heart and stomach. I could not have believed that one human being could so completely engross another.

It was for this very reason that I took another mistress. As King, I could not afford to love one of my subjects above all others. Because of this, Meg and I had parted, and it made our sacrifice valueless if in her absence I loved her no less strongly. I had to have another woman to distract me, not to replace her. But I found it exceedingly difficult to feel the least enthusiasm for any other girl, and it was not until I met the Earl of Angus's new mistress that a look flashed from her eyes which raised my excitement.

I would rather Janet Kennedy had been the mistress of any other but 'Bell-the-Cat'. It was an unlikely liaison temperamentally. Janet was too hard for a sensitive nature like Angus's, and she made him miserable so often and so obviously that even she said frankly that he would be happier without her, and I had no doubt whatever that she was right. And Angus seemed almost relieved to lose her, which comforted my qualms.

Our relationship succeeded because Janet Kennedy had met her match—and admitted it. I was gentle where gentleness succeeded, but with a warrior like Janet it was the firmest 'no' that brought results. Neither her tantrums nor her sweetness and cunning could move me, and she was game enough to yield and play it like a woman when she had to, in the hard male world she loved to fight. I think she loved me—in fact, she proved it, in the long years afterwards when she waited loyally at Darnaway or Bothwell Castles, preferring to stay unwed and lonely rather than sacrifice the five or six days and nights in the year when I would ride to visit her.

I felt at times that Time itself bore a grudge against me, for whenever the time was ripe for one thing to happen, everything else overtook me simultaneously. At a time when I should have been present in the North-West to ensure the smooth working of the Islands' administration under Argyll, I had instead to remain in the south of Scotland, where I was within easy calling distance of King Henry's ambassadors from London. This caused me considerable unease. My task, as I saw it, was firstly to unify Scotland; secondly to establish a comfortable working relationship with England; thirdly to bring Scotland into closer communication with the Continent. But faced with the alternative of attending to the Islesmen or to King Henry, I felt obliged to give preference to the latter: the Islesmen were my subjects, and therefore, I hoped, more to be trusted than England's King.

Throughout my reign I was dogged by the same problem: my two trouble-areas were set at opposite ends of my Kingdom. The peace along the Border was uneasily maintained at any time, and no sooner had I turned my back to give attention to the Islesmen, than there would be an incident of some kind upon the Border. Worse, I was playing a diplomatic game of considerable consequence at the Border, for the Royal Marriage was shaping itself around me all too fast for my liking, and I still hoped that, after using the match as the reason for the exchange of our ambassadors and the conclusion of a strong peace, I could escape from the marriage itself. I played my game of appeasement rather too cunningly, however, and found myself hooked in consequence. I was married by proxy to the English Princess Margaret, in King Henry's Palace of Richmond upon the River Thames by London, on January 25th, 1502. My as yet unseen wife by proxy was twelve years of age.

The year 1502 was the worst of my memory. For a moment it looked as if I might yet escape before the completion of my nuptials, when the heir to England, Prince Arthur, died in April. This was the worst possible thing that could have happened, in some ways, for it could make me second in line presumptive to the English throne; at the same time, it gave King Henry very good reason to think twice about the marriage. I took heart, expecting him to begin a graceful withdrawal from his commitment, and my alarm increased considerably when he showed no signs of doing so: what had the wily Tudor seen, which I had overlooked, that gave England the advantage over Scotland? I wracked my brains over it, even resorting to roaring at my Lords of Council that they were a pack of overtrusting fools when they tried to reassure me that the English merely wanted peace as we did. I told them flatly there was nothing King England ever wanted but the ruination of my Realm, however it could be achieved. I can remember standing by a window, looking down upon a greensward, and the knowledge ringing through my head as loud and clear as St Giles's bell, that unless I could stop this marriage before it went further, Scotland would one day have cause to curse the name of Stewart.

To add further to my troubles, the pestilence struck Edinburgh. All of that spring and early summer it had been festering in small pockets through the Lothians. At such times the atmosphere altered completely. I saw a boy of some eleven years collapse in a faint upon the cobbles in the market place of Edinburgh one day in 1502, due simply, I think, to lack of air in the dense-packed throng. In normal times a crowd would have gathered, some to be the good Samaritan and others merely to gape in hope of a morbid spectacle. Upon this day, the people about him turned their backs and in a moment there was a clear wide space around where he lay upon the cobbles tended by his mother and a sister. A ring of people, silent, some crossing themselves, waited apprehensively for a cry from the mother to announce the dread tidings that her lad was plague-stricken—and when no such cry came, they hurried off, each to his own business, none commenting upon the matter. When the pestilence struck there was no way to be kind to a neighbour, save by leaving him to God's mercy and hastening away before the contagion could be picked up and transmitted to others. The law was ruthless in this matter, and where a town was struck it was sealed off from the rest of the Kingdom. Forfeiture of possessions or death were the punishments which awaited any who traded from or with an afflicted town, and the same applied to any who sought or gave shelter in a town not yet stricken. Many who had taken the pest did in fact survive it, and thereafter rarely took it again, or if they did had it but mildly. These people were considered to be 'lucky', and it was a custom in times of infection for those hoping to escape to touch the garment or the arm of such people.

My duty was to shepherd my court clear of any town where the pest was raging. Had we taken the disease, our progressions would have spread it round the Kingdom. Yet it always worried me to stay away from my subjects who were suffering so wretchedly, and I would never go farther from the stricken towns than was absolutely required. Where there is the pest, there is nothing but the pest; foreign alliances, unrest in the Isles—none of these things mattered that summer in the Lothians. I was obliged to carry on my normal state business, but I did not go up to the Isles. I had been in the Islands during the outbreak of 1498 and to have been away on the second occasion would have suggested I was deliberately fleeing it. So I stayed where my presence was needed most, in the Lothians. I knew it would not look this way to those who lived beyond the Great Lochs and who had no knowledge of the pestilence; this I could not help.

Abstracted by these other worries, I did not see any way to extract myself from the threatening marriage. There were too many people harassing and hastening me toward its completion, and it was too much for my mind and strength to contend with. Nor was it a great deal of help that Janet was playing me up unmercifully because I had been obliged to chase her out of Stirling Castle before King Henry's emissaries took home reports of his new son-in-law's domestic habits. I gave her Darnaway Castle, by Inverness, and the son James whom she had borne me I made the Earl of Moray, but neither contented her, although she had known full well from the beginning that our liaison would be at best a temporary affair, to end the moment I embarked upon a marriage alliance.

Then, in late September, Margaret Drummond came to Falkland. She brought our daughter there, and lingered for a glance through the gardens where she and I had walked together. There it was I met her. I would say it was by chance, save that nothing in our relationship happened ever by chance, and my heart knew although my head did not that she was nearby, and where to find her. We walked together over a path spread like gold with autumn's leaves, until a corner hid us from all other eyes—and there was nothing more to be done, save to hold each other close in silence. They had been five long empty years, which now were ended. Meg at nineteen had been a lass incomparable, but at twenty-five she was a woman with whom I could have fallen in love yet more deeply had it been possible. For the first time in five years my heart and head were assembled together as one whole, and I awakened from my bad dream knowing clearly that Scotland's future no less than my own depended upon my having this girl for my Queen and none other.

My vigour and wits restored, I began to make my plans very quickly. Meanwhile, I began visiting Meg at her father's Castle of Stobshaw—and this may have been where a mistake was made, although I cannot say for certain. I had meant not to take her to me again until we had been wed, but we both found love too strong for us. Also, I needed her greatly at this time; together at night, with her head upon my shoulder and her long, dark hairs finding their way as ever into my mouth, I was strengthened by the knowledge that I was now back upon true, firm ground, and that I was right, whatever my Counsellors' good sense chose to advise me. I was myself; James Stewart, awake in a real world with Margaret Drummond to my arms, the Queen who would lift Scotland out of the way of its unknown peril.

I would have to wed her secretly. I knew it could mean war with England, but better that than a union which I knew Henry Tudor would never have contemplated unless it gave in some way more benefit to England than to ourselves. It was extremely unlikely, in point of fact, that King Henry would actually go to war, for to break a betrothal made in connection with an alliance was not regarded as an offence against the honour of either party; but there would be an edge of annoyance showing for some while afterwards. My foremost problem was to gain a papal dispensation before I married Margaret, putting aside our remote affinity. To obtain the blessing of His Holiness would be extremely difficult, in view of the fact that he had just granted King Henry a similar dispensation allowing me to wed the Princess. The only one of my Bishops whom I could take into my confidence was Robert Blacader.

Blacader listened as usual, his shrewd eyes never leaving my face as I talked at great length, giving him once again my reasons for believing it essential that Scotland and I should have Margaret Drummond as my Queen. I left out nothing. Blacader looked at me in silence for some while, then said merely that I would need to give him an excellent case for going to Rome, over and above my secret business, otherwise the lords would have his head for it before ever he reached the Papal Court. In the way I knew so well, Robert Blacader would make his stand against the world if he truly believed that I knew what was best for me and for Scotland. He was a splendid fellow.

It was late October and the equinoctial gales were with us, closing our harbours to shipping and the sea-lanes to the Continent. This meant that Blacader would have to go by the land route across England, requiring King Henry's permission, and as the Bishop had been one of the ambassadors negotiating the marriage with the English Princess he would need to have a water-tight excuse for going on a mission to Rome at a time when both the seas and the passes through the Alps were made hazardous by wintry weather. Diplomatic business between Rome and Scotland almost ceased between the months of October to February, and only the most urgent matters took a Bishop on such a journey. The covering business needed to be genuine, and the difficulty in finding it so harassed us that Blacader said he would chance his luck upon the sea-route rather than lose more time trying to justify a request to King Henry to cross England. No sooner had this been decided than the gales mounted in fury, continuing their rage into November, when as quickly as they dropped the mists replaced them as a new coastal hazard. An ominous dread took hold of me that luck once more ran against me; it seemed as if a contrary providence had set its blight upon the enterprise.

I had been at Stobshaw visiting Meg, and as I rode back to

Stirling I remembered suddenly my last sight of her. I had had some small matters to discuss with her father, and Meg had taken leave of me in the hall. She had taken a route which led her through the musicians' gallery, so that for a moment she passed again through my vision, like a pale moth fluttering between the shadows of the gallery. Her father, who had his back toward her, was speaking to me at that moment, so I refrained from interrupting; Meg caught my eye, and I saw her soft smile, impish, yet deferential to our male conversation, and her dark eyes looking down at me. Then she was gone. In the shadows the pale stuff of her gown had looked almost luminous, and the small head tilted in its backward glance had been strangely isolated from its dark background in a way I had not at the time thought strange. . . . Now upon the road to Stirling, my last glimpse of her came back to me in terrible and vivid detail. I reined in my horse, half-crazed with fear, upon the point of turning back to Stobshaw. But then common sense prevailed; had I turned back at every prompting of fear I had felt on Meg's account these past two months, I should never have been away from Stobshaw Castle. I continued upon my way, determined to lose no more time in making her my wife.

It cannot have been more than a day or so later, when I was stricken with abdominal pains so severe that my attendants panicked for fear I had been poisoned. Both my physicians were quickly summoned, but neither could determine what was the matter with me. The pains lasted until well past noon, some three or four hours all told, and then were gone as suddenly and mysteriously as they came. It was some while later there came a message from Stobshaw Castle. What I had felt were not my pains—they were hers. My lass was dead, together with her two young sisters, poisoned at the breakfast board. I can remember walking up and down, up and down, up and down by a table, wearing a brown surcoat with sleeves that swung to and fro across my vision. All I can remember are those brown sleeves, long and empty from my elbows, swinging as I strode up and down, up and down, beside a table.

We buried her before the altar in the Abbey of Dunblane, in

Perthshire, where I could be close to her at Stirling Castle. A great slab of blue slate covered her, and a plate of brass, so that none should fail to know how greatly I had cherished her. Her sisters, beneath smaller slabs of the same stone, were buried one upon each side of her.

Many people died by accident from eating meat improperly salted. Her luck, like my own, was bad; in after years, when I had seen more of it, I could well believe that fate could thus have struck her down when we were so close to our happiness. That she died precisely when she did suggested to many that she had been murdered. To this possibility I closed my mind. Scotland had to have its King, and if I let my mind play with the thought that Meg was murdered, I would without a doubt have killed myself. Lord and Lady Drummond, too, had to live with the memory of three daughters who died at breakfast, and life was more bearable if they accepted it as an act of God and not of man. I had three new links of iron put to my girdle chain.

It was a painless calm life after Meg was gone. In a way it made duty easier, not to have hope again, nor fear of hurt. My restless heart at last was still—laid to earth beneath a blue slab, with the bones of a girl called Margaret Drummond, whom I buried in Dunblane.

Within four months of Meg's death, my Court was in mourning for my youngest brother, John, Earl of Mar. I have few memories of my brother John—a dark, quiet, soft-spoken lad who smiled from the fringe of every family gathering. He was but nineteen years of age when he died, so he did not have time to make his mark upon the world. I remember him best as a magnificent swimmer; most people viewed swimming merely as a useful safeguard against death by drowning, and the few intrepid souls who, for pleasure, ventured with my brother into the icy waters off Scotland's south-east coast were regarded as eccentrics asking for trouble. It was, none the less, a great shock when my brother did in fact succumb to the fate of which he had been warned.

He took a chill after bathing and died of it within three days. I was severely criticized for refusing to let him be bled, but I had good reason for my decision—and the memory of another John, Earl of Mar, who had died of too much bleeding.

After Margaret Drummond's death, all others seemed but a changing stage in life's pattern. Where she was gone the rest, including myself, would follow in our turn.

I had signed the Marriage Treaty with England in St Mungo's Abbey, Glasgow, on December 10th, 1502. Still clad in black for Meg, who then had been gone less than a month, I went through the formalities like a man in a never-ending bad dream. I found it difficult to concentrate, and did not study so carefully as I should have done our respective Royal titles used upon the document, which I treated as the least important part of it. It was not until after I had set my signet to the Oath that I realized that Henry Tudor had perpetuated the old English fantasy of styling himself 'King of France'. This pretence I should have dismissed for the absurdity it was, except that it held to the same tradition which made King England wont to claim the Scots monarch as 'his vassal', so I could not afford to disregard it. I remembered that when His Most Christian Majesty Louis XII had succeeded to the throne of France in 1498 I had sent brotherly greetings at his succession—a normal courtesy, of no deep political significance. But when King Henry learned of it, he reacted in the petulant way of English Kings by seeking to exact a promise from me that as his new ally I would repudiate my friendship with France. This irritated me, for I saw no reason why our countries should not all three dwell amicably together; also it depressed me, for I saw in it then signs of the old claims which I had hoped might have ended with the Plantagenet dynasty. I credited Henry Tudor, I think rightly, with more sense than to renew King England's absurd pretension to the Crown of France, but he was obviously bent upon leaving the tradition intact for the benefit of future heirs who might wish to follow it.

I told King Henry's commissioners that I wished to have this title 'King of France' deleted, as he was not the King of France. Lord Darcy showed himself exceedingly annoyed and refused to accept the Treaty if the title were deleted. They departed in a huff back to London. As I did not care in the least whether Henry Tudor liked it or not, and indeed was secretly hoping that he would consider it grounds for tearing up our treaty, I drafted a new copy of the documents, omitting his style 'King of France', which I signed and despatched by Lyon Herald. To my chagrin, King Henry signed the Treaties without a murmur.

Preparations for the marriage took most of my attention for the next six months. I meant to make it a great occasion for the benefit of my Scots, who had earned a festival after our fourteen years' hard work to restore the fortunes of the Kingdom. Also, to spend money extravagantly in a good cause is pleasurable; my hall at Linlithgow filled with eight lengths of gold cloth held up like banners by its weavers to show for my approval, was a sight not easily forgotten. With the light from Linlithgow's yellow window glass shining upon it, it looked as if the hall had been filled with a river of molten gold. The greatest part we used to make the new Queen's bed-hangings, but I reserved sufficient to make two long robes for myself. These would have to last me for a lifetime.

We hurried to complete my new Palace of Holyrood, as I felt that my bride might not be so interested as I was to live with masons working round her. I had decided finally to move from our Castle of Edinburgh and all its discomforts, to the east side of the city wall where the Abbey of the Holy Rood, procured by a grant of land to the Augustinians, was now being rebuilt as a Royal residence. (The good folk dwelling upon 'the Hill' never forgave me for removing from the Castle the Presence which had made the area fashionable—and they were to like it a good deal less when they found themselves living next door to a furniture store and arsenal.)

Tam the smith vanished from my life. More taciturn than ever, his yellow hair and beard had greyed since the day he first made my girdle. He had adored Margaret Drummond—and, indeed, I had more than once felt a pang almost of jealousy when, in earlier days, she had so often begun a statement, 'Tam tellet me . . .' When, in the brief days of that unquenchable October, she had been again at my side, I rode with her once by the smiddy to show her off to Tam. Upon a later occasion, I questioned Tam alone beside the forge how our Scots commoners would take to one of their own kind as Queen? I had to know, and there was only Tam to whom I dared put my question. He said if it were 'yon lass o' Lord Drummond', she would have 'mukel laive' of plain-folk. He went ashen with rage and grief on learning she was dead, and when I wanted new links added to my girdle, he made a great clangour with his irons and asked me angrily why I saw fit to take on a heavier load than God—and my own lords—had already given me?

Some weeks before my marriage in August 1503, Tam disappeared. That is all I know. I sent to find him at Ardmillan, thinking his family there might know where he was; then I had horsemen search every mile of the Lothians in case he had taken a fall from his horse and lay injured somewhere—taking an active part in the search myself. Not a trace of Tam was ever found. Every man can have private reasons for wanting to disappear, but I knew 'the King's Smith' would never leave without giving me notice of his intention. I never resolved the mystery; Tam was my friend, and for that reason he may have died. To name any I suspected then would be unjust, for what I could not prove in 1503, I certainly cannot prove now; my Fool may have known something, although I did not suspect him of the act. But I will risk saying that somewhere below the level of what used to be the mud-bed of the old North Loch, where the mooring stage served the Castle, there may have been found—or could yet be found—a big man's set of bones, with the haft of a broadsword thrust between them.

Tam and I were as close as brothers. I was bitter about Tam for a very great while.

About this time I acquired a new friend—an Englishman: Lord Dacre, King Henry's Warden of the West March. Thomas Dacre was yet another of those men whom I recognized upon first meeting as though we had known each other for ever. He was one of the English commissioners appointed to discuss the Princess's marriage portion, and it was he who presented to me in the best light possible the reasons why the marriage was a good idea—I imagine he must have seen through my cheerfulness how truly wretched I felt about the wedding. As Warden, he knew better than anybody the savage butchery of the Border raids on either side; like myself, he wanted only to end it forever. He spent no words extolling the charms of my unwanted child bride; with forthright appreciation, he said, 'Your Grace hath done an act which maketh my task lighter, and shall have the thankfulness of many'. He was right: whatever dangerous potential existed in King Henry's crafty mind, time would discover it, and I—or others—could deal with it then; meanwhile, we had certain peace along the Border, during which we could begin to persuade Scots and Englishmen if not to love each other, at least to leave each other's life and property alone. It is Lord Dacre's figure I remember, when I signed the allotment of the marriage portion —bending forward at my side, tall for an Englishman, clad neatly in a surcoat of rich black damask, with the white pleated lawn frill of his shirt showing at the wrist and neckline, and his yellow-streaked fair hair swinging forward in a crisp curled edge at his shoulder. He had a down-curved moustache above a well-shaped mouth which widened to a smile when I laid down the pen—it was a smile meant for myself, with a direct look to my eyes, reassuring me that my sacrifice would benefit our Borderers. I had the odd feeling that I was completing this alliance with Lord Dacre, not with the King of England.

I had a portrait of myself made at this juncture to show King Henry what the man was like who would make or mar his daughter's happiness. There was a new Flemish limner called Hans Holbein who was reputed to be skilled in portrait painting, so I summoned him to my Court. He was a brisk, busy fellow, who set up his tackle while we were still engaged in our pre-liminary talk, and had my head-outline traced upon a screen of glass in a matter of moments. He told me this was the best way to gain accuracy with Royal sitters who tended to be called away, to return irritably indisposed to find again precisely the pose he had been drawing. All of his work was done at great speed, as though he had many other patrons waiting— which likely he had, this appeared to give him a right royal disregard for the importance of princes, as though it were his work and not theirs which would carry them through time's memory—and in this, too, I suspected he might be right. He did not suffer while he worked, like Jacques le Boucq—on the contrary, he chatted unceasingly, telling anecdotes about his other distinguished clients.

When the portrait was complete, I remarked how wondrously he had captured my likeness. He nodded briefly in agreement—then said with a sigh that it was a pity, however, that I had not kept to my original intention to let him portray me smiling. I was astonished; I had been smiling all the while—I knew I had been smiling because I had held my tongue pressed behind my top front teeth in the way my mouth set always when I smiled. It was Master Holbein's turn to show astonishment and he cried, in Flemish, 'But it is the saddest face that ever I have limned!' I was aghast, for I had been renowned always for my gaiety; I quitted the chamber without a word—although I made it plain later I was not angry with him for the liberty of his speech.

I never sent the portrait to King Henry.

Before I wed, I took the opportunity to test whether or not I had succeeded in the vow I had made when I first came to my throne in a strife-torn, lawless country—that I would make it so secure that even I might ride alone without fear of attack or robbery. I let my intention be well known in advance, also the route I would take from Stirling to Aberdeen, a distance of a hundred miles, across open country. I said that if anybody bore me a grudge for the stern way I dealt with our dishonest brethren, now would be their opportunity to call me to account for it. I set off, wearing my richest costume so that there would be no mistaking who I was, liberally sprinkled with jewels.

I met nothing but kindness on the way, and left my glove, for which she asked, to a shepherd's wife who gave me a breakfast of curds and bannocks. I rode at a great pace, changing horses where they had been posted for me, and it was shortly after noon that I reached Aberdeen. I decided therefore to ride on to Janet Kennedy at Darnaway (by Inverness) and came there by nightfall, having enjoyed the company for some minutes of a set of rough fellows who gave me a cheer when I left them—which pleased me greatly, for they were of the kind who fifteen years earlier might have thought more to have my ring and purse, and leave me dead for it. I had ridden two hundred miles in that one day, and for once even I had overtaxed myself. My knees wobbled when I came into the hall of Darnaway Castle, and I was so saddle-sore that all I could do was to flop down upon a trestle board they set for me.

It was the best night's sleep that ever I enjoyed, for all that my body ached so dreadfully. There were other lands richer, and other princes more powerful, but I could ride alone across my Kingdom fearing nobody. I had reason to sleep well.

9

My bride was small and plump, with a mass of flopping hair through which she peered at me. My heart sank at the full soft flesh of her, and the way her white shoulders showing above the square neckline of her bodice were as rounded at the back as was her bosom. I mean this not ungallantly, for many men would have taken a lascivious delight in her; my own taste, however, was for women of a totally different kind, and this lassie struck in me the dread of impotence —my first thought, because I had to beget an heir as quickly as she was old enough. She was neither handsome nor ugly—merely young, plump and plain; then I saw she had youth's legacy of three or four pimples on her face, and I felt a sudden flash of warmth for her. So young, and travelling so far, to wed a man she had never seen who was seventeen years her senior—life surely was hard enough, without the pimples.

She did not have much chance to shine, for the Earl of Surrey had been sent to be her sponsor, and he was the kind of man who makes instantly for the most important person in the room, wasting no time upon the others. He did this to me now, hailing me at once as though he and I were old friends—and totally disregarding the friendly greeting which the Earl of Angus gave him.

Surrey's Countess was another of that ilk, a large, commanding matron who seized upon a conversation like a pair of scissors and slashed it to pieces; there was no further contribution to be made, upon any subject, when she had finished with it. Their daughter I found the most agreeable, although she too bore traces of the family tendency to overpower—when I learned they had six of these girls, plus their sons, I had a horrible fleeting vision of what it would be like to meet a battalion of female Howards: dear God! To this one of them, singly, I took a fancy; she was about fifteen (I think), a jolly girl with a minimal sense of modesty, whose bright eyes sought mine in a scandalous fashion, to tell me plainly whose bed she would share without a qualm if fate had given her the opportunity. It had not, however; and I was the intended husband of the wee Tudor Princess the Howards were supposed to be attending. But I was grateful to the English lass for the frankness of her compliment.

The Surreys dominated the occasion to such an extent, I had to make a surprise sortie through the battlement of Howards to reach the Princess (now styled Queen of Scots). This seemed to cheer her; she had shown signs of sulking, which had worried me. I found, however, that she needed little encouragement to regain her confidence; Henry Tudor seemed to have been a father who had doted overmuch upon his children, and this lassie wanted all of the attention all the time, showing petulance whenever for a moment she was not the centre of attraction. She was ready to become a tyrant given half an opportunity, and worst of all—I was to learn—she gained her way by an affected helplessness, with upward childish glances through her long hair and a small toy voice which I found exceedingly irritating.

Altogether, I felt that I had paid a heavy price for peace with England. However, we were to live together as man and wife, and the only way to do that was to train the child to suit my taste, and train myself to please hers. At least she showed a grain of humour, and nothing is impossible where people can laugh about it. I kept to myself my thoughts about her, and I would not tell of them now save that our life together was the substance of which history would be made. Outwardly, I used all my charm to woo her—completely forgetting, alas, that when I made to win a woman I often succeeded beyond my requirements.

I knew when it was done—on the eve of our wedding, when she was tired, a plain, pimpled little Queen so close to tears that I felt for her as I would have done for one of my own daughters. Her own father, whom she loved well, was not a young man and London was a far way should he take ill; she knew herself the chances she might never see him again. And her mother, I knew, had been dead but a few months. 'Puir litel heart, puir Mairgret'—my deep voice, when softened, Meg had said, was the tenderest she had ever heard, and in this case it proved our mutual undoing. The next minute my future bride was a crumpled small girl in my arms, howling such tears, poor mite, I thought she would have drowned the pair of us. I held her thus for what must have been an hour, while she discharged her pent-up homesickness with a description of Henry Tudor which bore no resemblance to King England as I knew him. I might have liked him had he been my own father. In return, I thought this would make an excellent opportunity to tell her about my own family—about Alexander, who was but two years younger than herself; about Catherine, and James, and Jean (the daughter my cousin Isobel had borne me). The one of my children for whom chiefly I wanted her tenderness, was wee Margaret, now left motherless—a slender dark child, who fluttered like a moth about the dark passages of my castles; she had grown so like her mother, I knew she was not meant to have long days.

I had thought by speaking of my children to reassure my child bride she need have no fear of me. I remember telling her that I would not use her for a good while yet, and she could rest assured of none but fatherly embraces until I knew she cared for me enough to want those of another kind. She gave me one of her quick upward looks which I took to be grateful. It was not until afterwards, when I saw her jealousy of my children, that I realized hers had been a woman's feelings. I had secretly wanted my children to make a family with my new wife, but this plan miscarried and I had to house them separately. Alexander the Queen liked well enough, for he was a handsome lad almost of her age; to the rest of my girls she behaved well enough, but she was to prove a vicious wee madam in her treatment of Margaret.

I had not told her myself about Meg, but others did, and my Queen wanted nothing more than to dislodge Meg's memory from my heart. When she felt herself unable to do so, she vented her spite and jealousy upon Meg's child. Margaret Tudor was a girl who made her own discomfort; but she wed a man who was already a ghost, poor lass, and all the kindness in the world could not replace a lack of substance. I made her happy, but I never could give her the exclusive love she wanted.

But we did have peace upon the Border. Lord Dacre and I toured it together in company, showing all who dwelled there that he and I were friends as well as collaborators. At night, we sat together in my tent, talking almost until dawn. Poor Dacre found my sleeplessness a problem, for he was himself a man who retired early, slumbered soundly, and needed his rest. One night, to my surprise, he rose, and with his eyelids visibly drooping, made an apology for his breach of courtesy in asking, would I kindly dismiss him before he fell at my feet. I cut him short, saying that even for a king I talked too much and would ever keep him from his bed unless he had the forthright sense to tell me when he had had enough of it. Then he left my tent, and I watched a while at its opening, as his tall figure walked over the low grassy knoll which divided my tent from the rest. It seemed to me as if the hope for peace between Scotland and England had never looked so real as it did then, with a fellow like Thomas Dacre to be English Warden of the Marches.

I remembered how Dacre had saved the peace at my wedding. During the nuptial banquet, the Earl of Surrey, at my right hand, paid tribute to our Scots soldiery, by saying that under foreign commanders our Scots fighting men would make the finest mercenaries any prince could have to his service. I was stricken speechless by his English impudence. For a second I was tempted to renew the challenge I had left in abeyance five years earlier. While I seethed, I saw Dacre's eye upon Surrey, his shoulders hunched as though he choked upon the mouthful he was swallowing; it occurred to me, it was probably worse to have Surrey as a colleague than as an enemy. So I swallowed my wrath, and told the Earl of Surrey coldly that our Scots fought for love of my Realm, and not for hire by foreign princes. He asked my pardon, and I gave it.

My efforts to make happy a homesick young girl went not unappreciated by a doting father like Henry Tudor, and I well knew that the more kindness I showed his daughter the more tenderness was he likely to feel toward my subjects at the Border. Thus the mating of the Thistle and the Rose, as our heraldically minded age romantically called it, began to seem more useful than I had formerly supposed; and when as the months passed and Henry Tudor showed himself as willing as I was to implement the terms of our Treaty, I began to lull away my fear that I had brought peril upon my Kingdom.

It was as well we now had peace along the Border, for discontent had shown itself in the North-West between some of the Island chieftains and their Governor-General. In these times, loyalty was recruited mainly within the clan, and in order to find lieutenants whom he could trust Argyll not unnaturally chose his own kinsmen to support him. In turn, while administration was tied to grants of land, what the Islesmen saw was the Argyll family connections benefiting at the expense of their own folk. I had warned Argyll of this, but I knew as well as he did there was little else he could do until such time—it would be 1507 —as our new class of legal administrators emerged from university in sufficient strength to serve the areas where they were needed. Meanwhile, Argyll had to do the best he could through the feudal means available.

The Islesmen—or some of them—were not prepared to wait until 1507 for the King's futuristic notions to prove their value. It came to my ears that a few chieftains planned to raise the banner of a pretender to the Lordship—none other than my cherished protegé Donald Owre. I sent at once for Donald Owre, still at Tarbert. His long melancholy face was alternately troubled and charming, as he assured me that he had no intention whatever of succumbing to rebel persuasion, which I believed. My Lords of Council took the view that the only thing to be done with Donald Owre was to lodge him in custody. This at first I refused to do, for the unfortunate fellow had committed no crime save to get himself born the son of Old John's bastard. However, when secret messages began to arrive for Donald Owre at Tarbert, I saw an unwholesome resemblance to the pattern which once had set me up as a rebel leader against my inclination. I sent again for Donald, and told him frankly why I thought it best for his own sake to ward him in custody until the threatened rebellion had been put down. He was treated as my guest, rather than as a prisoner; and as soon as the emergency had passed (or appeared to have passed) I released him.

By releasing Donald Owre, I provoked much criticism from my Council—and when Donald Owre (I believed, against his will) next showed himself upon the side of the rebels, I was severely taken to task. They said, with heavy head-shakings, that Owre had badly repaid my generosity: to which I retorted that it was not my generosity he was repaying, but my lack of it in confining him in the first place.

The rebellion ended upon the death of its instigating chieftain. Donald Owre, his face more melancholy than ever, was hauled back to Stirling Castle as my prisoner. I wasted no words reproaching him for what he had done, and he wasted none in vain apology. In a way, I secretly approved Black Donald's response to his Island kinsmen, for he would have been of no further use to my plans had he shown himself a mere court sycophant. I could have hanged him, which he knew, and I liked his courage. All the same, it would be another ten years until the episode had been forgotten in the North-West, and I could risk sending him back there as Governor-General. Nor could I send him back to Tarbert yet awhile. I kept him at Court, where his elegance pleased the eye, and his charm brightened the life of the Queen's English ladies.

Although Argyll had done useful work in putting down several nuisance-makers in the Isles, I wanted none such to be able to claim they raided and killed for love of liberty: I went North myself to set my lands in feu to Islesmen I now knew I could trust. It was not a question of playing off one chieftain against another, but of encouraging those who were prepared to discipline their own territory. The chieftains I rewarded were men of vision who saw as clearly as I did that these were changing times, and life's pattern everywhere must adapt accordingly.

Among the reasons why, after Meg's death, I had decided to delay my marriage no longer had been the need to safeguard the succession. While I yet had two brothers each capable of wearing the crown, it had not troubled me greatly that I had begotten no legitimate heir; and while I might privately have resigned myself to the fact that John might not have long tenure of life, I became greatly alarmed when I saw manifest in my brother James that fatigue which I could now recognize as a trait common among the male members of the Stewart family. Quite apart from brotherly regard and the fact that he was Heir to the Crown, should anything happen to my brother James I would lose the man whom I relied upon to play a leading part in my plans for Scotland's future.

Upon the death of William Schevez in 1497, I had secured for my brother James the Archiepiscopal See of St Andrews. I had done this not because I wanted to follow the usual practice of securing a good living in the Church for the younger sons of royal and noble houses, but because James, Duke of Ross, was the most suitable candidate possible for that high office. He was party to my plan for Scotland's future when I asked him in his seventeenth year, would he be willing to take Holy Orders for his nomination to the See of St Andrews? What was most vital to me was that Scotland's highest ecclesiastical office be held by somebody who could work with me without betraying the spiritual authority of the Church. At the same time, I wanted a man who would think more in terms of *Scotland's* Church than could any of my bishops who had been trained to look to Rome for guidance in every detail. James held every qualification necessary for the task: conscientious, stubborn, trained to think as a prince, it looked as if James had been born precisely for this purpose.

I wanted to build on the privileges and the semi-autonomy we had obtained from Rome in my father's reign. While the Church, throughout Christendom, was urgently in need of internal reform —the behaviour generally in monastic houses, for instance, had degenerated terribly during the last decades, and many had fallen into disrepute (the Dominicans were a disgrace to their founder) —on the whole, standards in Scotland were a good deal higher than elsewhere. A reformer within the Scottish Church would regain the respect of the laity and could make easier my task of wider reforms.

When he took Holy Orders at the age of eighteen, my brother James might well, as others did in our day, have contented himself with the minimal amount of study; instead, in his usual stolid, thorough fashion, he set out to equip himself within the next two years with all the theological learning he would have acquired had he trained for the priesthood since the age of eleven. At the same time, he participated usefully in the administration of his See of St Andrews. When I warned him that he was taxing himself too severely, he replied, rightly, that there was no other way to win the respect of his subordinates, or to justify his holding the position. By the end of the two years he had attained his objective, winning the admiration of those who had formerly criticized his appointment, and setting such a high example by his industry that it was a warning to many of the lazier members of the clergy that a new zeal was expected within the ecclesiastical ranks.

In the initial stages of my grief for Meg he had given me great help, for a few days slipping unobtrusively into the role of unofficial Regent so that I might regain my senses after the shock by a few days' seclusion at the Franciscan House of the Observantine Friars in Edinburgh. Then, as unobtrusively, he returned to his place as Scotland's Primate.

(The House of the Observantine Friars had been founded in the reign of my great-grandfather and had remained under royal patronage ever since. The Order was well established in Scotland, where its tighter discipline and simpler ritual, together with its true dedication to the ideals of St Francis, had made it popular among a people whose religious faith was part of their natural being. The Observantine Friars I tended to regard as my personal as well as my royal protegés, for it was they who heard my confession and it was to one of their houses that I went in retreat when my punished soul needed respite. For the Edinburgh House of that Order I had an especially affectionate regard, and it was to them I gave my library of precious books to be housed in their Friary so that they as well as I could have the use of them.)

Then James took ill of a fever in 1499, and although he apparently recovered from it, he was never quite the same again. His vigour was spent. I pleaded with him to take a long rest from his responsibilities, but he insisted stubbornly that nothing ailed him, adding the qualification that he would rest from his obligations when he saw me do the same. It was hopeless to argue: our mother had reared us both to the same way of thinking.

James had been expected to join us at Court for the Yule festival of 1503, which was the time when traditionally the King held open house for all his lords and as many others as cared to present themselves; then a message came to say that the Archbishop had taken a fall from his horse and begged to be excused from our company. His servant assured me that it was 'but a mickel ill' being some bruised bones and a general discomfort, such as would benefit from some days' rest. From this I drew my own conclusions, that what ailed James was another bout of the melancholy to which these days he fell victim more readily, and I knew by my own experience that such a state was more likely to be aggravated than cured by the merriment of others. For all that, I was deeply troubled for I had had a presentiment at our last meeting some two weeks past that I had been looking upon my loved younger brother for the last time.

I wanted desperately to go to St Andrews, but my young Queen pleaded with me not to leave her during this her first Yule festival—and indeed it was virtually impossible for me to leave Court at this season, the more so as more elaborate festivities than usual were planned to honour the presence of my Queen. However, as soon as I could decently escape, I rode quickly to St Andrews—to find that my brother had died within hours of my arrival.

What had killed him had not been his fall, of that I was certain; simply, his overburdened spirit had been glad of the excuse not to rise from the bed in which his bruises had placed him. It was one more Stewart claimed by the constitutional fatigue which cursed our family.

The problem now was whom to appoint to the vacant See of St Andrews. William Elphinstone had fairly expected to receive this benefice at the time when I gave it to my brother James, and I felt badly about denying him the elevation a second time; but he was now a man in his sixties, grown old in service to Rome, and it was too late to bend him to my ways as Scotland's Archbishop of the future.

Elphinstone's real genius lay in his ability to organize any council of which he was a member—in fact he, like Blacader who was one of my most skilful diplomats, would have been far more use to me had he been a layman; the reason the Church had retained its power, despite its grossly apparent vices, was the fact that men of administrative brilliance almost always took Holy Orders. Elphinstone's great usefulness to my father had guaranteed his almost immediate re-employment by the next regime as Chancellor. Thus he had remained all the years of my reign. His dry, birdlike wit had livened many a Council meeting—and Elphinstone's impersonation of his own Dean hunting through the Bishop's papers for evidence of iniquities among the lower clergy had been the delight of my Lords in Council for years. The 'good Bishop William' could, in fact, be exceedingly malicious when he chose, and his frequent lapses from grace throughout his whole career were caused more by his unthinking cleverness than by his political opinions. He was a child in many ways, with a child's unthinking knack of wounding, for all his vast intellect. (He was born under Gemini, which excused a great deal in my eyes.)

It did not excuse, however, the mistake which he had made when founding our new faculty of medicine at Aberdeen University. I had made it plain to him that what we were establishing there was a faculty where would be taught the healing arts in a new way entirely different from the old. Under our then current system, all the student required was a knowledge of theology and natural philosophy, together with the ability to debate with his tutors in graceful Latin—which was all very well, to comfort the bereaved, but I had always the feeling that with less attention to the Litany and bleeding bowl my Uncle John of Mar might well have lived longer to recover from his fever. As two men who were neither physicians, bleeders nor apothecaries, we had to compose the curriculum of a university faculty never before attempted; therefore I had instructed Bishop William not to rely upon literary sources which could not then supply the information we wanted, but to go to the practical men who dealt in the healing trade—the apothecaries and barber-surgeons. This I had stressed, knowing Elphinstone's tendency to rush to a book when he could have learned more by using his ears to listen.

There was also the fact that any collegiate foundation had to have licence of Rome, and Elphinstone had a disposition to hug his cloisters—for which I cannot say I blame him, for it was a graceful life, but I meant to make drastic reform in the field of education, taking its responsibility more to the Crown and away from the Rota; Elphinstone's love for the old learning was no great help to me. The outcome was that our new foundation of Aberdeen fell squarely down the hole between the two traditions (although the new learning was not yet established as a tradition to my mind of 1494, and I use the word here in current context) —with hideous consequences in the field of medical study, as I shall tell hereafter.

This failure of Elphinstone's to see what I wanted in terms of Aberdeen's new medical faculty, led me to conclude that he was not a suitable candidate for the Primacy of Scotland. Blacader, I think, might have been the better man to choose, but it was out of the question to elevate a younger man over the head of Bishop William; Blacader made too many sparks fly among the lesser clergy who feared his sharp tongue and penetrating gaze, and who would band together in support of Elphinstone. I had to keep the peace in Scotland.

My young son, Alexander, at eleven years of age was a force to reckon with. He, like Margaret Drummond, was born upon the same day as myself, and he had all my vices together with (mercifully) my few great virtues. He proved himself later to have one virtue exceeding mine, in that he was chaste by inclination, but I was not to know of this when he was aged eleven. And I had made a terrible omission when I asked my Brother James was he prepared to take Holy Orders—an omission which I did not recognize until I lost Meg Drummond and he comforted me bleakly with the words 'Et es noucht gi'en ta all men, Sire, ta ha' comfort o' woman'. My conscience had never forgiven me thereafter, for consigning James to celibacy whether he liked it or not; I was determined not to make the same mistake with Alexander. I accordingly consulted his tutor, Patrick Paniter (whom I meant to have as my principal secretary when I could find another niche for Richard Muirhead—Muirhead was a good lad, but he did not share the ability of Andrew Forman, his predecessor, to think as I did without instruction, and which was the reason why Andrew Forman, now Bishop of Moray, was learning his way as my ambassador).

The ability in men to think as I did myself was the most precious qualification available to me in our times of slow communication. I must therefore take opportunity to tell of Paniter in more detail, for he shares with me the blame and glory of much that subsequently befell Scotland.

I was needing a tutor for Alexander in the year 1498, when Desiderius Erasmus paid briefly a visit to Scotland to see his friend of student days Hector Boece, who was Principal of Aberdeen University. Erasmus I knew as a kindred soul, and liked instantly; he was ideally suited to be the tutor to my precious, wilful son. Erasmus, however, had other commitments before him, and suggested that Patrick Paniter—another fellow student of his from the University of Paris—would be an excellent alternative to himself. Erasmus was as graceful in person as he was in character, and I had no hesitation in appointing Paniter my son's tutor even before I saw him.

My horror can be imagined when Patrick Paniter presented himself before me.

He was a small man, with a strange stumbling gait, and an odd way of tucking back his arms and thrusting out his chest as if he were a drawn bow about to discharge himself. When he spoke, he had a harsh voice, and each time he answered a question he would deliver a short lecture—although it had to be admitted that these uninvited lectures contained an enormous amount of good sense, and the penetrating hardness of his voice would as suddenly drop to the tenderest note imaginable. Also, he had an endearing grin which conveyed plainly that he had arrived with the best of intentions and therefore it was impossible that he should be unwelcome. What truly alarmed me was the physical aspect of the fellow. He had come to my court fully knowing—for it was known everywhere after eleven years, I would have thought—that anybody anxious to please His Grace should make some attempt to measure up to the standards of physical cleanliness required in those who served me. Yet he arrived wearing a surcoat of some mottled dark hue, over a doublet of the same, liberally endowed with food, ink and tallow stains, of unmistakably ancient vintage. There was some kind of nondescript mangy fur upon his sleeves and strapped across his chest—whichever animal had been its previous owner could hardly have complained at losing it. His hose were a faded orange colour, with what had been a huge hole cobbled together above the heel by a drawstring which had been tied off by a large knot and then both its end-strands left dangling. Nor had I ever seen a man so hairy. As a non-ordained cleric he wore the tonsure, in his case surrounded by a great halo of black wiry hair looking for all the world like a bird's nest with a hole in the middle, balanced upon his head rather than existing as a part of it. I was sure if he shook his head, his tonsure would fall at his feet—at which he would doubtless pick it up, clap it back, and continue talking. There was a second ring of hair encircling the lower part of his face, which, I strongly suspected, he wore to save himself the burden of too much washing. Nor did he even smell clean, for he carried the faint musty odour I associated with a pack of playing cards which had been overlong in use, or with the dark doorways of some of the vennel stair-houses of Edinburgh. It was not the strong reek of a man whose bodily habits were unclean, but simply the stale smell of a man who dressed quickly in order to press on with his work, and then found at the day's end that he had forgotten to wash himself. I was later to learn that this random judgement was exactly true of Paniter.

I had no idea what to say to the fellow. Some of the less well-behaved members of my court were secretly hiding their smiles (these would meet with a reprimand later) but the worst was that I had young Alexander with me, and I hardly dare look at that disdainful patrician profile when he saw the kind of fellow I had brought to be his tutor. Since the day he was born Alexander had been fastidiously clean; he was a graceful child who was irritated by clumsiness, and what he would feel about this shaggy goat-man's stumbling gait, I scarcely dared imagine. Children, however, are nothing if not unpredictable. Alexander, then aged six, had immediately stepped forward to give the stranger his impeccable low bow reserved only for the greatest among us, and thereafter took the hairy paw in his own firm, clean small hand, to present me with a *fait accompli*. Trust Alexander to appoint his own tutor irrespective of my approval!—yon bairn was the sole one of my subjects who made his own laws, having done so since the day he first wriggled out of my arms and crawled away across the floor presenting his back to me.

Since that time I had grown to appreciate how right Alexander's choice had been, for there was a greatly wise man hidden beneath the satyr's exterior. (I suspect, had Paniter been beautiful as well as wise, the rest of us would have found his virtues unbearable.) I came to seek his opinion upon most matters, for he had a useful way of furnishing me with practical grounds that explained what I knew by instinct, which was of great value when I had to show my counsellors by argument what the 'lang ee' saw to be inevitable.

What I wanted to discover from Paniter was whether he thought that young Alexander, now aged eleven, had the potential to make a bishop. Also there was the consideration of whether it was fair to consign him at the age of eleven to the celibate life. Paniter assured me, in cheerful pagan fashion, that if the boy sought to sow a few wild oats before becoming a priest, it need not undermine his ability to become celibate in the farther future. I let the matter drop at this point. Alexander was only eleven. More to the point, had Alexander a natural bent for the Church?—I had thought several times that he definitely had, but I was glad to have his tutor confirm my opinion.

Alexander at eleven was tall enough to reach almost to my shoulder, and his erect carriage would show off episcopal vestments impressively. His only physical defect was weak sight, but from the beholder's point of view, Alexander's mildly blinking eyes did a great deal to dispel his naturally arrogant air, which could otherwise be intimidating. He was, in fact, a Royal lad so fitted to become a king that I cursed his bastardy which denied him the succession.

When I told him of my plan for his future, subject to his approval, he was delighted—informing me graciously that I had made the best decision possible in order to exploit the regal talents which otherwise would be lost to Scotland. Alexander was not vain: merely he knew his true value. I hastened to tell him that we had yet to obtain papal sanction, and whether or not His Holiness and the Rota would approve the appointment to the See of St Andrews of an eleven-year-old boy of doubtful birth, not even old enough to be ordained, was a highly debatable matter.

When the Cardinal of St Mark's, who handled Scotland's interests at the Court of Rome, forwarded His Holiness's appointment of Alexander Stewart to the See of St Andrews, nobody was more astonished than I. It was true that the King of Scots was the one of the Pontiff's princely sons who traditionally gave least trouble, so that my choice of nominees had rarely been questioned; all the same . . . For once in my life, I truly felt my luck had turned, and gave thanks to God accordingly.

All I needed was *time*. Given peace with England, a mere twenty years would serve my purpose, to lay the foundations on which Scotland's future would shape itself naturally out of other men's work in centuries after my own.

10

M Y Consort's main interests were clothes, jewels, rich food, courtly pastimes—and my embraces when she came old enough to claim them. Her preoccupation with the trappings of royalty left me free to attend to its duties, which suited me very well. While my Queen presided over my Court, I was available to attend the burgesses' supper parties where talk was of ships, trade, crafts, and other matters to do with the development of my Kingdom.

Ever since my childhood when I first gave thought to it, it had seemed to me extraordinary that Scotland, which had the longest maritime frontier of any nation in Christendom, should pay so small regard to the size and quality of its fleet. A strong fleet was required not only for defensive purposes, but to bring us into communication with the rest of the world. So long as King England controlled our land route to the Continent, he had fair grounds for thinking himself entitled to shape our foreign policy, and our trade. I was determined to end this situation; throughout all my reign a part of my yearly revenue was allocated to finance the building of ships in the Royal yards.

In my day, a kingdom's navy was assembled in the same way as our land force was mustered—ships owned by and sailing beneath the emblem of the monarch formed the perennial core of a fleet, where over two-thirds of the vessels were the property of the king's subjects. These auxiliary ships were mercantile vessels, with their own or the king's cannon put aboard to convert them into warships, which meant that our sea power was provided not by the great feudal lords who supplied our armies, but by the new class of rich merchants, which had arisen to displace craftsmen and would in time impinge upon the power of the nobles. (It is significant that most of the magnificent houses upon the Castle Hill of Edinburgh were now owned not by our lords but by the city burgesses—and indeed, the cost of living upon 'the Hill' was so high, I doubt I could have afforded to live there myself had I not inherited the Castle property.)

While I confess to deriving good tempered amusement occasionally from our burgesses' excesses of grandeur, I knew and liked them well enough as men, and I knew also how exceedingly important they were to Scotland's future welfare. These men were my shipbuilders in a land which never lacked reasons to put its men to sea—as I had discovered in 1493, when a surfeit of idle fellows put the onus of their upkeep upon the burghs, which problem I suggested (to my Parliament) could best be resolved by giving the idle men work as boat builders, beneath the eye of a qualified shipwright, constructing fishing vessels to be owned by the burghs and sailed by the men themselves in the nearest coastal waters. In that way, each man would learn two new crafts; the burgh would have an added supply of cheap, fresh fish; and we should soon know which of the fellows were poor because they had no work, and which were inherently idle —it was, in Scotland, the Christian and the legal duty of the burgh to ensure that no man starved, but we were a practical people who did not believe that the industrious should supply bread for the children of those who lay in bed all day either sleeping or begetting more children. In the process of resolving this problem, I was also stocking my reserves of ships, sailors and shipwrights.

Now I had begun to enlarge upon this scheme; I needed ships of greater size to command our sea-lanes to the Continent. And this was where my own individual personality proved invaluable. My talent for winning men (and women) to my side was the means by which I built up Scotland's navy. The burgesses' supper gatherings were my field of conquest, and I used shamelessly the good looks, charm, and virility which the years, for some odd reason, had enhanced rather than diminished. In Scotland, unlike other lands (I was told), the womenfolk had strong character (they also had the Celtic talent for dressing well; their head-dresses were the admiration of any who came from the French or the Spanish Courts) and they were not dismissed the dinner table even when the King was present. At first it had been thought that in these special circumstances I would prefer to talk with the men, so the ladies had voluntarily retired—until I brought them back again, knowing full well that a flashing smile from me would cause many wives and daughters to implement my plea to their menfolk to build ships for Scotland.

I did not lack warmth from my own sex; indeed, as a man of 1500, I have to confess that we found the female talk of our times extremely boring, and we had not a great deal of use for women except as bedmates and the propagators of our species. I had, myself, a higher regard for the feminine potential because the women important to my life—my own mother, my aunt Margaret, Margaret Drummond and Janet Kennedy—were all human characters in their own right who merely happened to be women. Otherwise, I preferred male companionship. The trouble, however, in the case of these Edinburgh, Aberdeen, and Glasgow burgesses, was a lack of imagination—as with my Lords in Council, who pressed me to argue in terms of today, never perceiving that my own vision embraced the natural development of man through *centuries*. In consequence, they frequently considered me unpractical. When I proclaimed the need to build extra merchant ships, I was asked what would they carry? I had no idea; but a nation which supplied England, France, Flanders and the Low Countries generally, with all the smoke-dried or salted fish which those lands consumed (indeed, any kind of smoked or salted fish in France was known as 'poisson d'Ecosse' or 'poisson écossais'), not to mention their best hides and finest wool, had surely an unlimited potential as the provider of humanity's basic essentials?

There was also another commodity which our Kingdom's chequered history had never permitted us to exploit to the full—

the inventive resource of its people. The Scots are chief among the earth's prolific instigators, be it in terms of law or in practical invention; there was no limit to our native ingenuity, once free of war—a fact, I suspect, which King England had grasped centuries before I did, which was why he made continuous effort to enslave a people who had otherwise done him no harm.

The Scots are the only people who can say 'yes' in the negative. During those supper-parties, I had grown to dread the contemplative eye above the straight long nose and pursed bar of a mouth, emitting the long-drawn 'Ay, Yur Graçe . . . ay . . . ay . . .' meaning 'Ultimately, Sire—no!'

Which is why, when I left a burgess's house, having talked until the embers in the fire tumbled through their iron basket, I had cause to kiss my hostess, her daughter and the lady guests (together with any listening maidservant, for I omitted none from my human affections): the ladies were my lieutenants who after my departure would rouse their men to build more ships. And I would have kissed the men as well had it been the custom of our country; but our undemonstrative Scots way was to shake the hand, and all hands in that house were wrung, before I set out to walk alone down the hill to Holyrood. (I was known to my Scots by this time as 'ur Hiemmie', and I wondered often as I jumped a puddle on my homeward path through the dark, whether there was another prince in Christendom who bore as his proudest title his own Christian name bestowed upon him by his subjects. I doubted it.)

The Scots had never been slow to import the best of foreign craftsmanship; what was marvellous to me, in these great years of my reign, was the number of times that my host would show me with pride a silver quaiche wrought with Celtic patterns, or a rug woven of hemp in Fyfe, coloured with moss and heather dyes. Our craftsmen were emerging in times of peace and plenty. And not all of these craftsmen were of the artisan class; for when it was known that His Grace encouraged to Court all who could carve or paint or hammer metal, there began to arrive from noble families those sons and nephews who would fifteen years ago have considered such work to be beneath them. We were breeding a new generation of young men—and exceedingly tall young men, for our Scots diet had always made us famed for our stature among Christendom's less nourished people—who had never known days when the black timber houses showed closed doors to the world, with their valuables locked away against the thieves that roamed Scotland's wilderness as in my own boyhood. They were impatient that our land imported the craftsmanship of Italy, France and Spain, neglecting to encourage the quality of work produced by our Scots artisans. Having their own time free of the clan wars which had engaged their fathers, they themselves set out to show the world what Scots hands and Scots brains could produce between them.

At my Court the accident of birth was no obstacle to human progress. I collected a foster-family of these lads, of noble or of humble birth, who could work in wood or stone or metal. Their chief problem was to find good working light, to which end they commandeered the roof of my Palace of Linlithgow—which happened to be my own favourite walk when I had grave matters to ponder, and although I had every sympathy with their needs there were certain times when necessity obliged me to claim a few privileges in return for the tasks of Royalty. What finally caused their banishment from the roof-top was the litter of wood chippings that they caused to blow across the quadrangle lawn and block the waters of the fountain. So I took for them a house in the West Gait outwith the wall of Edinburgh, and there they dwelled and worked with hindrance of nobody.

One of my protegés was a lad called David Seton—of that ilk, and highly disfavoured by it, until I persuaded his parents and uncles that he had not betrayed his high birth by having talent as a sculptor. He had more than talent as it turned out, he had genius. He began with fine, tall, ascetic figures of saints in the mediaeval manner—exquisite work, though traditional. Then he began to experiment in the Italian style, and although his work then was charming to the eye, it was no better than many could have turned out who could round a nymph's cheek or a cherub's buttock. I saw myself small use for the Italian style in a climate inimical to thin drapery and bacchanalian fauna: our Scots angels

140

needed wool and oatmeal. We had many discussions on this subject, which may have been why suddenly in the year 1510 he came to see me in great excitement to beg two baulks of oak which he had seen left to season in a pile in my new dockyard on the shore by Leith; although I could ill spare Fyfe oak at that time, I let him have them.

Afterwards, I was not sorry. From the timber he produced two figures 'St Peter and St Andrew' at work hauling nets upon the Sea of Galilee. They were men of life-size, straining backwards, one standing and the other almost down upon his haunches —true fishermen, such as might be seen any day at work in our home waters, clad in their canvas jerkins, bare-footed, and with the enduring granite Scots faces of men wresting their hard living from the sea. When the work was finished, I had it brought from the house in the West Gait to set in the niche above my new square staircase in Holyrood—the first to be built in a graceful domestic style, for I felt Scotland was safe enough these days not to have a winding stair giving defenders the advantage to their sword-arm.

I appeared at first to be alone in my enthusiasm for these two Scots apostles. They were called crude and ugly—and indeed, St Peter's crouched splayed foot was ugly, in the way that most human feet are ugly, and its impact upon the eye as one came up the stair to its level was the stimulus to imagine the weight of the catch and the width of the waters of Galilee. It was called blasphemous, for these were not saints at all but common working folk—ay, so they were. And they were masculine as well—as was proved when I came up the stair to catch one of my Queen's ladies admiring St Andrew's muscular male forearm in a way that I am sure would not have pleased my bishops. However, to be a king is not always harmful to the interests of art; when it was known that His Grace heartily approved Seton's work, it was not long before many lords and burgesses were admitting to finding in it features of excellence which had formerly escaped their notice.

It was the burgesses who chiefly fostered the art of painting. Their town houses could be decorated in more homely ways than the stone fortresses inherited by our nobles, and there grew up a fashion to have ceilings, and walls where possible, painted with bright patterns of fruit and flowers—I knew one house where the artist had chosen as his subject the reed beds of the North Loch and the mallards and wild geese that throve there. And in the way that men do who have made their fortune for sons and grandsons to inherit, they were anxious to leave to posterity their likeness, thus creating a clientele for the portrait limners.

Much of the work was crude at this stage, but some of it was brilliant. I remember a portrait of myself, executed when I was about the age of thirty-seven, by a Scots limner whose name will be one of the several which float to the surface of my memory with their owners' personalities unidentified. Because it was a significant work, I have more cause to remember the art than the artist—for which he, being a true craftsman, would, I think, forgive me. He painted me with the direct gaze out of the picture, not commonly encountered at that time in portraits of princes, and he had me turn my head so that it appeared as if I were leaning forward about to address the observer. My hair he darkened with deep shadows, so that it swung, almost black, forward from my shoulders. When it was completed, the overall effect was to the life James Stewart—not a King of Scots; James Stewart, as the burgesses' supper gatherings knew me, eyes and mouth vibrant with enthusiasm, rousing the world with my own vitality. He had caught upon his board the quality of magnetism which made me able to achieve so much in so little time. It was the face of me that I would wish time to remember, when I had crept into line with the dusty solemn names and titles of my ancestors; I had it hung in the Tolbooth of Edinburgh to keep its eye on Scotland after I was dead. (Where is it now, I wonder?)

In music and heroic literature, Scotland's inheritance was rich enough before my time. The King my father had raised our musical art to heights which could never be surpassed, and barely equalled. His passion for music had helped lose him a crown, but as his son I was always secretly warmed to hear it said that we never heard these days the quality of music that rang in the vaults of the Chapel Royal at Stirling when I was a lad, with His Grace my father conducting a choir second to none in Christendom. And they were right.

In the verbal art, our inheritance had been carried forward by the Celtic bards and the makars of Scotland's lowland—great tales, and great poetry, needing only to be set to paper to make great literature. The bards and makars were performers, not scholars, and their skill with words lived only so long as did they themselves, or those whose memory held their singing and their recitation. But these were changing times; the new imprinting process made it possible for a poet's work to reach an audience wider than the group about the hearthstone. In England, France and Germany, they had just acquired imprinting houses; I was constantly impatient that we in Scotland should have this new means to promote art and learning. We had the poets, but not as yet the imprinting press.

There was a man, Henryson, now advanced in years, whose work I had been collecting since my youth when he was presented to me at my Court in Dunfermline, where he worked as tutor of a grammar school. He was a strange man, who gave me his verses to read as though indifferent to my reaction—they had marvellous visual sense, the work of a meticulous observer. I offered him a pension to stay at my Court and write for us, only to have my offer rejected in tones that made my courtiers shudder for his future. He poured out his contempt for sycophants, and demanded to know who would teach the young of Dunfermline to read and write if he came to waste his time among my courtiers? Abashed, I had no answer. At the end of his tirade, he gave me a sudden smile of incomparable sweetness, and added as an afterthought 'Yur Grace' . . . in a tone which made the word 'grace' sound more like a tribute to my character than the Regal style of Scotland.

His ways never mended. At times he would come through to Edinburgh, but there was small hope of persuading him to use a bedchamber in my Palace; invariably, he would choose in preference the hospitality of burgesses upon the Canon Gait or Castle Hill—although what he and they had in common remained to all a mystery. He would patronize the vennel howff—or tavern—where our younger poets congregated (and I among them at times); there he drank great quantities of ale and terrorized their gathering. Our argumentative Scots nature made poetry a battleground like all other vital subjects, and what the rival groups of these verse-makers had to say about each other could be heard at each end of the vennel.

One who came but rarely to the howff was William Dunbar—which was partly the reason why the rest of our poets foregathered there. Even I, who could find good in almost anybody, had nothing kind to say about Dunbar. I had endured his presence at my Court since the age of fifteen, when my boyish good nature had suffered his tale of woe, and I told him he was welcome to my Court 'fur sic time ye have need'. Twenty years later, I was still trying to get rid of him.

Envious, pompous, vain and sermonizing, he had no good word to say for living soul—except my Queen, whom he flattered excruciatingly. That was when I had made my second great mistake, by sending him down to London as part of my marriage embassy; I had hoped that King Henry would keep him. Instead, he managed to persuade the English Court that he was known in Scotland as our greatest poet—a fact of which we Scots until that time had not heard—and the crafty opportunist had come back thereafter to make himself 'the King's Rhymer' before I had realized what was happening. I loathed Dunbar. His saving grace was not his poetry; merely, he knew how to flatter a young girl who was pregnant every year with my children, and buried all of them save one.

He believed that as a poet he had no need to justify his existence in any other way. I pointed out to him that my great-grandfather, James the Lion, too, had been a poet of distinction, but *he* had seen it as no disgrace to work for his living in the Regal capacity. My Court of these days included several who could pen a verse as capably as they could break a horse, but they made no such fuss about it. Nor did I—and my verses written in the nocturnal, and unsleeping, hours, were no mean achievement; my trouble was, as King and as a man with a deeply private nature, I did not flaunt my verses, and most of them were consigned to the candle flame, once written.

I was, in fact, like all the members of my family, an artist manqué. The Stewarts were a dynasty of dabblers, and ours was a formidable history of poets, advocates, musicians, architects, astrologers and surgeons lost to the world through need to reign as princes. I was the arch-dabbler, even by Stewart standards, and the collection of experimental paraphernalia littering my *chambre de travailler* bore witness to the claim 'His Grace kennet yon' whenever news was brought to my Palace of somebody with a new invention. I had a smattering of every man's craft, which over the years had proved invaluable if only to sustain conversation with my subjects. If a man had a trade of which I knew nothing, I drank up the information he imparted like dry ground during a thunderstorm. Everything interested me.

When I was young, it had been the way of kings to deal with all matters while enthroned in their audience chamber or the great hall. I changed all that. Like my Aunt Margaret, I needed a glory-hole in which to potter, so that I could leave there untouched my pestle and mortar, the model of a ship, or a book open at the page which I was reading. Each of my palaces had one room set aside for this purpose, which none entered except on pain of banishment, and which, when it required cleaning, I attended myself with a dust-scrape and brush borrowed from the servitors. My *chambres de travailler* were a joke among my courtiers.

It was, however, accepted that even as a king my presence served other useful purposes. My row of flasks, whose contents I mixed together, never succeeded in presenting us with a cure for the plague, but I was not the only apothecary to fail in that quest, and my search gave incentive to those better qualified than myself to pursue it. My most often used implement was a pair of dental pliers—not unlike those used by a smith to extract shoe nails, but smaller; it had been found that my strong grip and steady hand caused less pain than was usual when extracting teeth. I had no shortage of patients. It was quite customary for a man to join my audience list whose swollen face gave him precedence before bishops and ambassadors; when I saw him, I would send for my tooth extractors and the flask of aqua vitae used to cleanse the socket, and we ended his agony while diplomats and petitioners looked on.

In 1506, Elphinstone's first crop of medical students from Aberdeen descended upon the suffering populace. In former days, it had been customary for a physician emerging from his course of study in natural philosophy, to set himself to learn the arts of bleeding, mixing medicine and surgery from those qualified to teach him. Youth is never slow to assume that it knows everything, and when we had created our medical faculty it had never occurred to Elphinstone or to myself that our new young physicians would amend the old custom, and assume that the word *medical* guaranteed their ability to wield the knife as though it had been a wand conferred on them by graduation. In consequence, I had an alarmed deputation of Edinburgh's barber-surgeons come to me with hideous tales of patients lacking limbs and bleeding to death at the hands of our bright young men from Aberdeen. I was furious with Elphinstone; I had told him to consult the practitioners and not the theorists when he compounded the curriculum for our new medical faculty. He never heard the last of it.

As it turned out, the barber-surgeons themselves had brought the answer. They were come to request a charter to form their own guild, to limit the practice of surgery to those whose ability had been examined and approved by qualified men of their calling. Such ruling applied to all trade guilds, but in this case there were complications; a physician graduated from university, could not spare time—nor had the inclination—to apprentice himself to a barber, to learn how to trim a beard in order to qualify as a surgeon. In the end we compromised, by having a training school set up and run by the guild, to teach anatomy and surgery to the graduate physicians. It was the practical manifestation of the dream I had in my head when in 1494 I told Elphinstone that healing art required to be taught in a new way. In this school of the barber-surgeons, who were lay-men, it was possible to do what would not have been countenanced within the ecclesiastical structure of the university, namely, to dissect cadavers and learn to manipulate the structure of the living body.

I was delighted. We granted our Royal Charter to the Guild of Barber-Surgeons of Edinburgh, upon October 13th, 1506. It was one of the few times in my life when I was conscious of making history in a way that had nothing to do with the fact of my being a prince—I was the innovator of a new kind of healing which would blossom in the years ahead of my generation. For all that. . . . I quaked inwardly. There was something in the thought of those dead bodies being cut to pieces by our students' knives which made me shudder. All my life, I had felt a terrible need to be sure the dead had proper burial. (I hated to gibbet the heads of felons, although we had to do it.) My Stewart 'lang ee' had seen ahead of me a peril which my intellect could not visualize. What was it?

These five centuries later I can tell you: not here—but in another document, I will.

Alchemy was another of my studies. A great change had happened in alchemy since my father's generation. Formerly, the quest had been for gold, and the pursuit itself had not been vital; incantation and magic played a part in it. Within my time all this had changed. There were two distinct schools of alchemy emerging in my day: the men who mixed substances to see what would happen, and the theorists who wrote out in detail what they believed to be the reason why the leadness of lead was different from the goldness of gold. And here there is a distinct change of thinking; we had left the climate in which humanity's problems were answered by the increase of gold, and entered a new day where knowledge about the structure of material was precious for its own sake. Our language did not have words to determine where lay this difference, but by our thinking and our efforts we made it plain to those who had eyes to see, that the world was changing.

My first alchemist, John Peddy, had been introduced to me by William Elphinstone—the Church had an ambivalent attitude towards alchemy at this time. Peddy was a practical alchemist, who held to the theory that if quicksilver could be heated sufficiently, its granules changed colour to become granules of gold. The problem was to create the heat sufficient to achieve this metamorphosis. In Damascus, it was known, they had some kind of process to heat iron sufficiently to make the strongest, finest steel imaginable, and Peddy's ambition was to discover a similar way to heat quicksilver in order to make gold. That he did not achieve his objective while he worked under my patronage was a risk taken when one employed an alchemist. He ended his contract with me, whereafter he would find another patron. It was easy to accuse an alchemist of being a charlatan—but then, it was easy to tell the difference between a charlatan and an alchemist: if a man promised to make me rich, I gave him his dinner and sent him away with my blessing; a man who barely mentioned wealth, but waxed eloquent about his method—oh yes, him I would employ.

The most remarkable man I ever encountered in this field was an itinerant friar called John Damian—a small fellow with warm brown eyes which betrayed the mixture of Italian and French blood in him. Damian had travelled everywhere and knew everybody. In Florence he had known Leonardo da Vinci, with whom he shared an interest in flying machines; he had also made a great friend of a fellow-mathematician called Buanaroti. Buanaroti had somewhat fallen in Damian's eyes because he had sold out his great mathematical gifts in order to acquire wealth as a sculptor and painter. I pointed out that Buanaroti, now called Michelangelo, had not done at all badly for himself by his work with chisel and brush—but Damian would have none of it; he was himself foremostly a mathematician, and felt that Michelangelo ought to have remained true to his genius.

The tragedy of Damian was that our world of 1500 had no employment to offer a mathematician. The best he could do was to become an alchemist—and to this end had followed across Europe a band of gypsies, whom he thought had the secret of transmuting matter that had been known to the Ancients of Egypt. This was how he came to Scotland, in the wake of a tribe whom he thought to be those gypsies he sought. He had already pursued his quarry across Northern Africa, and while there increased his knowledge of mathematics to such extent he could no longer communicate with laymen like me and my kind.

But he could talk in terms of alchemy. His theory was that all substance was composed of minute particles held together by the divine quintessence, the Holy Spirit. He had a great bundle of papers which he tried to show me, saying that these proved the truth of his argument, but they were covered with symbols which nobody in my Court could comprehend. He then tried by a physical demonstration to show what he meant—and here had more success, for he used sand and water to explain his theory. If, he said, he could loose the particles of lead, and then reform them, there was no reason why he should not reassemble them as gold. Knowing the trap, I asked—Did he truly mean that he could produce for me an unlimited quantity of gold? To this, he replied, with a straight look into my eyes, and then a downward glance, that any man who could loose the particles from the divine quintessence which held them together would be as powerful as God. He then lifted his eyes, which for that moment held unearthly sadness, and asked where was the man so pure of heart he could be trusted to hold the power of God?

I straightway took him as my alchemist, and to promote his labours gave him the Abbacy of Tungsland. Men serve God in many ways, and I had no conscience about using ecclesiastical funds to finance the quest for knowledge by men of such humility that the Creator might even be prepared to entrust them with it. It was for this very reason that I never gave a benefice to the poet Dunbar; and Dunbar thereafter became the sworn enemy of Damian.

Dunbar vented his spleen in a satiric poem about John Damian's attempts to build a machine on which he could glide through the air. Damian's theory—derived from watching sea-gulls—was that the air contained currents as does the sea, and that birds *floated*; he tried to build a machine of fine timberwork and feathers to emulate their flight. It failed. I expected it to fail; but that was no cause to say that flight by man was impossible, nor to snigger—as Dunbar did—at the efforts of brave men to try it. I never believed that my own generation was the wisest that the world had ever known; nor did Damian.

My courtiers expected gold. I was not terribly concerned about the gold, but we had to justify Damian's existence. Hence the flying machine which was wrecked upon a gust of wind from Stirling's plain, and nearly wrenched off the arm of its inventor. Beyond that, how could we prove him not a charlatan, when all that he ever produced were screeds of calculations which none of my courtiers, nor myself, could pretend to understand? Damian knew a great deal about the divine quintessence, I had no doubt whatever, but God had given His secrets only to Damian.

At the end, to try to make a place for the wee fellow, I collected a body of mathematicians such as taught in our universities—Aberdeen, St Andrews and Glasgow—and set them to examine him as a mathematician. I knew that none of the eight had sufficient knowledge of their subject to come anywhere near comprehending Damian, but at least their presence lent him credit in the eyes of my courtiers.

Or so I had hoped. What happened eventually was that the man from Glasgow—whose subject mainly was Greek and not mathematics—asked Damian, was he suggesting that the Body of Our Lord present at the sacrament was composed of granules of flour? At which I ended the debate. In three minutes more Damian would be accused of Lollardry, and I would be asked whether or not I supported him. Fifteen years earlier I might have turned the argument so that it would not matter, but not now; the whole of Christendom had changed its climate, and I kept peace among our Scots by not committing myself to any man's side in this particular argument. But it was not a world in which there was a future for a man who wanted merely to discover the identity of matter.

John Damian resigned his Abbacy of Tungsland as the most helpful gesture he could make in circumstances beyond our control. I gave him his bundle of papers, which he had offered me, to take away with him; they were more use to him than they would have been to me. His sad small figure haunts me yet, as he set forth upon the road: I think he may have been the one man closest to Truth that ever I discovered, and at the end I had to let him down. His mathematics were a menace to Scotland.

Our occasional failure to communicate with our own times had as well its comic aspect, as in the case of Maxwell's play.

The masque had taken hold at my Court, chiefly amongst the Queen's English retinue; it was a dismal entertainment in our Scots view, being merely an excuse for the performers to wear outlandish costumes at great expense, supported by a quantity of undistinguished music. In an effort to supplant it by something more virile and lively, I suggested to our poets gathered in the howff that one of them should write a play. Plays had been performed for centuries by the guilds' members upon holy days, but I was visualizing something closer to the style of the ancient Hellenic drama where the writer contributed more to the speeches than did the players using his own words. Maxwell accepted my challenge, asking me to suggest his theme—and I said 'Justice', thinking thereby to inspire him to shape a tale upon those lines.

Maxwell took the suggestion literally, and composed dialogue in the Platonic manner discussing the reality of Justice. It was not a bad effort, although the mummers we engaged to act the roles insisted they should add a great deal of horse-play of their own which, Maxwell and I felt privately, had not a great deal to do with the subject. However, it would serve to fill an evening of the kind that grew wearisome when the members of the Household were cooped up together during winter's dark hours.

Maxwell's play turned out to be the greatest Court entertainment of our lifetime, although not for reasons which its author had intended. The fun began when an elderly lord who was watching took exception to a statement made in the play by one of the actors, and rose to his feet with great indignation to join the argument. Those nearby at first tried to quieten him, pointing out that the object was to listen and not to participate—which seemed to this good and ancient Earl a suggestion not far removed from treason: he demanded to know where were the King's champions, when it was thus allowed in His Grace's presence that crude mummer fellows could argue that the King's Law was not a just law? At which the white-faced author of the play leapt upon his stool to shout that he had to give some of his characters foolish lines to speak, in order that these might subsequently be corrected by other players. This gave no satisfaction to the King's champion, whose vehemence had by now raised the native debating spirit present in all our Scots courtiers. The players, who had been provided with no dialogue to use in this emergency, stood lost in the middle of the hall, wondering whether to fight back, whether to bow their exit, or whether to continue with their own lines in the hope the debate within the audience might eventually die down. I was no help to them, being so convulsed with laughter that I rolled helplessly in my chair, tears streaming from my eyes, made speechless by merriment. Nor was I alone in my mirth, for the half of the Court which had not been caught up either in the argument about justice, or in poor Maxwell's wild efforts to quiet the audience and direct the players, was rocking with laughter at the unplanned entertainment.

All said afterwards that it was the merriest evening any of us could remember, and up to 1513 Maxwell was continually exhorted to write for us another play as hilarious at the one he had provided—but he never took this as a compliment, nor could he a second time thus oblige us.

Looking back, it truly was a great pity that so many more grave matters occupied my mind from the year 1509, for I think we had in Maxwell's play the beginning of an art in which the Scots could have excelled. We had poetry in our being, and we had that instinct for debate which wrecked this first performance of the play: drama should have been our *forte*. All of us who could have written it, and I include myself, went down into England in 1513 . . .

Even in 1506 I had the sense that our swift great achievement was foredoomed. Upon a hilltop or by a tower window often I would pause to regard our land of peace and plenty, feeling beneath my satisfaction that apprehension which had dogged my days. I who had come by my crown through an act of regicide ought not to have so well succeeded. My father's name had been these many years unspoken except to date an era, but he came constantly to my thoughts like a shadow thrown across my bright Kingdom. Was there somewhere retribution in wait for me? For myself I did not mind, but I shivered for Scotland.

I had sought absolution, which had been granted by His Holiness; yet the great fear persisted that I would at the end cause more harm to my Realm than benefit. It was useless for my confessor to tell me that Christ was merciful, or that I had paid my soul's debt through service to my Kingdom. I knew myself; James Stewart of the 'lang ee' who paid the highest price for everything. I decided to go upon a pilgrimage to Jerusalem. That journey in our day took heavy toll of pilgrims, many of whom succumbed to plague or fell victim to marauding Turkish galleys. Yet I had to go; and if I died, it would at least free Scotland from the danger it would inherit my worse-than-Stewart luck. If I could die for Scotland—now—I believed my death could spare her these unknown, dreaded calamities. For myself—och, since Meg died, I was not truly of this world at all; and I had done what I had vowed, as a boy, when I took the field by Stirling, which was to raise Scotland to her rightful place among nations. If I asked one thing more of God, it was that the blame for my transgressions be laid upon myself and not upon my Kingdom.

I had discussed with Robert Blacader this worry that I had, that a heavy penance was required either of me or of my Kingdom. He did not scorn my anxiety. I discovered that he many times had said masses to atone for the King my father's death, and to perpetuate our Kingdom's good fortune. He heard me out—and said, with a faint smile, that he, too, with the advancing years, had learned to be less sure of his welcome into Paradise than he had been when he was a young man with all of this world's opportunity ahead of him. These were strange words from my kinsman Blacader, who had always seemed to me one of humanity's most successful members, in that he had secured high position and amassed wealth without sacrifice of a single principle. I had always envied his knack of storing up treasure in heaven without diminishing his enjoyment of this life's benefits. It made me feel very old to hear him now doubt the success of this achievement.

He said suddenly—'Sall et please Yur Grace, ah wad da penance fur an King slauchteret, und gangend ta Jerusalem sall be my burden.' Then he gave a small, down-curving smile, and added, 'Ah hov gagend mony ways ta please Yur Grace, und lief wad ance travel i' sairvice ta God's Majesty.'

I was deeply moved by the offer that he would do penance on my behalf to spare the Kingdom; he was not a young man now, and the likelihood of his returning from Jerusalem was slight. It seemed to me that this offer of sacrifice made by a kinsman and a bishop, well might serve as an alternative to my own pilgrimage, if duty made that venture impracticable. I told him that we would talk of it again.

II

PRINCE JAMES, our Heir, was born upon February 21st, 1507. It was a propitious year for the birth of a future King, for in it we had everything. It was the year that our universities released their first full crop of the young men whose education began with the passing of the Act of 1496. Although they were not yet a great number, many were the sons of gentlemen dwelling in remote rural areas where the presence of trained law officers was most required, and for the first time we had no lack of qualified candidates for these appointments. And it was the year that printing came to Scotland.

Some two years before, at a supper gathering in a burgess's house close by the market of Edinburgh, I had seen a wee man tucked away in a corner, apparently overawed by the company he was keeping—the Lord Provost was a member of the party, with several members of the City Council. I left my fellow guests to share the Provost between them, and joined Maister Myller. I knew him as a glover, but it soon appeared that he had a string of other interests beside, including a fondness for writing verses. He lamented that we had not yet established an imprinting press in Scotland and casually mentioned that he had himself experimented with engraved copper plates, although not with any great success, owing to the deficiency of his knowledge. The outcome of it was that he volunteered to go to Paris, where his trade connections could give him an introduction to the printing house there, to learn more about the subject.

While Myller was away, I cultivated another city merchant, Walter Chepman, who acted for Bishop Elphinstone and Gawayn Douglas (the poet, third son to Angus 'Bell-the-Cat') as agent in the purchase of books upon the Continent. Chepman was a thin, dapper fellow, with a neat beard and the aspect of the successful merchant. On closer acquaintance, he proved to have a considerable depth of scholarship and to know as much about books as he did about prices. He was not slow to see that an imprinting house was a sound investment for his money, as well as a vital contribution to Scotland's learning. When Myller returned from Paris, I brought the two men together, and their partnership was formed during that evening.

Chepman bought a house in the West Gait, which at this time was a district imbued with an atmosphere of artistic experiment, for it was here the sons of wealthy burgesses had settled to do business on their own account; their youth made them venturesome, and they gave ready patronage to rising craftsmen. A printing press, constructed to Andrew Myller's specification, was installed upon the upper floor. Its weight and vibration when in action soon caused the store-room ceiling to give way, however, so that it had to be hurriedly taken to pieces and reassembled upon solid ground at the back of the shop, where new windows had to be made in the thick stone back wall of the premises to give enough light for Myller to see what he was doing. The outside staircase had to be taken away, too, to allow more light to enter what was now the main door of the ground-floor premises.

I can see that house yet, with the upper gallery, made of timber, overhanging the street. The doorway had a lintel and frame heavily carved with a pattern not unlike the bordering which Myller used at times to ornament the pages of his books, and instead of a sign above the door to indicate the nature of their wares, Chepman had the elegant and unusual idea of showing an open book upon a lectern behind the window which opened upon the street. It was a very small window, about a cubit square, with black pitched shutters fastened back to the wall each side. I went there myself to see the first imprinted book we ever made, set open in the window, and already there was a great press of people trying to get a glimpse of it. It was a set of Parliamentary Acts bound together in book form, for Myller's first and most vital commission was to print my laws to be circulated to the burghs, so that ignorance of law could no longer be used (as occasionally it had been used in the past) as a plea by the defendant's advocate. Elphinstone's breviaries had to wait—and indeed they had to wait rather a long time; they could, if necessary, be purchased from the Continent.

In the upper room, Walter Chepman kept the accounts and interviewed customers bringing their work to be printed. In the booth below, an apprentice served customers buying books, while Myller was at the back of the shop doing his printing. Poor Myller had a terrible time of it at first, for the customers were eager to see the press at work and pestered him with questions. In the end, they erected a screen, partly to spare him this nuisance, and also to protect their trade secrets as there was no guild to safeguard them, and there existed a very real danger that ignorant people might themselves set up as imprinters with insufficient knowledge of the craft to preserve its high standards. Myller had, if I remember correctly, at least three apprentices by the year 1513.

The house in the West Gait became a meeting ground for Scotland's literary population. Chepman's upper room might hold as many as a dozen at one time, sipping glasses of wine and perched wherever they could find a seat between the piles of new paper and the heaps of books—bishops, students, merchants, advocates, ballad singers—anybody and everybody who wanted something printed.

The vennel howff, however, still held its place in our affections —and particularly in mine, as I had made a friend there who revitalized me in a way I had thought could not happen again. Her name was Nan, and she served ale to the customers and at times would give them a song in a sweet, low-pitched voice, accompanying herself upon the Celtic harp. Other than the taverner's wife, few respectable women would work in an ale-house, but Nan had a way of quelling the lewdest fellow with a look so regal she had him blushing. All the young poets had tried at some time to win her favours, but had made no further headway than the rest of the customers. She was the widow of a sailor who was drowned in the early days of their marriage, and her heart was his alone. For all her gaiety, her eyes showed that she knew life as penance, and she and I knew as much about each other in five short sentences as most other people would discover in a lifetime. She was a bonny lass, tall and slenderly graceful, with a fine pair of hands and a thick, waist-long bunch of hair escaping down her back like a horse's tail from beneath her snowy linen cap. She wore her skirt girded to make work easier, showing calves and ankles that were much appreciated in the howff for all their dense covering of thick blue wool and the heavy shoes she wore. Blue-eyed, with a radiant fair complexion and curls of reddish gold escaping round her face, she made a picture. She carried herself beautifully—which to me was always important in a woman; but mostly it was the face which haunted me, her look of one who makes life bearable because she must, but who has no anxiety to extend it one day longer than necessary.

I did not go often to the howff, but I must have seen her three or four times—and she knew who I was, although it was an unspoken agreement in the tavern to act as though my other identity was something left behind at Holyrood—when one night I offered to escort her home, a spontaneous suggestion made because it was dark and she was a lady; in the same spirit, she accepted my offer.

It was dark as pitch in the labyrinth of vennels, with the wet, raw cold of a winter's night. The vennels were mere passages between the tall black timber houses, four and a half feet (three cubits) at their widest part, and narrowing by two feet where a stair jutted out from the wall. They were as steep as the bed of a burn where they dropped from the Castle Hill to the main thoroughfare at the bottom of the valley—and they not infrequently ran like a burn when the rain came washing down over their mud surface. (Eventually most of the vennels were paved with cobblestones, as the folk of each stair collaborated to lay a track alongside their communal wall.) They smelt of damp wood and urine, of cats and rotting vegetable parings. The rain had washed away the midden heaps to strand the ground like the forlorn hem of the tide; if one set a foot wrong, it squelched in filth up to the ankle. There was here and there a smell of supper, escaping through a pair of shutters—good smells, of a new-made pasty, or of fish browning in a skillet, the smell of common folk eating well. The day's din had quietened, for bairns were a-bed by this time, but the unglazed windows were like a row of mouths and ears lining the walls, from which a wife's voice to her husband spoke at my shoulder as though she had meant the words for me, and anything I said would have been heard within the room as plainly. I loved the vennels, for the sense of closeness to my subjects that it gave me; even as I liked the smell, which was a living smell, of human health and human filth in a world made warm by its company.

The only light came in filtering yellow beams from the shutters, and one was in danger of slipping on the steep, greasy surface, or of cracking one's head against the stair-frames which jutted out dangerously from alternate sides.

As the population of Edinburgh had expanded, a great many houses had been built upon the steep south side of the Castle ridge and, owing to the sharp gradient, many of these had fallen down. It was now customary for each house to be built partly overlapping its lower neighbour, thus creating an extra room, which native inventiveness soon turned into a separate dwelling, reached by means of a wooden ladder built to the outside wall of the house below. Within my lifetime this practice had become general, and Edinburgh's houses were built in piles of three or four, with a zig-zag wooden stairway up the outside of the structure, giving access by a small landing to each separate door. It was a phenomenon peculiar to Edinburgh; I was surprised when our foreign visitors expressed themselves amazed, and a little amused, by Edinburgh's stair-houses, for I should have thought other cities built over hills might have tried similar experiments.

Scots communal logic had bequeathed to the stair-houses a set of customs all their own. As it was in the general interest to have the roof, staircase, chimneys and so forth maintained in good repair, the inhabitants made a rule to share the work or the cost of the work. They required no law to make the occupants comply with these sensible proceedings, for the life of a rogue neighbour upon a stair would not have been worth living. Another custom was a meticulous regard for the cleanliness of the stair. Edinburgh was a notoriously windy city, and garbage flung out into the vennel frequently blew back to collect upon a lower neighbour's landing; therefore the housewomen decided between themselves to make a practice to sweep, and if necessary wash, the whole stair at least twice weekly. This duty they performed by rota, and so that none would forget or argue about it, they kept a token which was passed from hand to hand as a reminder. (Nan once showed me one of these tokens, which were round pieces of wood, horn or brass, with a cord loop by which to hang it up. I was delighted with this example of Scots good sense, and asked if I could keep it? Nan was horrified, and snatched it from me to replace upon its nail, asking did I wish to upset the governance of her stair?)

Nan walked ahead of me now, to show me the cleanest, safest way, and I may have had my eyes more upon her than where I was going, for I suddenly struck my head in the dark so hard that she must have heard the crack of my skull as well as the yelp I gave. After that we crushed together side by side between the jutting stairs, with her hand and arm locked close in mine so that she could guide me. I found it exquisitely exciting to go homeward bound in this fashion, like any couple among the stair-house folk, whispering and laughing close, and hugging to myself the glorious thought of what they would say at Holyrood if they knew what I was up to. My courteous gesture had brought me an adventure, and it was with a pang I heard Nan announce that we had reached her stair.

To snatch another moment, I said I would escort her to her door, and followed her up the zig-zag course of stairs and landings. At the third flight we stopped by the door of her own dwelling. It was then I realized my mistake in prolonging the encounter: what now was I to do, and what was she to do with me? Nan resolved the problem with instinctive skill: she flung wide the door, then dropped a deep curtsey—leaving it to me whether I took it as an invitation or a gracious dismissal. I entered, and stood looking at the fire's embers as she searched in the dark to find and light a smoky dip candle. I did not like to gaze about the single room as she replenished the fire, for it would have been like prying into her life. I felt uncomfortable and lost for words now the noise and gossip of the howff or the perils of the vennel no longer helped to bridge the distance between us. Then she turned, looking as uneasy and miserable as I felt myself, and for lack of ought else, dipped a slow, sad curtsey in the middle of her own dwelling-room. We had made a terrible mess of everything between us.

I clutched suddenly at the idea that she could sing a song for me, before I left, for music knows no barriers. She agreed readily, setting the single stool before the fire for me to sit while she changed her mud-soaked shoes for a pair with fine buckles of silver that she would wear for mass or festival occasions. Then she ungirded her skirt, shaking it loose about her ankles—and stood beside the fire to sing for me. I unloosed my cloak, while I sat enjoying her voice and the bonny sight of her. For the first time I saw that she was older than I had supposed, being about thirty—which pleased me the more, for she was a woman of my own years.

I felt free now to glance about the room. There was a table against the wall, set with her knife, cup and wooden platter for the next day; a shelf to accommodate her few culinary implements; a wooden chest which would hold her clothes; a bed without posts, covered by a blue quilt—above which, from a nail driven into the wall, there hung her rosary. The rushes on the floor were freshly strewn, and from one of the several hooks in a ceiling beam there hung a net which held rushes set to dry. The whitewash of the boards between the beams had been smoked by the back-blowing of the chimney, and coils of smoke wreathed out now as I was watching. There was a cold sliver of draught cut across the room from the crack between the shutters which took the place of glazing. It was an empty yet an ample dwelling for a widowed woman, and typical of the way most of my subjects lived who were plain-folk.

Then she sang a song which once I had loved, but since Meg's death could no longer bear to hear. I should have stopped her, yet could not. It was a lament for a dead love—and the girl sang it with terrible power, ringing out through each word her own real grief. It was five years my lass had been gone, and I had kept my feelings hidden all that while—now my pent-up anguish was released. I covered my face with my hands, but the tears poured through my fingers. I had no control of them. I was no more aware of the singing, and the next I knew was that a pair of arms encircled my head and shoulders, pressing my face close into the woollen skirt that stood before me. I wrapped my own arms tightly about her hips, clinging like a child to its mother as she cradled my head. How long we stayed thus I had no way of knowing; from the age of fifteen I had been father, mother, friend and comforter to my Kingdom; and this was the first time anyone had given me a place to cry.

Where could it end, as the fire burned low, save beneath the blue quilt with the rosary hanging from its nail above the pillow? We took refuge there together from a world which had used us hardly, two people with no other thing in common but mutual compassion and a need for human comfort. Our harmonious embraces lent sympathy a richness of expression, but it was not to them that I owed the deep warmth I felt toward this woman.

I may have visited Nan some eight or nine times over the next three years. She knew never to expect me, and on my side I was always prepared to slip away as quietly as I came if a head-shake as she opened the door told me she had other visitors. We would spend the two or three snatched hours of each visit in a private world complete of itself, unrelated to our other lives, yet entrancing them. Nan's way of styling me 'Yur Grace' in our closest and tenderest moments awoke me to the realization that my lifelong inward battle between James Stewart and the King of Scots at last was ended. Scotland, like a great fish scaled with silver lochs, rippling with muscular brown burns, had swallowed all of my loved dead, taking my heart down with them to hook into its guts: it and I had become inseparable. Nan, the solitary matriarch of the common stair, whose empty heart and life accommodated all her neighbours' troubles, was my Kingdom made compact for me to hold between my arms—leading me to the discovery that the Regal task, which I had never truly wanted, had been possibly my vocation.

As with Tam, I gave her no rich presents. I brought her at New Year a lover's gift, a jewel made like a heart, of gold, that she could wear without anybody asking whence it came. Another time it was a white woollen shawl I brought her, the closest I dare go to ladies' finery without causing tongues to clack upon the stair, for I cherished her reputation.

I would, had I the choice, have seen her more often, for this, I knew, was the closest I would ever come again to real happiness. But my Queen was a jealous young girl, and had it reached her ears that I went alone through the dark and filth of the vennels to visit a lady, she was capable of turning Edinburgh upside down to discover whose charm it was that so compelled me. Margaret Tudor was the last girl in the world to comprehend why I loved Nan. I kept safe my secret by sharing it with none—which made it exceedingly difficult to escape the court's vigilance. This was the reason why my visits to Nan's stair-dwelling were so few, and my calls at the howff dwindled in frequency—William Dunbar put his head in the door of the howff now and again, seeking acclaim as 'Scotland's Rhymer', and Dunbar was the Queen's spy.

The last time I saw Nan was upon a summer evening crossing the square to enter St Giles Cathedral, wearing a white shawl—doubtless the one I had given her. I was standing at the window of a merchant's house while the boards were being set for supper. It must have been that last summer, 1513, for the talk behind me was of the mustering for war.

It was in 1507, too, that I sent my son Alexander to the University of Padua where Erasmus then was a tutor. I thought he would have been delighted to have the opportunity to see the world and form yet more opinions about it with which to vex me, so I was exceedingly surprised when he asked morosely in what way had he offended that I should want to send him away from me? I hastened to point out that, as Scotland's future Primate, he required to see more of the world than his Regal father had done, to which he answered in his usual unabashed fashion, would I not then prefer to go myself to Padua and let him stay at home? Then he seized my hand and pleaded with brimming eyes that I would let him stay in Scotland. He was afraid, he said, that another would steal his place in my affections while he was away.

I suspected privately that the birth of a princely half-brother earlier in the year had not delighted my bastard eldest son so well as it had pleased the rest of my subjects. I could not blame the lad, for Alexander must have known as well as I that but for the circumstance of birth he was the one I would have liked to have care for my Scots when I was gone. I regretted it bitterly, which the young devil well knew and traded upon accordingly; but for all that, he was a sensitive creature who could be disarmed of his confidence by a single glance or a word of rejection.

The infant Prince whom I suspected to have been the cause of Alexander's jealousy died in February, 1507–08, aged twelve months. The Queen was again with child.

Several events at this time made me wonder how much value could be set upon the Treaty which had cost me in personal terms so dear. In response to a request from King Henry, I had dissuaded my kinsman the Duke of Gueldres from lending his support to a new pretender to the English throne put up by the Yorkists, Edmund de la Puile. (De la Puile had behaved rather badly, having been pardoned once for the same offence, and I had no wish to see my cousin of Gueldres led astray upon a venture which had a great deal less hope of success than my earlier foray with the Duke of York.) In return, the Duke of Gueldres requested my help against the Emperor Maximilian, and although I refused to send arms, I agreed to use my influence with the Emperor on behalf of my kinsman. Having made peace, it was annoying to discover, during a subsequent period of strained relations between the Duke of Gueldres and the Emperor, that King Henry was sending English mercenaries to fight against my kinsman. It looked very like the pattern of English behaviour that we of Scotland knew so well: England paid meticulous deference to the clauses of the Treaty where it suited her own interests, but registered surprise that her partner should want the same consideration.

The second discordant note was a Border incident of some gravity. My Warden Kerr was murdered by a group of men which included the bastard brother of the English Warden Heron, and there was no doubt whatever that the deed had the knowledge of the English Warden of the Middle March if not his complicity. This was a matter far more serious than an ordinary Border feud, for the Scots Warden had been slain on his way home from the Wardens Court after executing his duty; and if the English Warden paid no regard to the chief function of the Court at which he was a judiciar, the Treaty signed in St Mungo's Abbey gave protection to none of our subjects. Once more this curious English disregard for the rules showed itself. King Henry at first co-operated to the extent of delivering two of the minor culprits; a third was taken by Kerr's sons, who brought me the unwanted gift of his head in a basket; the fourth, the ringleader, Heron's bastard brother, was not produced at all. After some while, I took the English Warden, Sir Walter Heron, into custody in Edinburgh until such time as King Henry appointed a Warden who better understood why we had made a treaty; also, as hostage for his brother who was still at large. The bastard Heron was a trouble maker upon the Border who had, I suspected, earned his hanging quite a few times over even before the murder of Kerr, but for some reason King Henry showed himself curiously deaf to all my requests that he should surrender him, and seemed to think me unreasonable for insisting that justice should be seen to be done. I half-wished that it had been Henry Tudor who had received the basket with a head inside it, for he might then have supported me in trying to prevent these incidents which were a natural consequence of our failure to implement the law. The trouble was that London, unlike Edinburgh, was a very long way from the Border.

The third cause of my displeasure struck like an icy wind upon the year of promise which had looked the brightest in Scotland's history (for all that torrential rain had spoiled the harvest).

I had sent my cousin James Hamilton, now Earl of Arran, and his brother Patrick as ambassadors to King Louis XII of France (with whom England was at this time on friendly terms). On his return, delayed by bad weather, my cousin James in his usual impetuous fashion had decided to use the land route across England; for this, he ought to have requested a letter of passage from King Henry, but to my fury he had omitted this formality —the King's cousin had greater need than any other of our subjects to show punctilious regard for such matters. Henry Tudor seized Arran, which was reasonable enough, but instead of complaining to me about it and sending home my cousin to be dealt with by me as sharply as he deserved, he required my cousin to sign an oath confirming the Treaty of Perpetual Peace. (Arran was my heir presumptive, and this was a fair indication that King Henry did not himself regard the peace as being perpetual, but wished to make sure that Scotland did.) My cousin, having a higher understanding of Royal behaviour than the one-time Earl of Pembroke, refused to sign any such document without reference to myself, and was thereafter lodged in custody by the English King who refused to let him go until he complied with the instruction.

When this news reached my Lords of Council, the younger members were outraged at King Henry's extraordinary conduct in asking one of our Scots subjects to endorse a Treaty made by Scotland's King. It came, however, as less of a surprise to the older men who could remember earlier days when an English monarch had signed a secret agreement with my father's brother the Duke of Albany, to gain our Scots Realm in vassaldom. James, my cousin, mercifully, could be trusted: England's King could not. My loving father-in-law had slipped his mask, and behind it was the calculating face of King England which Scotland knew so well.

When the English ambassador came to Edinburgh, Scots fists were shaken and Scots voices raised in anger when he rode through the market place. He was a young fellow called Thomas

Wolsey, and the display of hostility perturbed his dignity; he seemed to think that our national affairs were none of our commoners' business, and I forbore to tell him that after four hundred years' acquaintance with King England's habits, there was nothing Thomas Wolsey had been briefed to say which my subjects could not have predicted as well as I could myself. We had grown prosperous and happy, with the chance to employ our creative talents: when England's ambassadors began arriving, we all knew what it meant.

I did not greatly care for Thomas Wolsey. What chiefly grated on my sensibilities was his constant reference to 'my master' in a tone which implied that he and I were disciples of the same Lord. I had no objection to a man bearing himself proudly on his own account, but I could never suffer kindly the sycophant who is pompous on behalf of his superior.

I did not greatly care for Wolsey's business either, although I believed him genuinely to be ignorant of the reason why King Henry wished the Earl of Arran to take an 'oath of perpetual peace'. I told Henry Tudor's diplomat to inform his master that if my cousin did sign any such undertaking, I would upon his return hang him at the Border—and I meant it. James Hamilton would know I meant it. Dearly as I loved my cousin, an heir to Scotland who had signed such an oath under duress was more use to Scotland dead.

As I had promised, when it became obvious that I should not be able to leave Scotland upon a pilgrimage of propitiation for my father's death, I told Robert Blacader that if he still wished to go to Jerusalem on behalf of the Kingdom, I would be grateful to have him do so. He had, as it turned out, for some time been privately making his preparations, and I noticed that he carried now a great serenity, as if he had shorn away all temporal cares. When I gave him his letter of passage, I felt strangely compelled to thank him for all his years of service to myself and the Kingdom. My heart ached unbearably to see him go.

The death of my son Prince James in the February, was followed in the July of 1508 by the birth and immediate death of our daughter. I had begun to see now very plainly where I had failed

Scotland in marrying against my instinct. I had squandered the years of my begetting while waiting for an English Princess to grow to womanhood. I was now thirty-five years old, and I knew in my inner heart that I should not live to a ripe old age. There should have been a Prince of Scotland, now the age of Alexander, to whom I could have been imparting all my plans for the Kingdom which he might well have to implement. Even had our infant Prince lived, he would have needed to mature with phenomenal rapidity to gain upon all our lost time.

I half-hoped that I would not have more issue. There was Arran—or Albany, if the lords would allow his greater claim—both of whom were grown men; I had myself the feeling that Arran would make a good King when responsibility had curbed his impetuosity. Either would have a better chance to hold the Kingdom stable than a bairn, with an English mother to be Regent and an unknown King England for his uncle. The kindest thing I could do for my unborn heir—and for my Kingdom—was to spare him his begetting; but this was more easily thought than put to practice, for my wife had a terrible regard for dynastic duties, besides being a warm-blooded lass with a strong appetite for her husband's kisses. Also, her distress at the death of two children would have made it cruelty to deny her the chance of another who might live.

In December, 1508, came news that my heart had known to expect, yet still it shocked me: Robert Blacader was dead. I had felt when I gave him his letter of passage to go on pilgrimage to Jerusalem, that I had looked upon this one of my henchmen for the last time. It had been as though when I handed him the letter a great slab of my life had torn itself away; the future, I had known, thereafter would be different. Blacader had been the man who tied a material weight to my spiritual endeavours. Now he was gone.

He had reached Jerusalem, and it was upon the homeward journey of the galley from Jaffa back to Venice that plague had struck the boat, slaying all but eight of the thirty-four pilgrims. I pictured the fastidious Bishop, whose crisp cleanliness had made even me at times feel scrofulous, lying with the stench of bubonic sickness upon him, crammed in the black hold of the galley with thirty others in like condition, or with them exposed upon the deck to the murderous heat of the sun. What a way for a man to die, who always had said it was the cleanliness of Glasgow that had spared it the pestilence. It was the nearest to martyrdom that circumstance could offer Robert Blacader.

Which proved my point: he always was a lucky fellow. Having enjoyed the best which this life had to offer, he had worked out a quick salvation to make him qualify for Paradise. And I will admit now what I could not have said then: he always was one of my favourite Bishops, damn his good fortune.

12

I COULD have done with Robert Blacader's shrewd eye to help me assess the complicated international situation that was now developing; Andrew Forman, Bishop of Moray, was now my principal ambassador.

When, in 1504, the College of Cardinals had chosen Guiliano della Rovere to be the Supreme Pontiff, it was fair indication that the Church had taken fright, for few of his fellow cardinals bore him sufficient brotherly love to elect him otherwise. It was said of him that he had once broken off his own celebration of the mass to crack together the heads of two of his acolytes whom he had caught misbehaving, and whether true or not, the tale bore witness to his character. When he became Pope, he chose his own name Guiliano to identify the pontifical personality, becoming Julius II.

The Turks were not the only menace to Christendom when the Cardinals elected della Rovere to be Pope: the Church had three crises to deal with urgently. There was its own sickness—like any ancient body which has outlived its health, it was badly in need of internal reform—aggravated by the pockets of heresy which were springing up all over north-western Europe as the new desire for learning, encouraged by the recently invented imprinting machine, developed questioning attitudes of mind; also Christian princes, like myself, had begun to resent the inconvenience of having to refer in administrative matters to the See of Rome. Secondly, Rome was but one state set within the disjointed Italian peninsula, and Italy had become a battle ground for all the great western powers, wrangling for possession of its richest provinces. The third menace lay in the changing spiritual values of our time—the rich merchants of the Venetian Republic, the Medici merchant-bankers of Florence and Henry Tudor of England were all exponents of the new philosophy that treasure upon earth is preferable to what may be stored in heaven. The Church by its own example had helped to propagate this philosophy and would pay for it dearly unless it provided a new code of behaviour for its flock to follow.

The new Pope began his reign with the announcement that he would lead a Crusade against the Infidel. His predecessors had begun in the same way, using the term as a figure of speech: Guiliano della Rovere meant to head the column in person. From the sound of it, we should be setting off the next morning —an attitude which I found refreshing; the Great Crusade had been the most urgent item on the agenda for the past two hundred years. The fact that Scotland lay furthest from the danger, did not lessen the peril to my shipping and therefore to my communications, should the vast number of Turkish galleys in the Inland Sea continue to increase their strength at the present rate. Thank God we had a Pope at last who was more realistically alive to the danger the Turks posed to our religion and our very existence!

I volunteered readily, requesting that I should be given early warning of the Crusade's actual date of departure, as I had to transport my army a good deal further than the rest of Christendom's princes. King Louis, I knew, had also volunteered, although his gout might prevent his taking part in person. My father-in-law King Henry would doubtless be totalling up the expense of the excursion, and whatever King Ferdinand replied would be known to be unreliable. The Emperor—'puir old Maximilian' as Paniter and I called him—would answer at solemn length, very much aware of his dignity and conscience compelling him to go on the Crusade and wondering how he would pay for it all. The Venetians would be promptly ready to go, if a Venetian were appointed supreme commander: anything in which Venice took part had to be a Venetian enterprise.

Although the language had not changed, its meaning was now quite different from that used by the old Crusaders, Barbarossa and Richard the Lionheart, three centuries earlier: the Turk had replaced the Saracen as Christendom's enemy, the 'Infidel', and the name Christendom itself denoted less a unit of faith than the area of western Europe which the Turk had not yet invaded. Since the Turk had crossed the Bosphorus in 1361, he had swallowed Serbia, Macedonia and Bulgaria, and by the year 1470 had conquered all of Greece. Eight years after I was born, in 1480, Turkish galleys had landed soldiers on the peninsula of Italy itself, in Calabria, who had held the city of Otranto for a year before they were expelled. The threat to our crowns was as real as the threat to our religion, for the Turk bore a missionary zeal to see Islam triumph over Christianity. We called our proposed campaign against the Turk a Crusade because, as in earlier times, our main target was Jerusalem, now strategically placed at the heart of an empire. It carried as it had ever done great spiritual significance for both Christians and Moslems, and its loss would undermine the morale and prestige of the enemy—besides which, naturally, we Christians were anxious to capture it ourselves. Viewed in military terms, Jerusalem was the only point in his empire to defend which the Turk would bring home his armies out of Europe—thereby giving the conquered peoples from the Danube to the Adriatic the chance to entrench themselves against his return. At this late stage, not all our armies united would have sufficient strength to drive back an enemy who had established himself behind a frontier as wide as eastern Europe.

There was never any doubt that Pope Julius truly intended the Crusade to set off within his own lifetime. His chief difficulty was, however, that he was a man in his sixties, brought to a task similar to that which I began when I was fifteen years of age with a lifetime ahead of me in which to complete it—and his was far greater. Also, he was an Italian, and while Italy desperately needed a man like della Rovere, the best place for him was not in the Papal chair.

The Venetians were Christendom's greatest sea-power, and

they were also the Christian state closest to the advancing might of the Turkish Empire. While Christendom's princes had been too preoccupied with their own affairs to respond to the repeated calls from Rome for men and money to mount a Crusade, only the Venetians were close enough to take alarm at what they saw. For their genuine, and understandable, interest in the Crusade against the Turk they should have been welcomed by the Pontiff; precisely the opposite was the case, however, for Venice had engaged in an orgy of conquest which had stripped the Holy See of its choicest provinces. What had started as a fight in self-defence against several enemies had ended with the Venetians attacking those who had been their attackers. Venice had made herself a Papal enemy, and Christendom had woes enough without its spiritual overlord having personal likes and dislikes among his princely children.

The Venetians were a people whose wealth everybody envied and whose manners were generally deplored. They had a terrible great love of property, and one heard of merchants' great palaces packed from wall to wall with as many pieces of sculpture and modern inventions as most of us would reckon sufficient to stock a kingdom. They were astute merchants, inventive craftsmen, and terrible gossipers. Their tattling caused almost as much damage as their galleys and their soldiers. They had no respect whatever for any culture but their own, and in this claim they were to some extent right, for the Venetians were the new men whose glory was their wealth and whose birth carried less importance; had they been less materialistic, they would have been comparable with the new generation of Crown administrators whom I saw replacing the feudal land-holders in the wilder regions of Scotland.

To regain the lost authority of the Church within Italy, the Pope began, moderately enough, by sending his ambassadors to request the return of the lost Papal territories of Romagna and Rimini. When Venice refused his request, he threatened her with excommunication. Once this would have troubled Venice (it would still have troubled me, for a nation under ban of excommunication could not properly bury its dead) but these were changing times. Venice continued to defy the Pope, who stayed the ban some while in the hope of bringing her to her senses, then finally applied it. It was the worst possible service that Venice could have rendered Christendom, for it sundered our unity at a time when we should have been gathering together against the Turk.

Pope Julius, having failed to restore order within his dominions by the use of spiritual force, discovered that it pays at times to use such persuasion as the offender best understands. Lacking an army of his own, he overcame his dislike of the French enough to take advantage of the presence of French troops in Milan. The French despatched the Venetians from Bologna with great efficiency, and thereafter entrenched themselves yet more firmly in Northern Italy.

It required no 'lang ee' to see that King Louis had dark forces building up against him. As a Cardinal, della Rovere had made no secret of his wish to see the French driven out of Northern Italy, where King Louis had claims to both Milan and Genoa—as well as to Naples in the south. Paniter and I debated whether Pope Julius was mad enough to make an enemy of a prince who could have aided him powerfully, not merely against the Turks but in stabilizing the spiritual balances within Christendom. (As I saw it, the jealously guarded autonomy of the Gallic Church, like the Celtic tradition now reviving in Scotland, were the most promising indications of how a reformed Catholic Church could function well within our modern states. It was in the lands which had not preserved some spiritual independence that the strongest reaction would follow if Rome chose to apply its authority more sternly.) Paniter thought Pope Julius was a wiser man than to let this happen, but I was not myself so sure. Twenty years' effort to put down tribal warfare among the wisest as well as the most foolish of my subjects had taught me never to overestimate anybody's capacity for acting sensibly.

In April 1507 I had gained a new title—'Christianae Fidei Protector'—together with the gift of a sword and a purple velvet cap from His Holiness. It was a title conferred by the Pope upon whichever of his princely sons had pleased him, or whom he required to flatter, and my private observation to Patrick Paniter was that this must be one of the few times when the 'Fidei Protector' truly had been trying to protect the Faith. The title I cherished a great deal more was the unofficial 'Rex Pacificator' used to describe me among my fellow princes.

My stately investiture at Holyrood, performed by the Cardinal envoy, was all very agreeable, but I was less than happy to be asked in tones of quiet significance how far I would lend my support to His Holiness against 'Christendom's enemy. . . .' I reassured the Cardinal that I was eager to lead my forces in the Crusade against the Infidel so soon as ever His Holiness gave the word—and I knew even without the Cardinal's flicker of hesitation before he smiled his gratitude, that the answer I had given was not the one which he had hoped to hear, and that by giving it I had robbed him of his chance to say what truly he had come for.

In the same month I had received from King Louis a request to send soldiers through Genoa to aid him in Milan against the Emperor. I had no intention of sending Scots soldiers anywhere, and certainly not to aid one friend of mine against another. Maximilian had accused King Louis of having designs upon the Imperial Crown, which he had not yet formally collected from the Pope. Maximilian had been universally recognized as the future Emperor for all the years I had been king, and it was ludicrous to suppose that the practical King Louis would want to take on the Holy Roman Empire—a shamble of fiefdoms spread over Germany, the Low Countries and Italy, where a need for vast expenditure was matched by the merest trickle of revenue. However, Maximilian cared about it very properly, and set out for Rome with a brave show of force for his belated coronation, only to be stopped by the Venetians, who refused to allow him way-leave, being themselves at this time interested in making a friend of France. 'Puir auld Maximilian' never forgave the Venetians.

(Tragedy had hit the House of Spain on a scale that made even his censors feel sorry for King Ferdinand. To the deaths of his wife and his heir had been added the degeneration into madness of his daughter, Juanna Queen of Castile, which left her son, Carlos, heir through his father, Philip, to the Archduchy of Austria, and through his mother's line, heir to Castile, Aragon, Granada, Leon, also to Burgundy. The thought of one man holding such a vast unit of territory disturbed all our thinking at that time, and the betrothal of Prince Carlos to King Louis' heir, the Princess Claude, now frightened even Louis. When the French King requested my advice, I told him to break the betrothal and spare us the possibility of France being added to the rest of Carlos's dominions. I had learned by my own bitter experience, it would be no more good to France than it would be to those trying to hold the balance of power in Europe. It was this fear that King Louis had too much interest in Maximilian's own grandson which had caused the Emperor to wonder if the French King might trade upon his service to the Pope to request the Imperial Crown ahead of the dynastic union which would almost certainly give it to the child of Carlos and Claude, if they wed. All of which convinced me, that my own 'lang ee' had been right to distrust this fashion of dynastic building favoured by King Ferdinand.)

I had learned by this time that it was no use sending King Louis lengthy letters of explanation, because he never read them properly. I decided therefore to send the Earl of Arran to France, with his younger brother, as my ambassadors. James Hamilton held other virtues beside being my cousin: he could hold his own in a debate with anybody, and his closeness to the Crown made him think at times with the mind of a king—also he knew my views upon most matters. While he was there, he could usefully strengthen his acquaintance with our other cousin, the exiled son of Albany.

What happened upon his return I have already told. King Henry seized him on his journey through England, and whatever information Arran carried which might have been used to avert a major war in Christendom was witheld from me in London while the whole situation changed to the greater peril of all of us.

In the Europe of our time, the pattern of alliances altered so rapidly, while information travelled so slowly, the chances were that everybody had changed sides again by the time news of it reached my far north-western territory. To counter this, Paniter and I, together with Andrew Forman, the Bishop of Moray, shared the knack of being able to predict events with remarkable accuracy. (Indeed, in our last years, when Scotland alone was left trying to hold the peace together, it became quite common for news to arrive after we had put in motion the required counter-measures.)

Venice's continuing contumacy provided grounds for other nations with interests in Italy to go to war for their own ends under cover of righteous indignation on behalf of the Church— a move as dangerous as it was hypocritical, in view of the fact that Venice, however improperly she had behaved, still remained the power with the greatest resources and the most pressing interest to lead the war against the Turk. A League formed itself at Cambrai in 1508, declaring itself the champion of the Church. The alliance included the Emperor Maximilian and King Louis (who had now made up their differences, with my help), while the Pope, King Ferdinand and King Henry of England blessed it from a distance. I was invited to become a member of the League, which kindness I rejected; instead, I sent letters to all concerned, including His Holiness and the Venetian Republic, pointing out that the argument as to who owned which vineyard in Lombardy was a matter which might be suitably postponed until we had secured Italy against the Turk.

At the same time I was making strenuous peace-making efforts in the Baltic, where the Republic of Lübeck had at Swedish instigation started a quarrel with my Uncle John of Denmark. I had strong political reasons for wanting peace in that area— quite apart from the fact that a good deal of my timber for shipbuilding came from Scandinavia. Lübeck and the Hansa had trade and feudal connections with the Emperor Maximilian, and as England always played for the Emperor, the last thing I wanted was a confrontation between him and my uncle which would have repercussions upon my Border.

It was now over a year that my cousin Arran had been held captive down in England. I refused to request his return, for it put my cousin under obligation to King Henry if I did so, and Arran was heir to Scotland now that both my children were dead. We had received no further news about the murderer of my Warden Kerr, either, and if I let pass this omission, it nullified the value of our Treaty upon both sides.

The Queen constantly begged me to arrange a meeting with her father. I agreed with her entirely that this was the best way to resolve our differences, but if we met it had to be *at the Border*, nowhere else. My wife pleaded that he was an old man, unfit to travel—to which I replied that if he were young enough to be contemplating a second marriage, he was young enough to mount a horse and ride to Berwick. In point of fact, King Henry's talk of remarriage, I privately suspected, was little more than an ageing dynast's last fling at the gaming board of his youth, but my dear young wife could not understand what a Scots King's visit to London could entail for his successor. However, my continued refusal to go farther south than Berwick, plus the embarrassment to both of us caused by the Earl of Arran's continued captivity, finally persuaded my father-in-law that a journey north was the best solution. Cheered by this moral victory, which proved what I had always maintained, that if the Scots were less willing to adopt King England's suggestions, he would show more willing to heed ours, we began negotiations for a meeting at the Border in the summer months of 1509.

All through April and May of that year, the Queen's English ladies stitched her finery—together with their own—chattering like a flock of happy starlings at the thought of meeting their relatives and friends after these six long years in exile. I cared enough about Scotland to understand why they were so pleased to meet King Henry's retinue at Berwick, which, although it was not far, was now upon what was reckoned English soil—bless their hearts, I would gladly have taken all of them to London, had I not required to consider my Scots. They sang as they sewed —and I remember twirling one of them about the waist as I passed through the Queen's apartments, to the great merriment of all. They were brief and happy days.

It was I who had to bear the news to my little Queen, so excited about the coming meeting with her father, that the messenger had brought word to say not when he was coming, but that he was dead. A new King reigned in England, her brother, Henry VIII. I am not sure which of us grieved the more, she for the kindly father she remembered, or myself for a man whom I had never liked but who was statesman enough to see through King Ferdinand's blandishments as he tried to inveigle King Henry into his own Continental wars. I knew nothing about the new King, except my wife's childhood memories of a small boy who cheated when playing games and then shrieked 'I have won! I have won!' so many times that he drove his brother and sisters half-crazy; and who, when he lost, accused all the rest of cheating. He would then go purple with rage, and stamp his foot, until given comfits to quieten him. He was now eighteen years of age, coming straight to a Kingdom in good order and with the richest coffers in Christendom if the tales of his father's avarice were true. Yes—I did know one other thing about him: I asked the date of his birthday, upon a sudden intuition, and my wife confirmed that he was born beneath the sign of Cancer the Crab. I wished now that William Schevez had been alive to explain what he had meant when he had told me to 'beware the Crab'; as it was, my own 'lang ee' had already told me more than I wished to know.

I suggested to my new young neighbour that we should continue with his father's purpose, and meet during the summer at Berwick. He made no response, and I realized what had been his preoccupation when in the autumn I heard that he had married his brother's widow, the Infanta Catalina, daughter to King Ferdinand of Aragon. I had for years been concerned about this Spanish princess, who had once been honest with Blacader and who, rumour said, had led a wretched life after her brief marriage of two months, in dire penury because the late King Henry had refused to disgorge her dowry, and her father had refused to have her back without it. I was glad to know that her young brother-in-law adored her so much that he had married her (with Papal dispensation) in the face of all the tut-tutting which would follow an incestuous marriage: but, oh dear God, what was my Scots future with an eighteen-year-old below the Border who was married to a daughter of *King Ferdinand*? I could give my brother-in-law a volume of good advice about King Ferdinand—I had been collecting it since I was myself sixteen—but I could hardly say to him, 'Never trust a word of that arch-fiend your *father-in-law*.'

I renewed the Oath of Treaty, as was required by the death of King Henry, and despatched it down to London. There, apparently, Henry VIII made a great deal of petulant fuss about having to sign his Oath before my commissioners, when I had not signed it in the presence of his. Technically, I was not obliged to do so, but if the laddie cared so much about his dignity, I was unwilling to cause trouble by refusing to humour it—he was new to his crown, and I had doubtless been overbearing myself when I was newly enthroned at the age of fifteen. I re-swore my Oath solemnly before King Henry's commissioners.

In the October of that year, 1509, a new son was born to me. With the hope of breaking the bad luck of the Stewart Jameses, I decided to call him Arthur. The Celtic King Artair had ruled what were now the Lothians about the time that St Ninian and his monks at Whithorn were fighting to preserve Christian scholarship through the dark years after the fall of the Roman Empire. He had been a great King, celebrated in the legends still kept alive by the Celtic bards, and two of his fortresses had been close by the sites of mine—one by Linlithgow, and the other upon the hill which overlooked my Palace of Holyrood. Since coming to live at Holyrood, I had fallen beneath the spell of this Celtic King who had ruled wisely what was then a great Kingdom. I had written a long poem about Artair, and in my own version of the legend I had brought my favourite Saint, Ninian, to his court, for it seemed to me impossible that the two men should have so much held in common and never met. I had ended the poem as the old Celtic bards ended it, with Artair falling in his last great battle, and being transported westward by ship to the Celtic Land of Youth, to regain his vigour for the battles to be waged on his return. It seemed to me that there was no better name I could choose for this son of mine, who had to continue the pattern I had started by reuniting the Saxon-Scots world of the Jameses with the Celtic inheritance of the North-West. It did not occur to me until I mentioned my choice to my Queen, that it was also the name of her favourite brother, who had been born beneath the same birth sign.

It was not long afterwards that the new King Henry released the Earl of Arran. Queen Margaret was so pleased that her brother had shown himself accommodating that I had not the heart to point out that my cousin was no more use to King England since the birth of my new heir.

I was more than pleased to have Arran back in Scotland. He gave me, very belatedly, the news of his mission to France. He had met Albany, who was apparently very different from his father: my cousin said, grinning, he would be prepared to put it to the toss, which of the two of them should rule Scotland. I liked this remark, for it meant the two men could think together if necessary. Another item of news he bore troubled me greatly: it was his private opinion that the Prince, now King Henry VIII, had been the one who had persuaded his father to hold him—Arran—prisoner. My cousin described the new English King as 'a mukel bonny' on account of his great size and ill-matching, high-pitched voice; I told him that King Henry, born under Cancer, was likely to be both womanish and a womanizer. When I asked James, was the new English King likely to be looking for an opportunity to show his youthful vigour in a war, I received the rejoinder, 'Verily—but noucht ane quhilk wad laus *hes* bluid ane drap!'

The Crusade which greatly mattered was progressing nowhere at this point. I did not like a very strange, and curiously disarming, letter which I had received from Pope Julius, justifying the reason why he had *forgiven* Venice. It was odd that the Guardian of Christ's Church should need to justify forgiveness, and it was equally strange that His Holiness the Pope should write James Stewart a letter so humble in its explanation of a Christian virtue.

Through all its suave pontifical assurances, there was a crying need to explain why he had done something of which he knew I would not approve. I pitied him—and asked Paniter, what has His Holiness *done*?

The fool had started the war with King Louis that I had dreaded ever since he gave me the title 'Fidei Protector' and I had sent Arran to France to beg my friend to collaborate with Pope Julius. And—oh, Christ, preserve my Kingdom!—he had begun a war which had our old ally France upon one side of it, and King Ferdinand upon the other, who was now father-in-law to the lad who ruled in London. The only hope left to me now was our Crusade against the Turk: let brash young King Henry swagger at the gates of Jerusalem, not in France; not upon my Border. Oh, God, spare the cry, 'Ye are my vassal!' ringing out again! We Scots had just made our Kingdom once more a land fit for men to live in—for the love of God, let nothing spoil it for us this time.

I brought the boys home from Padua in the year 1510. Alexander had been progressing marvellously under the tutorship of Erasmus (who must have known how to handle the lad!) and Paniter tried to urge me to let him continue his studies. But I wanted Alexander back in Scotland, for there was war in Italy. Young James—Janet's son, whom I had sent out a year before to keep Alexander from fretting jealously—would survive whatever the dangers surrounding him, but I was never so sure of Alexander: my eldest son was made of more fragile stuff, like a crystal goblet packed with pewter ware.

He returned home with a set of supercilious, cosmopolitan ways, and three chests of new clothes cut in the latest Italian style—the 'Padua gayre', I called it. The colours were dreadful, crude and gaudy, and I asked what was the point to have a doublet made and then to have it slashed to ribbons? He replied haughtily it was now the fashion to have the undershirt plucked through the vents like fishes' fins. I asked why? He said it was to show how many servants a man had available to dress him. I said that if that were the new principle dear to the Italian mind, he were better to have left it in Padua, for we wanted none of it in

Scotland. At which he burst out laughing, and hugged me, saying how homesick he had been. He was the same old Alexander, my son, for all his learning.

He did not look the same, however. The fourteen-year-old who had wept on leaving was now seventeen years of age, and half a head taller than myself. And handsome—dear God!—I wondered what on earth we were to do with an Archbishop who turned the head of every girl in sight, including that of my Queen, who became quite arch and coy when she gave him his welcoming kiss and placed him by her side at dinner. But whatever the fluttering of our court ladies around the new attraction, their hopes would remain unrealized, poor girls: Alexander played it all gently, with a marvellous blend of the priestly and the gallant, but it was plain to my eye if to nobody else's that Scotland's future Primate remained as innocent of women as he had been when he left our shores. Alexander had his true vocation.

He was eager at once to start making improvements in the educational facilities at St Andrews. When I told him to remember that he was dealing with old men who in the past had served us well, he smiled his warmest smile and assured me he would have gentleness and patience to win his way—and for a minute I felt I had known this lad before, standing in a scarlet cloak beside Lord Hume in Linlithgow Palace archway: I could have wept to see it all happening again.

Then, of course, we started to quarrel: Alexander had come back Romanized. Unknown to me, he had applied to His Holiness to change the ritual of St Andrews from the Augustinian to that which was used in St Peter's. It may not have seemed much to Alexander, but it was enough to upset all the balance I had so cautiously preserved these twenty years and more. I said that *in Scotland* we would do things *my* way, and I reminded him that he was not yet instated as Archbishop and never would be if I refused to allow it. He accused me of defying the Pope; I said I was the best friend Pope Julius had, and anyway, I knew best what was required in Scotland. Alexander was now ashen white, with two pink spots upon his cheeks: this time I had gone too far.

Heaven alone knew how I should restore myself in his eyes. I finished the argument abruptly, asserting my authority as his *King*, and stormed away, my surcoat sleeves lashing.

Although we were reconciled three days later, by Paniter who called a truce between us, the basic cause of our argument remained a vital issue for our Scots. To resolve it, I suddenly had the brilliant idea to take him to the house in the West Gait where David Seton had all but finished his statues of St Andrew and St Peter. Under the small window, amidst the wood-shavings and the smell of seasoned oak, while Seton worked in his casual way, Alexander and I sat and talked about Scotland's religion.

I asked, had he ever seen a better representation of fishermen-saints? He had to confess that he had not. I suggested that they might mean more to us than the statues of the same saints in the Vatican because they represented *Scots* holiness, of a kind we understood. He agreed. I asked, was it worth upsetting the clergy at St Andrews by elaborating upon a ritual which had contented them for a long while, merely because in Italy he had liked the style which suited the Italian temperament? Even if, as he assured me, there was not in fact a great deal of difference, it was enough to set the cat among the pigeons at St Andrews.

Given time and steered gently, the Scots Catholic Church would ride out a sea of troubles *in its own way*; the spirit of the old Celtic Church was struggling to emerge again, after its long submission to Rome. Let it emerge: for if we let Rome's pressure be brought to bear on one side, and imported heresy upon the other, among a people whose love of argument was matched by their depth of interest in matters spiritual, we should split the Kingdom in a way that neither King England nor our feuding clans had yet achieved. I remembered examining a pack of Lollard heretics in 1494, with Robert Blacader and others from the See of Glasgow, which turned into a thoroughly enjoyable debate in our best Scots style, resulting in a witty victory for the Lollards. I had, however, been less shocked by their unflattering views about His Holiness (each man is entitled to his own opinion) than I had been by their impractical sugges-tion that as only God had the power to make laws the laws made by temporal princes should be disregarded. I told Andrew Reid, their leader, that while God was occupied in ruling heaven, it was my business so to rule my Kingdom that at least some of my subjects succeeded in reaching His dominion; I did not hold that my laws were perfect, but they were useful in a less than perfect world. They could pray as it pleased them, Lollards, Jews—ay, even devil-worshippers—so long as they were law-abiding Scots subjects, allowing the rest of us, James Stewart included, to worship as we chose. Times had changed since 1494, all over Christendom, but we in Scotland, even yet, could argue about the bread's Divinity with a measure of good temper.

Alexander was thoughtful, and gave no answer. For once I had the good sense to know where to leave the subject when trying to persuade Alexander, and I dusted the wood-chippings from my clothes and went to see how David Seton was progressing. I felt like patting St Andrew and St Peter upon their wooden pates, for being such a help to me that afternoon.

We heard no more about altering the Augustinian ritual at St Andrews.

Alexander was instated in the Abbey of St Andrews at the beginning of the year 1511, and a nobler figure than his, with the mitre adding to his tallness and the crozier grasped in a firm hand, I doubt was ever seen at St Andrews. There were none now who said that I had bestowed the benefice unwisely; and if there were any left who secretly thought it, the charm of Alexander Stewart did the rest.

I wished we could have the same success in other fields.

Of my son James's return from Padua, I have but a single memory —of a scared wee lad, so unlike the cosmopolitan eight-year-old traveller who had set out from Scotland so assuredly, hurling himself into my arms and sobbing his relief. Alexander was as puzzled as I to know what ailed him. Eventually, I heard about the dream which had so distressed him on the night before they took ship for Scotland. In his dream, he had been standing upon the quayside with his brother, when a great black ship had sailed into the harbour, bearing upon its deck myself, my courtiers, and a very great number of my subjects. We stood in silent ranks, very still, staring before us. Then the gangplank had been lowered, and Alexander had walked aboard to join us, but when James had tried to follow I had turned glazed eyes upon him, shaking my head. Then he had been left alone upon the quayside, watching the black ship bear all of us away.

13

I HAD thought for a moment my peace-making efforts might yet have a chance to succeed, when the Venetian Commander of the Crusading Armies, Count Pitigliano, died. I remember meeting a small Venetian gentleman, the ambassador to England, secretly, beside a burn upon the Border. We liked each other, and he said he would fight to have me elected to replace the Count. I let him know it was important, because—apart from all else— the safety of my Kingdom depended upon my being able to speak with an authoritative voice for the Crusade. This should have been the Papal responsibility, not mine, but Pope Julius was fighting King Louis in Northern Italy and had temporarily forgotten the Crusade. Flailing a sword about him at the head of his Swiss mercenaries, the old lad had found his true vocation; but it was a tragedy for Christendom.

Now I heard that the Captaincy of the Crusading Armies had been given to the Marquis of Mantua, another Venetian. It was no more than I could have expected, I suppose. The little russet-cloaked Italian I had met beside the cobbling burn had fought his hardest to get me elected by the Doge and Senate; it was simply a pity we had failed. I wrote to the Marquis of Mantua, offering all of my assistance to his cause. I sent another round of letters to Christendom's princes, urging them to do the same. I sent to Venice, asking for them either to build my galleys in their shipyards or to send me Venetian shipwrights to work in

Scotland—I wanted them to ship my army to Jerusalem. I sent King Ferdinand a list of my wants—ships' anchors and cordage for my sails, both items for which Spanish craftsmen were renowned. (We could have had the same made as well in Scotland, as it happened, but I was hoping that King Ferdinand might pass news of the order on to his new son-in-law, perhaps to bring to Henry Tudor's mind the pleasurable vision of himself campaigning as Christendom's leader against the Infidel.)

The war between His Holiness and King Louis had now so deepened in bitterness that Pope Julius refused to accept French ambassadors. King Louis was indignant because the Pope had also refused to accept the nominations of several clerical candidates sponsored by the King—an attack upon the autonomy of the Gallic Church which alarmed me exceedingly. Furthermore, His Holiness was now openly referring to all non-Italians as 'barbarians', a contemptuous reference which put back Rome's thinking full fifteen hundred years. I asked Paniter and Forman, had the Christian Pontiff gone completely mad? The Bishop of Moray said he thought Julius had just confused himself with a former Roman Emperor of that name.

Forman had a dry, tolerant regard for the Papal peccadillos. I decided to send him to Rome to try to reconcile the Pope and King Louis. Then it occurred to me: why not send another ambassador to help Forman, my cousin, the Duke of Albany? The Papal Court would accept a Scot, but not a Frenchman; and Albany was a Scot who had been born and reared in France. He could argue King Louis' interests better than Forman could while at the same time he was indisputably a Scots subject. Forman, who had been most warmly received by Pope Julius, introduced the Duke of Albany into the Papal Court with no difficulty whatever. I drew a sigh of relief, seeing now a glimpse of clear light behind the clouds.

I had other reasons for wanting to bring Albany forward. If he bore himself well on such a delicate mission in our interests—and Forman seemed greatly pleased to have his new colleague's assistance—it was the first stage towards reinstating him among our Scots lords as Heir Presumptive to the Crown. Only the memory of his father's treason in my father's reign disqualified him from taking his rightful precedence over Arran, and if we laid that sour old ghost he would be welcome back to Scotland. I had always felt sorry for this poor cousin of mine who had paid so hardly for his father's sins, while, so far as I knew, committing none of his own. Moreover, the question of the succession was crucial again: our infant Prince Arthur was dead by the summer of 1510.

Relations with England were no better. The latest crisis was a family matter to do with some jewellery of her mother's which had been left to my Royal wife by her father at his death the previous year. By the summer of 1510 the new King Henry's reluctance to obey his father's wishes and let his sister have the jewels, had made it gruesomely apparent that Henry Tudor had inherited his father's meanness as well as his wealth. He was known to spend lavishly upon his own amusements, but my wife's few jewels were a treasure he could not afford to spare. With a fellow of that mentality, I had no desire to argue: I told my wife that she had her mother's love to remember as a keepsake, and the cost of the gems I would give her myself. Unfortunately, my sweet wife had inherited her own share of the Tudor love of property, and she meant to have those jewels if our Scots Kingdom had to die for it. And as she was carrying my fourth child and had just seen buried the third of three dead ones, where could I let her gratify her whims. So long as the sibling squabble did not draw my Kingdom into it, I could not insist upon justice for my other subjects and deny my Queen the right to hers. I politely requested King Henry once again to let his sister, my wife, have the jewels left to her by her late, dear father. Since when I had heard nothing from King Henry about the jewels, but I heard about them from Queen Margaret morning, noon and night.

The impression I had now formed of young Henry Tudor's character led me to suppose that peace upon our Border would continue only so long as it suited him. I must supplement my peace-making with the preparedness for war.

I made my cousin James Admiral of my fleet, for a special reason which I kept to myself, and I took him down to Leith and the Pool where my new warship, the *Margaret*, lay at her moorings. He was critical of the *Margaret*, saying she was too heavily walled for her size: that we had already discovered. He did not ask me, as others had, why she was so thickly walled; he enquired instead, with a sly grin, after which Margaret in my life was she named? I told James rather curtly, I had called her 'Margaret' after my mother, which was near enough to the truth, for my Viking ancestry had inspired me to name my next ship the *St Michael*, after the saint in my mother's portrait. It no longer mattered which of the Margarets in my life had given her name to this ship—she was built to defend my Realm, in my devotion to which all my earthly loves were now comprehended.

Some people criticized the appointment, including Sir Andrew Wood, Scotland's veteran sea-captain who, I will allow, had fair reason. I had several grounds for doing so, however, among them his seamanship. My cousin had the sea in his veins—he had proved it at the age of five when he stole a boat in the Firth of Clyde and shipwrecked himself on the smaller Isle of Comrie, whence a fisherman rescued him half-dead of thirst, when his parents had already had a mass said on his behalf. Since that time he had sailed everything, when allowed, and at the end had a perfect master of navigation and the ability to trim a sail with the best of them. Even Sir Andrew grudgingly admitted that his seamanship was not impaired by his noble birth.

We began to lay the keel of my new ship, the *St Michael*, along the shore from Leith, where the flat blue thistle with holly-shaped leaves grew in abundance among the sand dunes. It was an isolated spot, by the flat sanded track of the coast road between Leith and the Queen's Ferry, with only a group of four or five fishermen's huts built around, which made a hamlet too small to bear a name. We cut a deep sand berth in the dunes to fit the shape of a ship so great in size that folk came to look at it, refusing to believe that such a ship was possible. (I knew she was possible, for we had made three wooden models of her built to scale—so far as I knew, a new idea, begotten out of the need to build a ship so costly that I could not afford to have her fail.) We heaped there all the oak timber cut in Fyfe and seasoned in readiness either for this one great ship, if peace failed us, or for smaller ships if the unity of Christendom went forth upon Crusade. (I always made every plan with an alternative in mind.) Beside the piles of timber grew up the workmen's huts, and we made a small stone jetty to accommodate the galleys bringing more new wood across from Fyfe. In times of storms, inevitably, fishing boats put in there for shelter, and my unnamed second dockyard upon the Firth of Forth became known among local fishermen as the 'New Haven'.

She was to be the biggest ship the world had ever known, two hundred and forty feet long and thirty-six feet wide, her walls built of Fyfe oak made in three shells to a thickness of ten feet. Nobody could fathom why I wanted her walls of such great strength, or why she had to have a double set of canvas, and four small galleys to be stored upon her deck. I had great difficulty to justify certain of her features—certainly the expenditure of oak to an unneeded thickness of ten feet caused much puzzlement and head-shaking when we were so short of it and had more ships to build beside the *Michael*. What hampered me most was that although I was not myself a marine architect, I had to design a ship of a kind never built before to do a specific task which I dared mention to nobody. Only if my peace-making diplomacy failed would I resort to the action for which I was preparing the *Michael*. Therefore I had to trust entirely to my own judgement in assessing every possible hazard she was likely to encounter on her mission, and make provision to counter it.

The 'New Haven' and the great ship we built there—we changed her name very soon from *St Michael* to *The Great Michael*—is linked in my mind with a black horse, Balthazar, who came to Scotland from Poland with the only man alive who had ever been able to handle him. He was bought for stud, but I took one look and said I would have him to ride. My courtiers blanched as we held our distance in the stable court at Stirling Castle. He had a gleaming coat the colour of a damson, and hoofs like polished jet. He was the handsomest horse that any there had ever seen, and the most arrogant, and he flashed temper from his teeth and eye in such a way it was not surprising he had daunted even Poland. His groom, who had known him since he was a foal, stood holding him—a wee fellow, with a toothless smile and wisps of straw-coloured hair on a smooth pate, who spoke no tongue but Polish. Even our tough horsemen begged me not to go near the brute—and, indeed, they had good reason, for we had not a King of Scots to spare at that moment. But I too had my pride, like Balthazar, and there was never yet a stallion that had the better of James Stewart.

Balthazar, with his gleaming coat and gold-and-scarlet harness, and I, thundering together along the shore-track down to the 'New Haven' were to become legendary figures within our own lifetime. Some old wives, whose doors I passed, used to say he was the Devil's horse—at which I always laughed, and said that I would have more respect for the Devil in future, if the Devil could ride him.

In November 1510, at the end of the most harassing year in my memory, upon a dark night with a winter's moon, there came some Bordersmen to Holyrood, all patched with blood, to say there was a reivers' battle being fought upon the river hard by Jedburgh. All the ladies of my court, who had been watching a masque, thought the Turks had landed at Leith and were come to rape them. Disappointing their hopes and fears, I stormed from the hall, calling any who would come to help me put down a reivers' fight upon the Border—and there was a great flurry of ladies' sleeves waving us upon our way as we thundered out from Holyrood, as though we had been setting out to storm Jerusalem. (Jesu—how I wish it had been so!)

I was in a rage—and Balthazar's flying hooves shared my anger. We had a Pope leading Christendom to its death, a King of England who was dangerously half canny, half foolish—and now we had a bunch of cattle thieves making hell merry at the Border. In our fury, we had outstripped the rest when we reached the scene of battle and found there a second skirmish taking place between those of both sides who had returned to collect their dead and dying. We stopped to wait for nobody. I rode Balthazar into the middle of the pack, clouting heads to right and left with the flat of my Toledo blade—the only good thing that Spain had ever sent me. My Toledo sword and Balthazar's fore-hoofs raised for action brought the quickest end to a fight that ever I witnessed. It was all over within the few seconds before the others joined me to pick up the stunned, the dead, and the dying. I can remember myself dragging a fellow by the collar of his jerkin across the grass, unknowing whether he lived or was dead, and not much caring.

Those who survived we brought to the Justice-Ayre at Jedburgh. It was the usual tale of cattle-reiving, but worse mixed with it, for there had been somewhere a conspiracy with Englishmen. One of those we sentenced to be hanged, shouted that Englishmen were never to be trusted. Some we hanged, and gibbeted along the Border; some we clapped into the dungeons of my Border fortresses. At Jedburgh we rendered justice, not mercy—there was no mercy now to spare, with my unconciliatory Tudor brother-in-law now on England's throne. My Scots subjects had to live by Scots law, whatever the pernicious ways of Englishmen.

It was Andrew Bartoun's mischief that finally unmasked my Tudor brother-in-law of all pretence to be a statesman or a friend.

There were three Bartoun brothers, who had become close friends of mine through my cousin James—Andrew Bartoun being the kind of company James kept while he occupied the 'Princes' House' in Edinburgh (where my Aunt Margaret had once lived) which had given it a bad name among the gentler residents upon the Hill. Their father had been one of my father's sea-captains, who lost his ship, the *Lion*, to the Portuguese a lifetime ago. Many were the times I had wished the Bartoun brothers would let yon auld tub of their father's sink into the pool of old, forgotten things. It was customary, if we had not received satisfaction from the Sovereign of those who had wantonly plundered our vessels, to issue *lettres de marque*, which is to say, licence to plunder any vessels of that flag met upon the high seas. The custom had its uses, for the offending Prince was usually forced in the end to make a legal settlement with the other country, but what dire complications it could cause in days when a ship bore her identification upon her mizzen topsail and her mainsail, or upon her taffrail! Half the time it was impossible to know whose ship was being chased and plundered, for the colours endured badly in the teeth of the salt, wet gales, and replacement work was costly. Had King Emmanuel of Portugal realized that it would be twenty years before the Bartoun brothers had avenged their father's honour at the expense of Portuguese merchantmen, he might have thought it wiser to hold a proper legal enquiry into the loss of the *Lion* in the first place, and pay reparation accordingly. Periodically the Bartoun brothers lost a round to the Portuguese, which subsequently had to be avenged as well, and so it dragged on.

I used to grow angry frequently against the Bartoun brothers, but I had to uphold their rights in a callous and mercenary world. There was Robert, whose huge size and prodigious strength always left me expecting to see him pick up a culverin and nonchalantly walk off with it beneath his arm down the ramp of Edinburgh Castle, scorning an oxen team to drag it to Leith. His younger brother, John, was a slight, quick fellow, whose chances were evenly balanced between dying respectably in his bed like Robert, or ending in a noose from the yard-arm, which seemed the likeliest end for the eldest brother, Andrew. I dearly loved Andrew, but he was a fighter for just causes who became a rogue animal during times of peace. I had lent him to my Uncle John of Denmark in place of the men-at-arms and fleet for which he had asked me, and I was sure the Lübeckers would come to rue my decision.

What had happened—I heard afterwards from my Uncle of Denmark—was that Andrew had tired of fighting Lübeckers, and slipped away to renew hostilities with his favourite enemy the Portuguese. He had not merely absconded from my Uncle's service, but to worsen matters had made off with a ship which I had sent as a present to the King of Denmark, and was using this vessel together with his own to raid the water around Biscay and the Channel.

I did not know this when I learned that King Henry's gunboats had seized two Scots vessels and killed the man whom I had meant to captain the great ship under construction in the New Haven. I was livid; the more so for being informed of the fact in the rudest letter that could ever have been received by one prince from another within my lifetime. He was obviously trying to copy my own style from twenty years earlier, when his father's ships had preyed on mine, but the clumsy Tudor substitute for dry Stewart humour had a graver side: what Henry Tudor had forgotten was that in the days when I had kept his father's ships as prizes and sent home their captains with a letter for the King, there had been no Treaty between the two Kingdoms providing legal machinery to deal with such occurrences.

Andrew Bartoun's two ships had *allegedly*—there was no court ever tried the truth about the matter—been plundering English vessels on the plea that he had mistaken them for Portuguese merchantmen. The mistake could in fact have been genuine—but none of this excused Andrew Bartoun's presence in the Channel chasing the Portuguese, when he ought to have been in the Baltic fighting Lübeckers. He was not such a fool—I would have thought—as to plunder English vessels deliberately, when I had already warned him that I would knot his neck-rope with my own hands if he ever gave me cause for argument with England.

What King Henry should have done was to despatch to me the complaints he had received, so that I could send out a vessel to escort home my subject Andrew Bartoun; I would have delivered him to the Border Wardens' Court to be tried, and if found guilty, then handed him to the English Wardens for suitable punishment. King Henry, however, being a young laddie over-full of his Royal importance, on receipt of his subjects' complaints, had at once sent out two gunboats under the command of the two Howard boys, sons of the Earl of Surrey (the elder was his Admiral)—with orders to capture Andrew Bartoun's vessels. Our Scots had not unnaturally resisted, and the result had been a great sea-fight in June, 1571, in which Andrew was slain, and the lighter-armed Scots vessels captured. King Henry had imprisoned and terrorized their crews with threats of hanging for piracy, until he had them upon their knees telling him what a noble and merciful prince he was for sparing their worthless lives. (The English seamen we had captured in his father's time

I made sure first had their dinner before setting them loose, and their captains I had allowed to stand during their brisk lecture.)

Long ago, when I had been about to sign the Treaty in St Mungo's Abbey, I had put down the quill, and asked the English Commissioners was it truly agreed that the Wardens' Court had power to try any of our subjects, irrespective of rank or any other condition? They assured me it was so. To test the matter, I had put it to them that in extreme circumstances the law might require *me* to appear before the Wardens' Court, in which case I would present myself there: would the Majesty of England do likewise? Lord Darcy had laughed, to flatter my strange sense of humour; but I had replied quietly, and without smiling, as I took up the pen, that Kings' Law meant the power to try a king no less than any other of his subjects. This was the way I meant the Treaty to stand, and I hoped they would carry this message to their master. Darcy, somewhat embarrassed, gave me the dignified reply that England's King was mindful of his honour. The solemnity of the occasion forbade me do other than accept this statement.

I therefore now made test of the Treaty's value by requesting King Henry to submit the Howard brothers to examination by the Wardens' Court to determine the true facts surrounding the death of Andrew Bartoun. Quite apart from the fact that Andrew Bartoun was a subject of mine whose name should either be cleared or his guilt proven, I was taking a hard line with this laddie who respected neither his sister's right to have property left her by her father, nor the terms of a Treaty made to protect our seas and common frontier. I confess it came as no surprise when my request met with a great show of Tudor and Howard indignation that I should dare to suggest that an English Admiral of noble birth was answerable to *law*. By this time I knew all that I need ever know about young Henry Tudor's character as a man and as a prince.

All through that summer the English were strengthening their Border garrisons. On the Continent, King Henry had sent English soldiers to help Savoy annex lands held by the Duke of Gueldres

—he had no interest there, except to flatter the Emperor and to give annoyance to myself. In the meanwhile, Andrew Forman travelled patiently between Italy and France, trying to bring about a reconciliation between Pope Julius and King Louis. I used my own time riding between my Palace and the New Haven to oversee the building there of a great ship needed for a purpose that I dared confide to nobody. In the *chambre de travailler* Paniter wrote our letters, and when I could I joined him there for dinner, which we had served separately from the Court.

Christendom's crisis of that winter and summer I remember best in personal ways: the huge oaten bannocks which I stuffed with meat and fed to Paniter while he continued working— he let me wait on him in the same way he left me to pick up the sheets of paper scattered round his feet; I remember it for the times I soiled my velvet and silk helping to shift a baulk of timber in tune to the Celtic work-song in the dockyard—I was the more 'licht o' foot' than Andrew Wood or Robert Bartoun when we saw a hitch in the work below our surveying platform. And best of all, I remember it for a black horse with its groom which stood outside the great gate of Craigmillar Castle. . . .

I used Craigmillar as a bachelor establishment, to be close to the dockyard when the Court was in residence at Falkland or Stirling. I would ride back from the New Haven to my dinner, and when I emerged there was a black horse with red and gold harness waiting for me at the gate, held by a grinning, toothless groom whose excruciating effort to wish me well in Scots needed all my self-control to accept it soberly. I would clap his Polish shoulder and say 'Ah love ye, mon!' which was the nearest I could give to a relevant answer. And there they stand yet in my mind, outside the gate of Craigmillar Castle, the Polish groom and the gleaming black stallion called Balthazar, waiting to take me back to New Haven.

There was not a great deal else in that year to cheer me. In November a letter came from the Emperor, bringing me the news that I least wanted to hear: King Ferdinand had formed an alliance with the Venetians against King Louis. His Holiness, too, had been persuaded to become a member. They called it by the usual name—the Holy League. *Holy!* Mother of God! Denouncing King Louis as the chief impediment to the departure of the Great Crusade, they were going to war to remove this obstacle to their own devout enthusiasm for the Christian cause. I had not thought that even King Ferdinand in his enthusiasm to have the French possessions in Italy—or was he this time to get Navarre as well? —would have the sacrilegious impudence to call these intentions 'holy'.

Maximilian himself seemed doubtful of the holiness of King Ferdinand's purpose, and this new arrangement of alliances he viewed with alarm, afraid lest certain of his fellow princes more happily situated might continue to disregard the Turkish presence creeping closer to Vienna. The Emperor's letter urged me to help him persuade other princes to abandon their way in Italy, and unite for the Crusade against the Turk. It was, in fact, in its request, a replica of all the letters I had been despatching to Europe's princes over the past seven years, and I was so delighted to find a fellow enthusiast after so many years, that I wrote at once to assure the Emperor I would do all in my power to follow the lead which he had given.

I did not need to be told whether King Ferdinand had been pressing his English son-in-law to share his holy work—that I could take for granted. The other thing which I could take for certain was that when Henry Tudor joined the League against France, his only interest in our Border Treaty would be to make sure that I kept to the terms of it, and especially the one which bound me not to form an alliance contrary to England's interests. Pope Julius had inherited his predecessor's role as guarantor to the Treaty, together with the power to excommunicate whichever of us broke it. I would not have dreamed of asking for King Henry to be excommunicated however many times he breached our terms of Treaty, but the laddie who had won his nursery games by cheating would not hesitate to ask for the ban to be applied to me if I did not support him and his allies against France. I wrote to Pope Julius, informing him that the English King had so many times breached the terms of Treaty, that he obviously regarded it as invalid, and I was therefore making a formal announcement to the effect that I no longer considered myself bound by oath to honour what had become honourless.

In January of 1511–12 I received King Louis's ambassador, Cordier, bringing the suggestion that France and Scotland might profitably renew the Auld Lyig for mutual defence purposes, with the inclusion of an agreement to make joint attack upon the Turks within a year of the cessation of hostilities between Pope Julius and King Louis. King Louis's gout was troubling him again, so he was unable to say whether he would be able to lead an army in person; however, a levy upon his Kingdom of men, money and materials would be set at the disposal of myself and his fellow princes. He was extremely anxious not to widen the breach between England and Scotland, but to mend it, and for that purpose was sending my own ambassador Forman through England on his way to Scotland, to negotiate with King Henry in the hope of persuading him that friendship between our three Kingdoms was the most constructive contribution we could make to the safety of Christendom.

I waited to hear what Forman had to say before I committed myself to a renewal of the Auld Lyig. Andrew arrived a week or two later, with the news that King Henry had been pleasant, evasive, but a willing listener, until King Louis's name was brought into the conversation. He had then in a censorious tone delivered himself of a lengthy dissertation upon King Louis's sins as the 'enemy of Christendom', and, turning his noble profile to face the east, had solemnly stated that his 'duty to God's Majesty' bound him to take arms against the French in order that *our* Crusade might prosper.

Paniter and I had guessed correctly: Henry would be a great lad for crusading, now the symbolic crown of thorns had turned out to be King Louis's solid gold one. That Tudor instinct never made a blunder where the value of property was concerned. After a grab at King Louis's crown, whether it succeeded or failed, the next would be mine. It was our old acquaintance, mask removed—King England.

We were now at a crossroads where matters were too serious to be settled without further advice. My Lords of Council were mustered to hear Forman report upon the whole of his mission, covering the past years' negotiations between Rome and Paris, and his more recent conversations in London.

Julius he described as adamant in his determination to expel the French from Italy. King Lotis's indignation against the Pope had been at first another barrier, but he was a practical fellow who had at last said he would withdraw from Bologna and make other concessions in the hope of peace, as Julius had demanded. But the Pope's Swiss mercenaries had then scored a victory over the French, and he had at once refused again to accept peace proposals. Andrew's patience had been matched by his determination, for he had twice crossed the Alps in the depth of winter in an effort to bring the two sides to agreement—a journey upon foot and horseback which made my Lords in Council shudder. And our wondrously patient Bishop, with his undaunted view that it takes time for morals to develop, expressed himself willing to return again to try what he might to resolve the deadlock.

There had been, apparently, a strong body of opinion within the College of Cardinals that His Holiness's policy was lunacy in the face of the Turkish threat, and that his active soldiering was not precisely the business of a Pontiff. Then, during the summer, the soldiering Pope had taken a chill which at his age had been expected to be fatal. He had, however, shaken it off, and regained his health so marvellously—he was now in his seventies—that it was viewed as nothing less than a miracle; and a 'miracle' was all it had required to persuade many of the doubting Cardinals that Julius II was destined to a purpose which, although it might be unfathomable to others, was comprehended by Julius himself and the Almighty. (Forman told me privately that what had brought the old lad back to life was his personal hatred of King Louis and sheer determination not to let the rebellious cardinals have the last word in the matter.)

Opinion was divided within my Council over the renewal of the Auld Lyig with France. The majority favoured it, but some disagreed—amongst them Elphinstone. He was for appeasing King Henry by letting pass without more words the breaches of our Treaty: Elphinstone considered peace more vital than legal technicalities. So might I have done, had there been assurance that the Tudor could learn better ways through kindness. Tudor was a bully. To appease a bully is to create a tyrant. It was I, not Elphinstone, who at the end might have to fight King England.

14

ON my thirty-ninth birthday, the Papal nuncio, the Spanish ambassador to King Henry of England, and the new French ambassador, le Sieur de la Mothe, were all at my Court. De la Mothe had arrived to tell me that King Henry had declared war on France and was threatening to invade: could I let him know precisely how far I would support France, and if we renewed the League, could my uncle, King John of Denmark, be expected to support us? The Papal nuncio and the Spanish ambassador, on behalf of England and Spain, were bent on telling me that our most vital Christian business was the Crusade against the Infidel at present being delayed only by the evil intention of King Louis toward His Holiness. My reply to their masters assured them of my brotherly goodwill at all times, and pointed out once more that Christendom's Crusade was precisely what concerned me most and that I could not see how it could be better promoted than by ending the war in Italy. All I should get for my pains, I knew, was a lofty reproach from all of them. The fact remained, however, that England could not invade France with a hostile Scotland at her back: Scotland held the balance of power in Europe.

On the 10th April, 1512, my Queen gave birth to a son, whom I did not hesitate to baptize in the family name of James. This one would live. He was not thin and wailing like the others. He was a bonny bairn. My heart sank at the sight of him. I would be dead before he was much older (the 'lang ee' knew it) and what chance did the poor mite have, as King, with an English mother—a warm wee lass, but not with the head to make a Regent—and King Henry VIII for his enemy and uncle? I felt like telling him to hasten back whence he came, before the Crown of Scots broke his heart as it had all but broken mine.

When the weather came warm, I had him well wrapped in blankets and rode through Edinburgh town with our wee future King perched upon the saddle bow before me. Folk swarmed at the windows to bless both our heads, and they seized my hand to shake it from the street side and the upper window ledges, and I cannot say yet whether as King I was sad or glad: but I was proud to be the father of such a bonny baby.

That sad-sweet April brought back another glimpse of happier days. Lord Dacre came to me on embassy—bringing with him another fellow, West, who styled himself Doctor. West was a dreadful creature. He had Thomas Wolsey's way of smirking the phrase, 'my master'; it would have driven me half-mad had I been his employer, but the unctuous obeisance likely suited Henry Tudor. He was totally devoid of humour. He was devoid of all ambassadorial qualities except a mindless determination to strip every word to pieces until he had made it meaningless. He had a dreadful mannerism, drawing back his head like a pouter pigeon and smirking over his collar at the end of various points he made, as though to say 'There!—what do you think of that, Scots fellow?'

We discussed the war at sea—for it was now open war, with English vessels preying upon my ships. My Scots too were inclined to like a sea-fight, but when an English vessel attacked one of ours, the English seamen would yell a war-cry, 'For the Pope!', which was neither tactful nor accurate since Pope Julius was still upon the best of terms with myself. Nicholas West, however, proceeded at interminable length and in scrupulous detail to out-line the history of Europe in the past eight years (damn the fellow's impudence, I was one of the kings who had made it!) ending with the triumphant statement that it totally explained why King Henry's seamen attacking one of my ships did so 'for the Pope'. Dacre was looking at him incredulously, as though amazed that he should find himself in such company. I almost laughed, remembering Dacre's choking shoulders at my wedding feast when Surrey made his reference to Scots mercenaries: poor Dacre always seemed to be burdened with colleagues who were worse than enemies.

I was very careful during the five weeks the English commissioners were at my Court never to speak to Dacre except when West was present or when others of my courtiers were there to hear our conversation. I had been given no cause to think it, but my instinct told me that Dacre's future, and possibly his life, depended upon my not showing him particular friendship. My suspicions were confirmed when, one evening just before he left, he took advantage of the surrounding general conversation, to lean across my chair and whisper, 'Your Grace hath mended me in the ears of my master. I thank you, Sire, for the loving attention of a noble prince and a true friend'.

By this time I knew Henry Tudor's character well enough to guess why Nicholas West *had* been set to spy upon him: he could not bear his subjects to show warmth to any other Sovereign. Poor fellow, what an attitude to carry in a *princely* mind! I pitied Dacre, too, who had to humour the fellow. I was glad I had acted correctly—but, oh, sweet St Ninian!—what a way it was to end the high hopes for peace that we had shared yon summer night, ten years ago, when I had watched Dacre walk over the green knoll to his tent, exhausted with my sleepless hours of conversation!

Scarcely had Dacre gone away, taking his muzzle-hound West with him, when the French ambassador, de la Mothe, arrived again, sailing into the Port of Ayr with a dozen English fishing vessels towed in his wake. He must have looked like a mother duck trailing home her ducklings from their exercise upon the pond. He came to tell me all about it, how he had made his collection sailing through the Channel, and then had auctioned the English vessels in the market place at Ayr (leaving their disconcerted merchant-purchasers with unexpected crews of cross English sailors requiring transport to their homeland)—

and he was so proud of himself as he gallantly laid at my feet the purse of gold profit he had made by the venture, that I had not the heart to tell him that I did wish God would stop sending me other people's ambassadors who became addicted to my cause. Fortunately, as England had declared war on France, King Henry's lost fishing-boats would not be a subject raised at our Border Wardens' Court: but I was apprehensive all the same. I knew it would not come amiss to him if he succeeded in embroiling me in war with England—indeed, he had to urge again the renewal of the auld alliance.

What had I to lose?—a Treaty with a King who broke it as and when it suited him, and whose respect for truth and principle was no stronger than the grass-blades trampled down by an army. What I had to gain was the support of a King whose inherited distrust of the English neighbour was as justified as our own, who knew that our only hope to deal with such a fellow, was to take advantage of the fact that his territory lay between the two of ours.

I signed the renewal of our Alliance with France on the 10th day of June, 1512, in our Palace of Holyrood. When I had done so, a great burden rolled from my shoulders as though I had come to my senses at last after a ten-year effort to achieve the impossible. I just prayed God that I had not found the path too late.

My subjects shared my relief at regaining our Scots sanity. When I rode with de la Mothe through Edinburgh's streets, there were cheers and shouts of welcome as they seized his hand or mine to wring it warmly. (My English wife had sobbed in my arms that night of the 10th of June; then she had said, in the Scots tongue which she spoke, scarcely aware of it after these ten years, 'Ah aime content ta ha' yur ain love, Sir, an' et maket mee Scottesh'. For which I kissed her tenderly, and truly meant it.)

The French ambassador returned to France in one of my own warships, with two more for covering escort, commanded by Robert Bartoun and David Falconer. I knew King Henry's ships would be under orders to sink him and the Treaty if they could catch the vessel, and they lurked beyond the Isle of May— that islet in the Forth estuary I would have blasted out of the seas these many times had I the powder to accomplish it—and gave chase. But they only sank one of the escort vessels, Falconer's, and took its master to London where Henry Tudor kept him in prison under threat of hanging as 'a common pirate'.

Robert Bartoun brought grave tidings back with him from France. The French had lost their great commander in the field, Gaston de Foix, immediately after a victory at Ravenna, and had been driven back demoralized by the Swiss and Venetian forces. They were now back upon their own side of the Alps, but even this was not enough for Julius: triumph can make the best of us greedy, and His Holiness was no exception.

Bartoun also reported that an English army was now encamped outside Bayonne, waiting for a Spanish Army to join it. The King of Navarre, who knew better than young Henry what was Ferdinand's true objective, had been in Paris signing a Treaty of mutual protection with France upon the day the Spaniards marched into his Kingdom. The fate of Navarre's courageous Queen was as yet unknown, but she had sold her husband's little Kingdom as dearly as she could. While King Henry's troops still waited at Bayonne, wondering what delayed their Spanish allies from helping Henry Tudor win 'his' crown of France, his fleet, returning empty, had blasted the Breton coast with all their guns. All in a true Crusading spirit. . . .

King Henry himself now sent to tell me that my ally King Louis was supporting the younger brother of de la Puile as English Pretender, which he thought I ought to know in view of my own proximity to the English Crown. Privately I reckoned the whole tale to be another 'holy' invention to justify the attack upon Guyenne, but I replied diplomatically that I would mention it to King Louis if it truly troubled his Majesty of England.

It was a screaming windy night in autumn, its dark lashed with rain, when word came to Linlithgow that a foreign vessel had been driven up the Forth to shelter off Blackness Point. The *Great Michael*, now completed in all her magnificence, was anchored off Blackness—together with the *Margaret* who looked dwarfed by her towering companion; we had them brought there for safety during the equinoctial gales. Nobody could identify the foreign ship with certainty, but I knew de la Mothe was due—in fact, overdue—to arrive; I wanted action after weeks of frustration. I took Balthazar, and rode the four miles to Blackness, exhilarated by the wind and dark and rain. I am not sure whether my escort liked it as well as I did. There was a full moon dipping its face behind the scudding clouds, and the huge black outline of the *Michael* rolling at anchor, with the *Margaret* close by, loomed enormous out of the dark each time the moon cleared. Their horn yellow riding lanterns showed their position, and the Frenchman's own lights showed he had made safe anchorage close by.

There was now a sixty-oar galley tethered to the *Michael* (replacing the four small ones which I had previously intended) but I wanted no state progress over the water on a night like this, so we hustled out two fellows from a fisherman's hut by the Castle, father and son, to ferry me across in their small boat. It was a choppy black sea made oily by reflections, and we shipped a lot of water—my clothes were soaking by the time we reached the wall of the *Michael*.

De la Mothe came aboard a while later—he too had taken a soaking. To sit talking with him in the gilded and painted State chamber, with its polished oak table locked to the deck, reflecting the swinging brass lantern's yellow light upon its surface, gave me greater comfort and security than I had felt for a very long while. De la Mothe was a big, solid fellow, his loquacity, and exuberant energy undimmed even after his gruelling voyage through November gales. He made France seem real and solid and closer to our shores, reducing Henry Tudor's grandiose delusions to the myth they were. (He was now boasting that he could conquer Scotland and France simultaneously.) I can remember becoming drowsy upon a single glass of wine, with sheer relief, feeling secure within the great ship from all the world of wind and rain that lashed outside.

Seated in the state chamber of a vessel which had cost over

£43,000, le Sieur de la Mothe may have wondered privately why I was so glad to receive his gifts from King Louis—powder and ball, some cannon, kegs of French wine and fine gold cloth for my wife. I could hardly tell him that almost my whole wealth was comprised in a string of palaces and this magnificent ship. But she was worth it: a French king who coolly saw that our alliance was in our mutual interest was a stout defence, but to be upon the safe side, our Scots had built the *Michael* to save our necks when all else failed.

While Henry Tudor could impose upon his grumbling subjects the heaviest levy ever known in Europe's history to pay for his glorious war, I had to pay my own way. It was an excellent method to ensure that Scotland bred no glory-lusting princes, but it made devilish hard work to equip an army and a fleet for our protection. I had written to my Uncle John of Denmark asking for ships and soldiers. His war with Lübeck now was ended, partly as the result of my diplomacy, and I felt reasonably confident that he would aid me in my turn.

Some of our ordnance, together with a great many of our spear-heads, we imported from Flanders—a country which had long been recognized for its skill in forging cannon, though there were new pieces being turned out by Borthwick's men in my Castle of Edinburgh which challenged any made elsewhere for beauty as well as power. In place of iron, we had been using brass, and the three gleaming culverins set within the arched entrance to Malcolm Caen Mor's banqueting hall would have made the Great Chief as proud as I was. (I was not so sure, however, he would have approved his Castle being turned into an armourers' workshop—only Queen Margaret's chapel had been spared, because it was no time to be giving annoyance to any of our national saints.)

We also were experimenting with a new arrow head, of a different shape entirely from the old, flat, barbed head. It was triangular in section, formed of three fins; its aim was more accurate and it gave deeper penetration; it was also extremely effective against armour plates. It was more likely to kill than to maim, and if the recipient did survive, the new head could be extracted with less damage to the surrounding flesh—anybody who had been wounded by an arrow and lived to tell the tale appreciated these considerations.

The dockyards at New Haven and Leith were no less busy. Many adjustments became necessary in the *Michael* herself, as could only be expected when such a ship had never been built before. Her main mast (of all things) was found to be too tall, and it was a considerable undertaking to get it down, shorten it, and build it back into position. Her foremast had to be replaced, for it was faulty timber, and she lost an anchor when a storm drove her aground in the autumn, so she had to have another anchor cast.

God alone knew where I could find the money for it all. The worry so far reduced my ability to sleep that most of the time I existed in a feverish state, buoyed up by an energy whose source was as mysterious as that of my revenue.

Then, suddenly, there came from Rome the first gleam of real daylight I had seen for many a murky year. Letters had reached Pope Julius from Ragusa—Cyprus being our last Christian outpost in the East—which had alarmed him exceedingly. A usurper, Selim, now ruled Islam, having murdered his predecessor, and this young lad sounded like the Moslem equivalent of Henry Tudor. He boasted that Crescent banners would float from the dome of St Peter's within another year, and the Knights of St John of Rhodes were in imminent danger of attack. This, not surprisingly, had made even Pope Julius wonder if the French were his most dangerous enemy, and I was delighted to have him suggest that my services as arbitrator between King Louis and himself might after all be useful.

Henry Tudor refused to let my ambassadors cross his Kingdom. I had sent request for them to have way-leave, and he despatched Thomas Dacre to tell me that it was unlikely that King Henry would grant them passage. He did not even have the courage to set his own mischief to paper. What there was of Henry's letter concerned the evil of King Louis, against whom he felt morally obliged to warn me. He would be happy to welcome Andrew Forman as my ambassador to London. . . . And I thought grimly, ay, true enough he would: with Forman held fast in London, my most experienced ambassador was rendered valueless to Christendom. At times I wondered, did young Tudor honestly suppose me to be as naif as himself? With regard to my imprisoned sea-captain, King Henry 'in his great mercy' had pardoned the offence.

I can remember Dacre as he took leave, standing before me with his eyes cast down thoughtfully upon the cap he hardly ever wore, its brim revolving slowly through his fingers as he spoke. Then he looked quickly upward with the strangely sweet smile that put his goodness plainly for a moment's glimpse upon his face. He dipped a knee, showing me the well-shaped head of hair which had been my first sight of him. Then he was gone. I think I must have known that I had looked my last upon Thomas Dacre, the best of all the Englishmen that ever I encountered, who might have held the peace upon the Border had Heaven and King Henry given him more help. He was a princely gentleman.

I wrote myself to Henry Tudor, explaining that the ambassadors for whom I had requested way-leave were being sent at the request of His Holiness to treat for terms of peace between himself and King Louis, and between England and France. I drew his attention to the closer presence of the Turk. His reply some while later stated that as he went to war with France in a holy cause, he was in no position to discuss peace terms without permission of His Holiness. As for my so-called brief from Pope Julius to act as his intermediary, he, Henry, had recently had other letters from Rome informing him that His Holiness had changed his mind about wanting the King of Scots to treat for peace, and therefore my despatch of ambassadors was no longer required. (He made no offer to show me these alleged letters from Pope Julius.)

My fury left me with a headache lasting several days. Also, I was truly alarmed, and a little incredulous, at this new kind of diplomacy. King Ferdinand's lies had at least been plausible; the Tudor laddie had cast even this poor rule aside. My father's generation had valued their honour, however little it may at times have rated in God's eyes; within my own lifetime, the code of values had altered to a new pattern set by the King of Aragon—but if we were to adopt this new style set by the Eighth King Henry of England! I felt very old, quite suddenly, and very weary; I no longer cared whether Christendom survived or not. It stank worse than the vennel midden-heaps: leave the Turk to sluice it away. I had worked to clean it up long enough.

I wrote to His Holiness telling him that King Henry continued to refuse passage to my peace-making envoys and was now all but openly at war with me upon the high seas. To counter whatever slander the English Cardinal Bainbridge might be spreading about me in Rome, I asked him to believe nothing told about me until he had my confirmation for it. (Cardinal Bainbridge now had the Pope's ear—which doubtless explained why we heard no more about Andrew Forman's elevation to the cardinalate, which had been strongly in the Papal mind as reward for his great services to Christendom. Since Bainbridge had arrived in Rome, too, answers to my letters to Pope Julius almost never arrived; King Henry was rather a rich young man.) It was humiliating, after twenty-five years' recognized service to the Church, to have to plead my case in this fashion because a lad with too much money had bought his way to the front rank of influence in a bare four years.

Poetic justice still had its moments, however, as I learned later: his troops, rotten with fever, boredom and poor food, had mutinied at Bayonne and had to be transported home, having waited all through the summer for their Spanish allies to arrive. King Ferdinand held Navarre and was smiling sympathetically.

Then the pestilence struck. We had been waiting for it all the year, but when summer passed without a serious outbreak we reckoned to be safe from it. For it to hit full strength in winter was a novel and ominous sign. There were those, needless to say, who called it God's vengeance upon the King of Scots for renewing the French Alliance. Kings were accustomed to being blamed for the weather by the superstitious peasantry of my generation, but I had thought to have better sense from Aberdeen's Bishop than to blame my acts for the visit of the pestilence.

Elphinstone had worse for which to answer. The Papal nuncio had taken it upon himself to travel from Rome to my Palace via Aberdeen. The letter conveying the Pope's hope for peace reached me with its seal unbroken, but I had no doubt its content had been discussed with Elphinstone. This I would not tolerate—nor would any other prince. It was one of the few times in my life when a foreign ambassador, and my own Bishop, received the full weight of my Royal indignation.

Also, I was hurt. I was not a man who took hurt easily, but it pained me greatly to discover that my old friend Elphinstone had been saying that *for my own glory* I was trying to displace His Holiness as Christendom's leader. I knew I had a terrible load of vanity, and that once or twice when I had finished writing a letter pleading for peace, I had approved the ringing phrases and my own sagacity, as though for a moment it had been my own wisdom and not God's wisdom lent to me—but I did penance for it afterwards, always. And when I thought of Pope Julius slashing his sword gleefully at the pates of God's French enemies, with the Turk close by Vienna and a lout like Henry Tudor as King England, I knew that whether God liked it or not I was more upon His side than the Pontiff was. Somebody had to pull the other way. Elphinstone had never considered whether his words caused pain or damaged a cause, and with the English Cardinal Bainbridge present in Rome to bear false witness against me, whatever Elphinstone had said to the Papal nuncio it could be reckoned no help to me or to Scotland. His light words would be taken at face value.

My grief at Elphinstone's conduct and my despair at Henry Tudor's mischief were matched by the pall of gloom which lay everywhere upon my Kingdom. To be stricken in winter by the pestilence was a new, baffling kind of misery; the death-cart rumbling its heavy wheels through the mud and greyness of the late afternoon, seemed some way worse than ever it had done upon a June night when the air was mild and sleep was welcome to the bereaved. It must have been agony to put out the dead at five o'clock with supper still to be made and eaten by those who were left. I saw these rattling wet loads of dead more than once in 1512, for the plague made small unheralded attacks everywhere at once.

I took the idea to go to Cambuskenneth Abbey, to see if a prayer at the grave of my father would do some good; I had never lost the feeling that we owed a penance for his death greater than my iron chain-girdle could pay. On my homeward ride, I made a detour to pass Stirling, which had been stricken by the plague for the first time in my reign. It was not a walled city; merely a broad street of houses with a central market, and it looked more wretched with its grieving emptiness displayed thus nakedly to the world, than ever did Edinburgh in the same straits shut in behind its gate and walls. I sat Balthazar at a distance, looking at poor Stirling, shunned and left to its misery which nobody could help. And I can remember thinking how incredible it was that we should covet crowns and have to fight the Turk, when we had not yet found a means to cure the plague. A good grave-digger who could last ten days at his job before he died of it, was more use to Stirling than the 'Rex Pacificator' of Europe.

I turned my horse and rode back to Linlithgow, weeping.

At Easter, more weary than devout, I went into my customary retreat with the Observantine Friars—this time at their House in Stirling, as the Court was in residence at the Castle; nor did I want to risk bearing the pest through to Edinburgh. My wife was angry about her jewels; Elphinstone wanted to appease King Henry—God alone knew in what way; the work of armourers and shipwrights required more money; there was no news reaching me from Rome; and as the ultimate threat to my sanity, King Henry was despatching the clucking, jerking, smirking Dr Nicholas West to 'treat for peace', whatever that meant. (I had already written to King Henry offering to cancel all grievances and reparations due to my subjects, if he would only join me in the Crusade against the Infidel. He never replied to my letter.) The prospect of my tiny bare cell in the monastery, with its stone bed covered by a slatted wooden frame to lift my single rug above the damp, was paradise by comparison. The night's cold and my chattering teeth when I rose early for the first day's mass was a small price to pay for the privilege of confining my thought to God.

I saw my fortieth birthday in the Friary of Stirling. The figure had a round, final ring that told me it would be my last, although I tried to persuade myself that the number forty had biblical overtones and that was why it struck a note of such significance. I can remember how I crunched my jet beads within my clenched hands as I prayed in chapel that morning, kneeling at the prie-dieu in my stall within the circle of light cast from a taper set within its ring and socket at my side—Easter was early, and the March mornings were dark in our northern Kingdom.

It was barely daylight when Robert Bartoun, who had docked his ship at Leith, came riding through to tell me the latest news: della Rovere, Pope Julius II, was dead. He had been dead for a month, and a new man occupied the Chair—His Holiness Leo X. He was a Medici, one of the Florentine merchant family: the thought struck me, he belonged to the same sort of world as the Tudors. I wept for old Julius. Even if he had taken the notion he was Caesar, he had *meant* well, in a world that now no longer cared about the quality of intention; and he, like King Louis, had been a giant among the tribe of lesser men. The news of his death arriving with my fortieth birthday was a heavy blow: my time was over. I knew it.

At Holyrood, my Queen had been entertaining Dr West during my absence. The silly girl, contrary to my advice, had immediately begun to question him about her brother's intention regarding those jewels, and I came in to find her in tears while Nicholas West quickly cut short the rest of his words. It was a good thing he did, for had I known what he was saying to my wife (again with child) it was unlikely that Dr West would have returned to his master alive. I heard later that he had told her that Henry would not give her her jewels while her husband continued the enemy of England.

I was a patient man, especially with my wife when she was with child, but I had had enough; it was well known that Queen Margaret of Scotland had more finery than any queen in Christendom—and certainly more than Henry Tudor spared his own wife Katherine—but her constant clamour to have her jewels had given Henry Tudor an excellent excuse to imply, through his ambassador, that I could not keep my wife in the state to which she had been accustomed. She promised now that she would write to her brother and tell him that I myself would give her the value of her jewels, but I only wished to God she had accepted my offer at the beginning, when I could better spare the money and before we had wrecked our Treaty for the sake (among other things) of that handful of gems.

Nicholas West had brought me a letter to King Henry from Pope Julius, written just before he died—and West's way to deliver a letter was to open it, underlining every sentence with his finger as though I could not read. It was the only time I ever snatched a letter out of anybody's hand. His Holiness had also sent a letter *meant for me* direct to King Henry, for delivery by his ambassador, informing me coldly and briefly that the Church would not tolerate my hostility toward his 'beloved son in Christ, Henry of England'. Pope Julius was also very surprised that I should wish thus to impede our Holy Cause against the Infidel.

By this time I had gone almost past caring. I remarked that King Henry was fortunate to have had such a Pope to guard his interests. The rest of the correspondence consisted of briefs to King Henry assuring him that His Holiness would certainly put the ban of excommunication upon me if I continued to break the peace with England. West must have been waiting for my reactions of fear and anguish, but I refused to gratify him. I leaned back in my chair, concentrating my attention on my hands curling over the ball-and-claw ends of the arm-rests. I wanted to ask him why Lord Dacre had not accompanied him upon the embassy, as I had been led to expect, but it would not help Dacre's future to put such questions. It was Dacre's absence which made me conclude that Henry's 'peace mission' was nothing of the kind. He was too great a moral coward to attack me unless he could claim 'provocation' and the best way to provoke me into provoking him was to send the man who most irritated me and not to send the one man who could be relied upon to make peace between us. Either that, or Henry Tudor was too incompetent to choose his ambassadors properly. Whichever it was, the result would be the same.

What West had come to ask of me was my promise that I would not invade England while King Henry was away invading France. What he wanted, in fact, was my blessing upon his enterprise. Whether the preposterous West and his no less preposterous master honestly believed that I would give my word on this, I never knew. All that I would say—and West had my answer on the first day, had he been content with it—was that I would not invade England so long as England did not invade France. West considered this an unpardonable (and incomprehensible) limitation of his master's ambitions.

I sent Andrew Forman by sea to Rome to salvage what he could of our one-time good relations there, and to acquaint the new Pope with whatever of the truth he cared to heed. Meanwhile, I had to endure West's presence for a month. I dared not send this wearisome fellow packing, because Henry Tudor would then triumphantly send to Rome, through his Cardinal Bainbridge, the information that I had rejected his peace-making ambassadors.

West and I spoke no language that held common meaning, but he doggedly remained at my Court seeking the promise I would never give. Everywhere I went, I would hear his quick bouncing pace at my heels, until I had begun to hear that dreaded footstep in my sleep (such sleep as I had). I had seen his name so often at the head of my list for the day's audiences, I instructed Lord Hume to add it no more. Whatever the group of my court friends surrounding me, West's head would appear at the fringe, and work its way forward ring by ring, until I fled to a fresh circle. He followed me to dinner, to chapel, and to my bed at night: I had become a fugitive in my own palace, hiding from his importunings. He was driving me insane. The only light relief that I remember came one day when Paniter and I watched through a window the indomitable Dr West standing patiently in the rain-sodden garden of Holyrood, hidden within the bushes, cowering in the wet as he waited for me to leave by a door which I had not used because I had been warned that he was waiting for me upon the other side of it.

Getting no satisfaction from me in answer to that question, he put another: would I lend to King Henry the *Great Michael*? I said 'No'. This time he added insult to presumption by saying that 'had I need of money', I would do well to accept his master's offer, who would buy her at any price I cared to name.

Sell the Michael?—and to *Henry Tudor?* I remember the red haze coming up before my eyes: I had my grandfather's temper (he had stabbed a Douglas when provoked too far), and although I had spun a web of patience around it for safety's sake, this offer to buy the *Michael* almost broke my self-restraint. Sell the *Michael* —which had stripped Fyfe's woodland of all its oak, when I had ridden in those oak-glades with my bonny, precious lass of Perth? Sell the *Great Michael*, built with our Scots strength and skill? *Sell the* Michael—built for a purpose known only to myself? And—Christ preserve us! sell it to Henry Tudor? *King England?* The only thing that saved Nicholas West from the sharp steel at my waist was the patent lunacy of the suggestion: I laughed. (Oh, I knew why King Henry so much wanted it: it was the biggest, finest warship afloat and—incredibly!—it was not *his*.) Being cautious not to give the matter too much importance, I said that I had agreed to send my warship to France—which was true.

Then West asked me (oh, Lord, that smirk and preen of his!), what would I do if 'his master' pressed for my excommunication? I replied laconically, that I would appeal to 'an Higher Authority', meaning, to God. Again he tucked his chin into his collar and asked, to whom would I appeal, there being no higher authority than the Pope? I remember looking at him, baffled to know how one answers a man so dense. Then my mind flashed from the late Pope Julius to another (renegade) priest who had made a name for himself by his warlike vigour—the pirate called 'praistre' Jean by our Scots sailors: I said I would appeal to 'praistre' Jean. As it happened, Prégent de Bideux (his nickname was a pun upon his name and his abandoned career) was a Frenchman, so Dr West asked me solemnly, did that mean I meant to join France in making war against England? What upon this earth, can anybody answer to a mind like that?

15

MY answer to King Henry rode at anchor in the Forth: if he continued to harass me, the *Great Michael* was to sail up the Thames and blast Tudor's riverside Palaces of Westminster and Greenwich clear of the earth. Alternatively, she could land a thousand men upon his doorstep, who could cause him more distress within one hour than centuries of Border raiding. I meant to teach King England such a lesson he would leave my Scots in peace for the next five hundred years. And if I could make my blow at the right time, we could avoid all the miseries of a protracted war across our Border.

That was the reason why the *Michael*'s walls were built ten-foot thick of oak from Fyfe. Her timbers had been tested by my own cannon at close range and their balls had barely dented her, which made it fair to suppose she could sail through whatever gun batteries were mounted in the Thames estuary. Her great size and the depth of her draught had worried me, but a smaller ship could not have carried the weight of her armoured walls (as we had discovered when we built the earlier vessel, the *Margaret*); she had made good distance up the Forth, however, a river which they said was not unlike the Thames. I had tried to think of everything. She had a complete set of spare canvas, if her sail were set alight by fire arrows; and if the winds failed her, she had a sixty-oar galley to tow her into position and help get her away after her mission was completed. She was built like a fortress, and her walls mounted thirty-six guns, together with small arms to repel boarders: there should not be much left of 'Placentia' and Westminster by the time she up-anchored and left their rubble and dust to settle.

This was a very improper and unchivalrous plan, for royal property and personages were customarily given due respect, and it was the duty of our subjects to pay the price of our princely ambitions. I was going to *earn* my ban of excommunication by the time I had taught King England the cost to others of his recurrent stupid claims to the crowns of Scotland and France. What the rest of Christendom thought of my dastardly behaviour I did not greatly care, but I did care very deeply what my Scots subjects thought about me after I was dead. I had based my life and my reign upon one principle, that love resolves all other troubles—and my twenty-five years' rule had shown our formerly disunited Kingdom that this principle would work. If I now became branded as an aggressor, it gave the lie to all I had said, done and achieved. My own Scots now living knew me for the man I was, but I could see dark days ahead, when my people would need to remember the proud, prosperous, amiable nation which at the end had gone to war because there was no other way left to her. There were few enough good times in our past we could look back to for inspiration.

This was why I had to be very careful that my terrible stratagem using the *Michael* was known to nobody but myself, until all my efforts to resolve matters by other means had failed. I had to measure winds and weather against minutest details of diplomacy, trying to judge by my own guesswork what was happening everywhere in Europe so that I could time the despatch of the *Michael* to strike a demoralizing blow to the enemy precisely at the moment when he could be seen to be in the wrong.

I had been greatly worried to have no reply to my last detailed letter to my Uncle John of Denmark. I hoped the silence meant that he was equipping ships and soldiers to send to my aid. Daily I expected to see ships' sails bearing Danish colours appear upon the skyline. In May I discovered why there had been no answer from my uncle: John, King of Denmark, was dead. I stared incredulously at the letter from my cousin, the new King Christian, explaining why he could not send aid to Scotland—he had just regained Sweden, and his interest for the present lay all in Scandinavia and not in Northern Europe. It ran true to our Stewart luck that my uncle should die just at this moment; he had been my last relative alive who could have been expected to care what happened to myself and my Kingdom.

De la Mothe made safe arrival at the same time that I learned of my uncle's death. King Louis was insistent that my fleet should be present in the Channel before he released any of his army to come to my aid in Scotland. This was understandable enough, for he had war on two fronts and was in imminent danger of invasion upon his Channel coastline. But I was reckoning upon the likelihood that King Henry would divide his forces, sending one army to invade Scotland, while he himself took another to invade France simultaneously. Our Scots population was not nearly as numerous as that of England or France, and France's king had reckoned on help reaching me from Denmark, for he had not known that my Uncle John was dead when de la Mothe had sailed. Also, I needed trained gunners, for all my best gun crews were to go aboard the *Michael*; Pat Paniter was having a lovely time practising with the ordnance from the Castle, but I was not sure he would be as skilful with the ramming rod of a culverin as he was with his pen.

De la Mothe bore some comforting news: God's Champion, Henry Tudor, was not enjoying success all the way. His fleet had clashed with the French in the Channel and had taken a severe mauling. In the fighting, England's Admiral Howard had been slain; the English ships had holed back to lick their wounds. That would delay his invasion project for a while.

The French ambassador's second good piece of news, although not so spectacular as the defeat of the English vessels, carried great diplomatic significance. King Ferdinand, having now possessed himself of Navarre, had begun to lose interest in the 'Holy' cause. He had put out feelers to know if King Louis were interested in treating for peace. . . .

My hope leapt at this news, for I had heard recently that the

Venetians were also becoming restless within the League, as Sultan Selim's galleys were sighted in yet greater numbers, viewing Italy's eastern coastline at their leisure. Their presence would not make Pope Leo any happier, either. Which left only the Emperor as signatory to the League—apart from King Henry—and I knew 'puir auld Maximilian' would be out of it as fast as his allies let him go: his Diets would not give him the money he needed, and he had only been kept going by subsidies from King Henry—they had signed a special agreement the month before.

It looked as if Christendom's rulers were about to recover from their madness. We had no haloes to show in our portrait gallery, just a row of crowns—and not all of those were come by honestly (*pax, O mei patris anima interfecti!*), nor honestly maintained. But we had enough sense between us to accommodate a vain lad like Henry Tudor—who was heading soon for the discovery that his great wealth and vainglorious character had served their purpose while Julius wanted to put down Louis and Ferdinand had seen his way to get Navarre; but he would find England was a very little king indeed when his usefulness to his allies was ended. (Scotland was a very little king, too, and by knowing it usually contrived to win more friends than enemies.) He would learn the error of his ways.

Full of hope, I stopped all work upon the *Michael* and other war preparations and sent a letter to King Henry, pointing out that as Spain and France were anxious to make peace, and the rest of the League had similar inclinations, there was nothing further impeding Christian unity but his own determination to make war upon King Louis. I begged him to join with the rest of us in a Crusade against the Turk. I also requested him to let pass my ambassadors to France, Spain and Rome, in order to pursue their negotiations for a general peace—the sea routes were unusually storm-ridden that summer.

He wrote back to say that he could not make peace without the permission of his allies(!) and that he would not let pass my ambassadors going anywhere for any purpose. With solemn piety he contrived to lay responsibility for the situation entirely upon God.

The man was a devil. I began to realize that this new Tudor dynasty was the greatest threat to Scotland since the days of Edward Plantagenet 'The Hammer'. If I did not put it down within my lifetime, there would be none after me that could.

I had wasted precious time—over a month of it—laying off my war preparations while I negotiated with a man too contemptuous of peace even to be hypocritical in his replies: King England wanted *war*. He never wanted ought else but war, and, by St Martin, he would get it! I cursed myself for the time I had wasted, as I galloped Balthazar between Craigmillar Castle and the New Haven. All Scotland knew me: the man in the red cloak, whipped like a wet blood-soaked sail about my ears, thundering the coast road upon the fierce black stallion they called the Devil's charger. I was frantic with haste. I had begun to feel that I would haunt this coast road forever, if the freak June weather persisted and we failed to make ready the *Michael* in time for the job for which I had meant her. I would wave to old wives gathered at their doors to see me pass, and laugh my greeting. *Laugh!*—dear God, with the squalls of rain so dense at the New Haven, we once nearly rode straight into the *Michael's* side from the jetty because the murk was so dense and Balthazar had the scent too late (it was the only time I ever knew weather defeat the senses of an animal). What re-caulking, tallowing, and loading could be done by men who were wind-borne shapes in the day-time darkness? Living memory bore no record of such weather in June—and it appeared only above Scotland, for it was said they prayed for rain upon the parched hot lands of Southern France and Italy; which made me feel that even God had joined the 'Holy' League.

Nothing any more was on my side. Every silver piece which came miraculously to hand, now paid arrears. I never put men to work unless I could pay them—so there were fewer kept upon the task than I would have wanted. Many would have worked who wanted no pay, but I dare not let it be known the King was so desperate for funds, or why the purpose of the *Michael* was so vital.

There was a blanket of silence between Henry Tudor's Kingdom and mine, so that it was as though we were two lands with half the earth's surface lying between us. How far he was progressing with his own preparations for the invasion of France I had no means of knowing.

At the last, a chance visitor to my Realm kindled a new flicker of hope—although I knew it even then to be a ghost fire, like the marsh lights likely to be seen upon his native Irish bogland. He was the Prince of Ulster, Sir Hugh O'Donnel, who wanted my help in trying to unite the whole of Ireland in one nation. It would be an aggressive war, for he would have to combat chieftains who valued their independence, but Sir Hugh's reasons were not to gain power for himself but freedom for Ireland. His father had avowed himself my liege in earlier times, and Ulster remained Scots in allegiance and influence at a time when Ireland was so torn by chaos that King England had managed to capture all the chief ports along the eastern coastline (needless to say, these bases useful for an English invasion in the west of Scotland were never a comfort to me).

The meeting with Sir Hugh O'Donnel was one of the strangest I ever had, for—as with Dacre—I *knew* this man whom I had never met before: his crinkling black hair and his rolling brown eyes, which gave his nod of agreement a doom-laden air. And I knew why he was known to me: this was the *other* ally, who had been waiting all these ten years upon the *other* road I would have taken had Meg Drummond lived to keep me true to Scotland's more vital destiny. I should have looked west, not south nor east, to the Celtic fringe of the world which had once linked with Scotland before to preserve wisdom through the dark ages. At last I saw clearly that the answer to the Border problem was a Celtic alliance, between the three lands who shared these islands with an aggressive Saxon neighbour. The Celts were a peace-loving race, who fought between themselves; the English fought to gain power over others, which was a very different matter, and they were the last people in the world whom it was safe to leave unguarded. Ringed by three Celtic strongholds, King England long ago might have been trained to better manners. It was now too late, as I knew it was too late—but Sir Hugh and I talked of it all the same, in a last fleeting hope that time might turn back to aid us.

We agreed, we had to strike together now or within a hundred years Ireland, and possibly Scotland as well, would be under English rule. I gave him guns to bear back to Ireland, in the hope he could use them there against the English before King Henry sailed for France. I doubted this threat to the English-held forts would be sufficient to alter England's plans, but it might cause him to ponder a little longer whether it was wise to leave his Kingdom unattended with so many enemies around her: I was taking it for granted that King Henry cared about his English subjects.

It was a mistaken assumption. Barely had the Prince of Ulster left me, when the news came that King Henry, in person, had landed upon French soil. He was capering about on his horse before the walls of Thérouanne, challenging 'the enemy of God and Christendom'.

It was several days more before I learned that Sir Hugh O'Donnel had left behind the guns which I had given him. He had received my word that King Henry had invaded France; in which case, he said, I would have more need than he for the ordnance I had given him. He left me his blessing, *'Beannachd Dhei leibh, mo righ'*.

Time had been my enemy all through my days; either I had seen too much of it, or not enough. Now it had dealt me a blow too great almost to bear. With all man's ingenuity, why had we not invented a way to know what was happening in other parts of the world without a month's delay? It would be fatal to send the *Michael* to destroy King Henry's palaces during his absence, so that he came home hot with anger to see the damage, bringing his entire army north to exact retribution: it would be a different matter entirely if he were present to see and hear and feel the power of my guns. The problem now was to bring him across the Channel and then send in the *Michael*. For that, we would need to have a sufficient show of force upon the Border to convince him that we presented a greater threat than a mere Border raid.

The final work to make ready the fleet continued by night and day at Leith and the New Haven. The weather was no more help than it had been earlier, for it was now July, the month in which a dense sea-fog covers the east coast of Scotland, making some of the days as dim and dangerous as November. I had always regarded the haar affectionately, but now even Balthazar found me an ungracious and morose companion as we galloped through the greyness, our hoof beats muffled and the two of us shut off like ghosts in a world where no news reached us nor a glimpse of life until we clattered on to the cobbles of the quayside where the yellow horn lanterns burned to give light to the workmen. The sense of urgency and excitement had passed now that King Henry had sailed, and it was only the grim, desperate need to have the fleet upon its way as quickly as possible which bore me along.

On the day before the fleet was due to sail, I sent out the proclamation calling all my lieges to assemble with their men at Ellem, the traditional place of mustering in Berwickshire, or upon the Burgh Muir of Edinburgh. And upon that same evening, I had the Earl of Arran to sup with me privately.

After we had eaten, I sent the servants away, and I told Cousin James the purpose of the *Michael*. I then presented him with his sealed orders, which I had written out and been carrying within my shirt next to my skin for the past fortnight. These he was to study when he was aboard, and then destroy.

James took it all very quietly, contrary to my expectation, merely giving me his thanks that I had entrusted him with such great responsibility. I was greatly cheered that he did not think we would strike too late: he felt that we stood to gain by having to recall Henry from France, so that his fleet would be in the Channel to be sunk there or scattered by the combined French and Scots force, leaving the *Michael* to chase home the King's vessel and complete her object unimpeded. He immediately started to check my calculations of the *Michael*'s chances of completing her task and getting away safely, taking into account the winds and tides and the chances of the South-Easterlies blowing him off-course with all the Irish easterly ports in English hands.

He wanted to know whether the Thames River had sufficient depth to take a large vessel the size of the *Michael*, and whether, if she grounded, my provision of a sixty-oar galley would be sufficient to tow her off. He made my head ache with his eager, tireless questions—to him it was all exciting, new, a challenge, whereas to me, who had pondered these matters for over two years, it was a wearisome venture of which I had already had enough. I cannot remember whether I ever instructed him that the essential point was to destroy London, and that whether or not the *Michael* got away again safely was immaterial—though I know that I wrote in the orders that if all my precautions to get the *Michael* away were foiled by elements beyond my control, she was to be fired alongside the city, close inshore, so that her blazing oak and her powder magazine could take up with her so much as was left of London.

That same day I sent my final challenge to King Henry, stating simply why I knew there was no hope that he would ever mean well by my Kingdom and why, therefore, I had decided to attack before he did. I said that I had lost faith in him—a statement most people use many times but which I had never made before. Always until now I had had faith in people—that they meant well, and would do better upon the next occasion; I never hoped much, but I hoped. In King Henry's case, I had no hope left whatever. He was a weak, silly lad, vain and a natural bully, spoiled by his father and brought without princely knowledge to a throne where nobody could say to him 'no'. He should have been whipped as a child for his tantrums and warned that the world was too small a place to allow for such a big head.

The next day, a glittering assembly of the entire Court gathered at the New Haven to see the fleet set sail for France. All decked out in their best attire, my Queen and her ladies viewed the occasion as a naval tournament, wanting to be ferried across to see over the *Michael*. I had to deny them the pleasure, for the main job was to get the *Michael* away, not to have a flock of shrill, fluttering lassies playing hunt-the-sailor round her decks. I had not a great deal of patience left for feminine attitudes to war. Anne of Brittany, Louis' Queen, had sent me a ring to wear when I invaded England, which was a pretty gesture, but I should have been a good deal more grateful had her husband sent me instead some soldiers.

For all that, even my heart lifted as I saw my three great ships hoist sail, and the first swell of their white and painted canvas as they caught the air current. The *Michael* looked splendid with her simple decorations: her oak rail gleaming with its wax and oil coating above the black-pitched hull. Her mainsail carried the royal crimson and gold of the Lyon Rampant, but she bore no other device upon her sails. Her poop gleamed with gilt around the carved Lyon between whose claws fluttered the blue and silver banner of Scotland. Best of all was the glint of brass and iron gun-barrels like eyelets winking in her sides. She was lovely to me because—God will!—she took with her Scotland's answer to King England.

Surrounding the three great ships (the *Michael* dwarfing the other two) was a flurry of smaller vessels—half a score of these bearing my own insignia and the rest covered with as many crests as they had owners. The long evenings I had spent persuading our Scots merchants to invest in shipping had brought ample reward. I took heart this day that my fleet had persuaded not only the wind to moderate but the sun to shine in its honour: the great white streamers of cloud in a washed blue sky suggested God's galleys went as escort with the *Michael*.

Cousin James had dressed himself in white and yellow, entirely unsuitable for the venture, but in keeping with his rank (knowing James, he would be in a canvas jerkin, swarming up the rigging himself before he was out of sight of the courtly gathering upon the quayside). He came to kiss my hand. He looked terribly young; but when he dropped to his knee before me it was reassuring to see that his scalp was now faintly visible beneath his hair: if James were going bald, he was old enough to command the fleet. Then he bowed himself away, three or four times, before he jumped into the waiting galley. He stood among the oarsmen, facing me, to the moment he boarded the *Michael*— the white and yellow details of his doublet and the gold chain around his neck, from which hung his seaman's whistle, still clearly distinguishable. I had looked my last on Cousin Arran, I knew already in my heart—I would be dead before he returned. He would secure and guard my Realm for the safety of its infant King when I was gone. I felt a pang to take leave of Cousin James: we had squabbled and understood each other for a long time—forty years all told.

Their sails filling, the great and the little ships headed for open sea. I saw the sun's light flashing on the windows of the poop cabin of the *Great Michael* so that she seemed to have an aura of golden light about her stern in whose radiance the figures of Arran, and Robert Bartoun beside him, were lost. The amazing thing about the *Michael* was her gracefulness; for all her huge bulk and thick walls, she floated like a bird, making the rest look like tubs rolling in her wake. We had built a great vessel, the finest ship on earth; it would be a pity if she had to end as a blazing pyre in England but, for all that, it would be well worth it to achieve the job for which I had built her. As her sails disappeared over the horizon I felt unbearably lost, with all of the activity ended which had made busy my days for the past four years: I suppose I had realized my dreams, in my head since I was a wee lad, and a dream realized can make the heart quite as forlorn as a dream lost. I left the Queen and the Court to return to the Palace for dinner, and I rode back to Craigmillar to eat there alone.

There was no time to indulge the sense of anticlimax. All thought now was to muster the army. My tournament pavilion had been erected on the Burgh Muir outside the walls of Edinburgh. It was of bright blue canvas stretched over a wooden frame, with small oval glazed windows set one in each side and a matching velvet curtain lined with scarlet across its entrance. It was my girding room, and the place where I rested or received visitors when taking part in a tournament. It was a pretty thing, belonging to happier occasions, and it seemed incongruous set down by the armourers' sheds where the last of the pikes were being assembled ready for distribution to the volunteers—but I could not have afforded to have a new, more suitable pavilion made for the purpose, for I had no money to waste upon show and toys. It was all needed to buy the more deadly accoutrements of war.

For my battle emblem I had chosen the falcon—the bird I had loosed so many times before upon the Burgh Muir to catch fat wood pigeons. It was not depicted in the customary heraldic way, but in a new style of my own which marked me as a hunting man not an armorist: with wings stretched back and pinions down, as it plummets to make a kill. In outline, it was not unlike the Saltire crossed low, with claws added, which gave it deeper meaning for my Scots. But even I had not expected it to have such potent effect upon all who saw it. It was as though every man who knew himself as Scots had seized upon it as *his* sign. It was easy to draw, and I found it limned everywhere—marked upon walls and scratched wherever a piece of bared earth showed itself beside the path.

The pigeons now had mostly fled from the great oaks of the Burgh Muir, to take refuge in the denser woodland, and beneath these oak trees were now pitched the small tents of the men from the Lothians, from Renfrew, Ayrshire and Argyll; from Perthshire, and all from the North and North-West. The men from Fife and Angus, the Bordersmen and those to the south-west of us would go direct to Ellem; all others mustered to their King.

Alexander had at last the privilege of being recognized openly as the royal favourite. He was the most precious human being I had left to me, and he would go to war beside his father like all other beloved sons of proud fathers. I took him everywhere beside me; he knew my reasons for all I did—for we discussed them, as we loosed our falcons beside the woodland while waiting for our men to gather, or wandered quietly, talking, between the trees. He was to fight at my right hand, in the middle of the front rank, like any of our men. (I had never asked any of my subjects to undertake a task I would not do myself, and when a Kingdom has been built upon that principle, and through it achieved harmony and greatness, there is no way at the end to alter it if what is to be preserved is more important than the death of a King or Archbishop.) It was a strange kind of happiness we shared during those days of the mustering on Burgh Muir. I can see him now, as he stood once by my stirrup, speaking up to me: the dark, curly hair around his tonsure above the collar of his white silk shirt worn under the gaudy blue and yellow doublet I termed disparagingly the 'Padua gayre'. Then he grinned and leapt away to mount his grey mare; we always raced back to the pavilion to dine, Alexander and I, and he always lost whatever handicap I gave him. It was a question of principle with Balthazar, that he and I should never lose a race.

While he had been in Padua, Erasmus had made for Alexander an optical glass, and the lad had great benefit of it when reading; unfortunately, however, it did not make things at a distance more clear to his weak eyes. I worried how he would see when he had to wear a helmet, for the vizor was a curse to any, let alone to those with poor sight: I wondered whether his viewing glass put inside a leather band and strapped across his eye would help, but he said not. We would have to rely upon my sword arm to guide his vision, I said—and it would to some extent shield him, although I dared not mention this to Alexander.

The most splendid thing in these weeks since he came from St Andrews to join me was that for the first time we could talk together upon any subject without quarrelling (I had always grieved that although I could come easily to terms with almost any man alive, yet I had such great difficulty in holding peaceful conversation with this son of mine who was more like myself than any). Our thoughts were now attuned to one another. For instance, Alexander said that we would need a song to unite the marching feet of the many who came from such far-flung territories. I told him that I had composed one for that purpose, and I sang it, in my voice which had never found its right note since I was a lad of thirteen. (He never would believe that I once had a voice as good as his own.) He liked the words, if not the rendering, and said he would compose a new tune for me. I said we would have *my* song sung to *my* tune—which I heard well enough in my head, for all that my voice failed to deliver it correctly. He said we would have *our Scots* army song sung to *his* tune, and proceeded to sing it exactly to the melody I had in my head when I composed it. It was his tune, my tune, who need argue about it? It was a splendid tune—and, it was true, he had improved it by repeating the last line three times: 'Ta wrest King England's creuwn. . . .' The rest of the words I have forgotten, but it is ironically the tune which has lingered in my mind.

We had need of a rousing marching song. The Earl of Hume had undertaken to raid the Northumbrian Border Marches to clear the English forts along the Till River—those same forts which had caused us so much lost time and unnecessary impedimenta in the war for the English Pretender. News came up now from Berwickshire that he had lost a third of his men in an ambush by English bowmen: some five hundred slain and his two kinsmen captains taken prisoner. He was furious, for it had been his own fault for not beating down the gorse and bracken lairs upon the apparently empty field where the English were hidden. His men had fought off the attack ferociously, but the first storm of arrows had taken a heavy toll of their numbers. The loss of the men was bad enough, but the effect on the morale of the army so early in the war was worse.

Next was brought to me the extraordinary news that my fleet was back in harbour at Ayr. Ayr was upon the west coast, and the route to France from the Firth of Forth was through the eastern sea-lane to the Continent. Dismissing the report as a rumour, I wondered in alarm if King Henry had landed upon my shores from Ireland.

Hard upon what I called a 'rumour' came confirmation that it was indeed the Scots fleet which had put in at Ayr, having—oh, Jesu, Lord of Mercy!—sacked Carrickfergus upon the north-east coast of Ireland! What could Arran have been doing at Carrickfergus, when my orders were that he should sail to France? I confess, I went near mad with rage. I sent at once to call out Sir Andrew Wood from his house on Castle Hill—he was an old man, but he had served my father well—and we rode furiously together, without escort, through to the west.

We reached Ayr in the early afternoon: to look out over an empty skyline. I knew what had happened: there had come a good wind, and my practical cousin had seized it to advantage. The tide was high. I can remember standing with Sir Andrew beside me, upon the harbour side, amidst an extraordinary collection of small cannon—not mine—powder kegs, crossbows, long bows, halberds, casks of wine, barrels of flour and fishing nets, and looking, baffled, at the empty ocean.

It was not until later, in Edinburgh, the messenger arrived whom my Cousin James had put ashore to ride to me with the news that he 'asked my pardon to have tarried, then gone hence with mukel haste', but there had come a 'fine and gentil brees quhilk I see as good to blaw mee to France'. So he had gone, leaving behind such supplies as 'I knaws, gud cosying will be abundyng to yur lack'—which he had brought thoughtfully from the plundered fortress of Carrickfergus. He told me that all of my guns were in sound working order, and that he had proved beyond doubt that the *Michael* could achieve the purpose for which it was built. Also, he could now 'mak with licht heert to our matter', there now being one port upon the Irish coast where he could shelter, had he need, without fear of English guns.

I might have known that what would defeat me would be not Cousin James's vices but his damnable clear virtues. I had given him a task to perform, and he had given it the detailed thinking which I gave to my Kingdom. He had tested the *Michael*'s guns and her manoeuvrability in an estuary not unlike the Thames; he had stripped clean of guns a base for which he could make if the South-Easterlies blew him off-course when he was heading back; he had supplied me with some valuable equipment for my land force; and—if it were of any real concern to King Henry— he had done his best to create the threat of attack upon his Irish bases. To sack Carrickfergus was a masterly stratagem.

The one thing he had overlooked, was that what happened to his men, himself or the *Michael*—or to the King of Scots—was irrelevant, so long as we put down King England's menace for the next five hundred years. That was what I had told him—I thought—when I had said that in the last resort the *Michael* and her powder store must be fired to take up with her what was left of Henry's palaces. And he, a competent king of his floating kingdom, had lost ten precious days in order to achieve what, so far as Scotland was concerned, did not matter. If only he had used the time he had to spare in waiting at anchor in the channel where—according to my own plan—he was more likely to cause King Henry qualms about the Kingdom he had left behind.

I could not fault Arran. I had given him his command because he had an independent and a practical mind. All he lacked was a quarter of a century of kingship, which would have taught him that the only life to be considered was that of *Scotland*.

But I could not be philosophical upon the harbour wall at Ayr. I could only take off my cap to let the cool wind blow through my hair and my head, and wonder if the fleet would reach the French coast in time to double back to the Thames if we managed to entice King Henry home to London with our assault upon the Border. I think I must have known the end, as I looked at the empty horizon. I know, I put up the forefinger of each hand in turn to dash the tears from my face.

I never learned what happened to my fleet—my precious fleet, that was designed to make Scotland safe for ever and a day.

There had never been a mustering like it, upon the slope of Burgh Muir. I could stand then upon the height of the Muir beneath my flying falcon standard and see all of the moorland, reaching down to the sandy beaches of Cramond and the winding road along the strand to Leith. Upon a clear day there lay only the waters of the Forth beyond it, and the clear brown earth of Fyfe now stripped of its trees; and beyond it again, when it was very clear, the hills of Meg Drummond's Perthshire and the faint blue of the line that ran to the north. I thought often it was like looking upward through the heart of my Kingdom.

And there were all of its men around me, where I could see them face to face. Nearly every man in Scotland between the age of sixteen and sixty. In the midst of my great despair and desolation, it was strange to have the most powerful sense of happiness that I had known in all my life. I saw for the first time, gathered into one great harvest, all the fruits of my twenty-five years' labours—like apples carpeting the ground beneath the oaks of the Muir. Felons I had won to better ways came forward grinning to show me their enlistment pike. Clansmen mixed there who had feuded for longer than living memory, prepared to bear with one another while they fought together in our cause. All of my neighbours, from the vennels and the modest mansions of the Canongait, and the rich folk who had complained about the armourers' noise upon the Hill, all sought me out to let me know that they, too, came with me down to England. Out from their wee turf cottages they came, and from the common stair. All of our young lads from the vennel howff who painted or sculpted or wrote poetry—young David Seton among them. And there was Donald Owre, to fight with the Islesmen volunteers. There had never been a mustering like it, in all of Scotland's history. And the thing which awed me was that they came not in their hatred of King England but for love of me.

Some days before we set out, there came late of night to Holyrood a message that there was an unholy disturbance close by St Giles. I sent out the Guard to see what was the matter, and they brought back an old woman whom they knew as 'the old *faidh* who sings among the rushes of the North Loch'. I knew the old *faidh* too, for she was an Edinburgh character, as mad as the March winds, but she had the 'lang ee' right enough. She had demanded to see the King—none other would suffice.

She came pattering to me across the tiles of the hall, a scrawny wee figure with straggling yellow-grey hair and the hooked nose of a witch above her empty gums. She grabbed my arm, and stared up at me with her narrowed pale eyes. Then she said, 'Da noucht gang deuwn ta England, Hiemmie, da noucht gang deuwn! Fur ye sall noucht cam hame the mair'. She kept on repeating, 'Ye sall noucht cam hame the mair'.

I sighed, for I knew that myself—and said so. Her lang sicht and mine had no secrets hid between them. But she seemed greatly distressed and began trying to tell me about 'the Crab sall eat up the Fish . . . and there sall be twa gauld rings maket ane . . . und ur seed sall be despersit ta mak a' lands green save ur ain'. What held me was her mention of the Crab. I asked her, what did she know about the Crab and the Fish?—for there was nobody knew what William Schevez had told me those years ago. But she would only reiterate over and over again, clawing at my arm—'und ur seed sall be despersit to make green a' lands save ur ain'. I asked, what did she mean, 'twa gauld rings maket ane'? But she only repeated it, without further explanation. It clung to my memory a long while before I had the answer.

I was very tired, and it was late. Also, she frightened me because she knew what I knew. I did my best to explain that I had no choice but to go now down to England. Then, suddenly, she said, 'Gi' me feel o' yur banes'—and clutched my arm so tightly in her claw, I winced as much with pain as with foreboding. She muttered, 'We sall noucht hauld yur banes i' this lond, Hiemmie, we sall noucht hauld yur banes i' this lond, lad!'— and then she darted away from me towards the door. I cried out to her to wait a moment, but she was gone, only the quick patter of her departing footsteps answering me.

And with the memory of 'yon auld faidh' is linked a picture of Alexander, on the last evening I remember of Scotland's great days, when, as our Archbishop, he said a mass for us in Linlithgow's chapel of St Michael. I am standing in the new gateway, waiting, as Alexander followed by his clergy pauses to adjust his mitre, with the fountain of the Palace playing in the green quadrangle behind him. He was twenty years of age; and I remember thinking how good to me life had been, to give me such a glorious son.

Upon the next day, we took the road down into England.

16

WE marched in the rains of autumn from the slope of Burgh Muir—an endless host of us, pikes shouldered, with those who were the captains claiming the privilege to have their weapons go with the baggage train. (It was the only privilege we had.) We set out from the Burgh Muir in our many companies, our banners and small pennants flying, to defend against King England the Scotland we had forged together over the past twenty-five years. Alexander and I, in the while the men camped in waiting upon the Muir, had taught each small group our marching song. We needed the one song to bind us all together, in Scots and Celtic, for we had no other that everybody could sing, and now we had it all together: 'Fur to wrest King England's creuwn. . . . Fur to wrest King England's creuwn. . . . Fur to wrest King England's creuwn!' (What I really meant to wrest from him was his signed promise that he would make no more preposterous claims to *my* crown, but that was too elaborate to explain in an army chorus.)

All who could make the journey came to see us leave the Burgh Muir. Only two of our lords we left behind—my wee James, Earl of Moray, and Angus 'Bell-the-Cat'. It had been a terrible decision to leave Angus: he was old and he had earned his retirement but, as he pointed out to me, almost wrecking my table beneath the slam of his fist to prove the strength of his right sword-arm, he was as able as any in the land. I knew that;

what was worse, I had a terrible, superstitious feeling that all of us should go together who had shared in making the Kingdom what it was. I was frightened that if one of us were left out of it, some vital part of the pattern would be lacking for success. But I had small choice in the matter. My wife—bless her—was no fit person to leave alone in charge of my Scotland. True, she had Bishop Elphinstone, but the two of them did not too well agree. She had begged me to leave with her Angus, and I felt she was right, that the Kingdom needed one strong person to hold it while I was away—and who else but the guardian of all our emergencies, 'Bell-the-Cat'?

He stood watching now as we marched and rode past the waving bonny lasses and the old men who grinned with toothless gums and banged a gnarled first on a palsied hand to show us how to treat King England. My eyes met those of Angus—and he looked away. I wished later that I could have read the message in his eyes before it was too late.

We rode in the rains of autumn, with the pest to harry our ranks. We should have known we would bring it with us from one of those festering pockets of infection spread across the Kingdom. Men would step out of the marching column and waver to the roadside, where they sat, vomiting and groaning, with a hand tucked into the armpit—and there we left them, to march on. Usually, when a man fell by the wayside, some companion would stay to tend him—which always moved and amazed me for there was no social readmittance for these men who had tended a plague-stricken comrade, although they themselves might live; who were they and how many, these folk who stayed behind for a cause dearer to God than even our Crusade? We never stayed to learn; there is nothing can be done when the pest strikes a marching army, other than to flee it.

Alexander changed his clerical robes once more for the gaudy blue and yellow of the 'Padua gayre'. I talked with him a little about this matter of bishops and the lower clergy fighting with spears to kill like other men. It was a contemporary custom—but I liked it less since Pope Julius had set such a warlike example. I asked Alexander what he thought about it, for he was not a lad to enlist without he gave it thought. He seemed surprised by my question. What else was there to be done? In Henry Tudor we had the greatest evil contributed to our Christian ranks in many a long day. He had foiled every effort of my pen, leaving the sword as the sole alternative. Thus reasoned Scotland's Primate, Alexander Stewart, Archbishop of St Andrews, with a quick tight smile, and his armour following in the baggage with my own. His warlike road led him, as he saw it, to Jerusalem. Then he cantered away very quickly not to let me see his eye wet with regret for all the better things he could have done.

We marched in the rains of autumn, with the pest and sheer damp misery to thin our ranks. It was a diminished column by the time we joined the rest at Ellem. I stood upon a cart to look above the sea of heads. I never had seen before so many of my Scots assembled in one place. They cheered me—which was nice of them—and the only reply I could find, was to shout 'Ah love ye!' across their ranks, and then to start our battle song.

We crossed the Tweed. At Twizelhaugh, in England, Paniter, who had gone ahead with the guns, rode back to remind me of a piece of work left undone by our last Parliament in Edinburgh. I knew it was to do with the list, which we had with us—what on earth became of that list, after the battle, of every man's name who fought in Hiemmie's cause? The list had been a new idea, to replace the fashion of the old days when every man from a small community was remembered by his lord or by his comrades; on the Burgh Muir men had enlisted to me personally, not to my feudal lords, and how could I remember each of the thousands by name who came to my banner, so that I could inform his widow of my intention to help support his children? So we had made a list, as we gave each man his pike, and for the first time in the world's history a prince had recorded every man's name who fought by his side. We had that list in my baggage, I told Paniter. And then I remembered: we had not made it law that widows and orphans be safeguarded—for the reason our last Parliament, in Edinburgh's Tolbooth, had much other business to conclude, and we were not expecting heavy casualties when we went down to England.

At Twizelhaugh we formed a square upon the grass—my lords to my right, our commoners to my left, and facing me the clergy, with my son Alexander in the middle, his mitre upon his head. And there, upon the 24th day of August, 1513, as we had done for a quarter of a century, we members of our Scots Parliament enacted the ruling that would spare widows and orphans all taxes to the Crown in the event of their breadwinner's death. I think could I have chosen that last day's parliamentary business conducted in my reign, I would not have had it other than it was. Our last Scots enactment of Law was in our Scots tradition.

After Twizelhaugh, there followed the seizure of several Border fortresses. We needed to finish the work of the 'ill raid', and we needed time to let the fleet reach the shores of France. Then we came to Ford Castle, where, with some satisfaction, I set up my headquarters (it had been the home of Sir Walter Heron, whose bastard brother had slain my Warden Kerr). It had been left in the charge of Heron's young wife. Lady Heron, poor lass, had a dull solitary life in the country, and a romantic nature. I had hoped to be able to drive a straightforward bargain to leave Ford Castle lands undamaged if she would arrange the return of the two Hume kinsmen taken prisoner, but she meant to have me to her bed first. I had a war to think about, and when I said 'no' to a woman, I meant 'no'. At the same time, I had to retrieve the two Hume lads, who might have useful information of English intentions. In the end, it took me two weeks before I managed to persuade the sweet lady that I meant what I said and that if she complied, her fields and woodlands would still be there for her pleasure long after I had departed. We parted upon good terms, all considering: I had kept my virtue, she had her lands, and I had our hostages.

Having thus allowed a fortnight, it was surely time for Arran and the fleet to have reached the coast of France?

On the English side of the Till there was a great square hill called Flodden Edge. It was not unlike the Castle Hill of Edinburgh, and a bonny site for a stronghold if we ever saw one. We decided to camp there while waiting for the Earl of Surrey's army, which was approaching from the South. We were not in any hurry, for our objective was not to invade but to tease: if the entire Scots army were to camp upon English soil, it would surely bring Henry home to London and make decisive the *Michael*'s guns.

The hill was thickly timbered upon its west side, so we cut down the trees to make a fortified escarpment such as we had built at Linlithgow when we were quartered there as rebels. The trees were huge here, however, and it was a great business to drive them as staves into the milder slope of ground. And— oh, dear God!—how clearly I realized now why all of my life it had depressed me to see wood chippings blown by the wind and trampled underfoot into the mud of winter ground. I had been waiting for these days, when I would stand upon the high escarpment of Flodden Edge, looking down upon the trodden mud and raw wood spikes and those slivers of white blown by the wind—knowing that I was about to die. What a long time it had taken for the 'lang ee' and my mortal eyes to meet. I was waiting and watching for the appearance of my Herald, bearing King Henry's answer to my last challenge. I had bade him before it was too late to turn home from France, but I had not yet received his reply.

Instead arrived the Earl of Surrey, to take up the challenge to a combat eighteen years later. This time I knew my luck was out, but there was nothing I could do about it. He was rude and blustering as ever; having sent me his challenge for September 9th at the latest, which I accepted, he then sent his herald to accuse me of cowardice for escarping my army, and challenging me to descent to the Millfield below (where the Earl of Hume had met his ambush). I told him I would stay where I was, for it was not seemly that a mere earl should dictate to a king when and where we met each other. We could have continued in this fashion until the appointed hour, but then Surrey's army, massed below us, began a sidelong movement which looked to me dreadfully as though he meant to cross the Border into Scotland. And there there was nobody left to defend the homesteads and fields and women and children save the lads younger than sixteen and the old men. It could have been a feint—and I knew likely it was—

but beyond the line of his advance lay my Kingdom, open and undefended. I was its King. I could take no chances.

We piled our camp rubbish and those of the tree-trunks we had time to dislodge and set fire to it; behind the smoke screen we moved out of our impregnable fortress, sending the guns to new positions where they had no chance to select their aim upon an enemy who was still moving below the pall of smoke from our fire. I cursed this factor but there was little we could do about it. From this time onward it was all a desperate effort with expediency taking the place of careful planning. (Those who later would hold theories as to why the Battle of Branxton Moor ended as it did may know more of it than I, for I fought in the front line, on foot, and I died early. Of what *I* saw and knew, I can tell: nothing more.) We had to move blind, and there was a groping to find the enemy and the best position simultaneously. By noon, my force had to be prepared, for thereafter, until three o'clock, according to the terms of the challenge and chivalrous usage, we were open to immediate attack from any side. It was all poor, rolling ground, either marshy or sloping, and we had to find the best of it in a very short time. We decided to take the upper level of Branxton Moor, so that at least we had the gradient to our advantage.

There had been constant rain for over three weeks, and although it managed to clear a little upon that day, the ground beneath us was soaked deep, to make a greasy mud surface which gave no grip to the foot. I had a quick meeting with Huntley, Argyll, Lennox and Hume to decide if the upward or downward slope gave best tread, and it was decided to use the downward—we would then also have a better view of Surrey's men approaching. The ground, however, was so bad that we gave orders for all of our men not steeled—steel bit to find a surface—to remove their boots and fight in their hose. It was hard for them upon the littered surface of a battlefield and there was some growling about it, but it was better than death.

Nobody liked the battle ground. The two middle battles were composed of spearmen in a phalanx, and the phalanx fights best on level ground. (The Scots fought, like the Swiss and Germans, in the old phalanx formation; its advantage for undisciplined soldiers was the sense of solidarity and comradeship given by the lines of long spears resting upon each shoulder, which compensated for lack of experience.) There is nothing on earth can resist a phalanx of men armed with spears—other than a stone wall—but only if it holds together. If it breaks, each rank is vulnerable, and mounting up the hazard for those behind as it falls; and as the rear ranks come forward, they are left to thresh at close quarters with first ten, then fourteen, then eighteen- and then twenty-foot spears, useless weapons in such circumstances. A phalanx of spearmen did not go into battle assuming it would break; it assumed it would hold steady and that it would have time to choose its ground. We had no time to choose our ground carefully because we had agreed to the opening of hostilities at twelve, and we took the best of the bad ground available.

At a meeting upon Flodden Edge, we had already agreed our positions for the battle—although agreed is not the word for mine because I was the only Scot, with Alexander's support, who held the view that the King's position was in the front line of his men. I have given my reasons, as I gave them then to those who tried so hard to dissuade me—and they did try hard to make me stay upon the hill, out of danger. But had I the choice to make again, I would still take up the position which I held upon that day: while rulers fight in the front rank of their men, they will not go to war for any but the best of causes.

I did, however, make one great mistake. I put my nation's leaders together in the front and second ranks beside me, instead of scattering them between the other lines. If the men had taken their positions regardless of birth, there would have been a better chance that a balance of brain and brawn would be left to carry on the Kingdom whatever befell.

What I most regret was a clash of personality. For twenty-five years, since the day we stood, red cloak beside red cloak, in the entrance to Linlithgow Palace, Lord Hume and I had waged constant struggle. We had worked and achieved great things together; we had also quarrelled as frequently, and huffed our way through separate apartments. On Branxton Moor, Hum

was at it again—giving orders to everyone in sight and irre-
pressibly taking the command upon himself. Many liked it
no more than I did, and I should have stayed to cool their ruffled
feelings—as I had had to do throughout my reign. But the English
would be upon us any moment, we thought; and in my im-
patience to meet the enemy and have done with argument, I
felt my temper begin to rise. There was a moment's danger that
I might lecture one of my earls before his men, and to guard my
tongue, I walked away. I did not speak to the Earl of Hume
again. I had meant to remind him to watch his men and keep
them together, away from chances of plunder (I remembered
how, in our fight for the English Pretender, they had shown
themselves to be thieves first and fighting men second). Whether
it made a difference I cannot say, but I regretted my omission
afterwards.

We lined up on the height of Branxton Moor to await the
English. An hour passed; another hour, and still we waited tensely
for them, spears lined up on shoulders in the offensive position.
When it had gone three, our tense expectancy and our tense
muscles began to relax. We stood our spears since the cavalry
scouts reported no sign of Surrey's army. By the rules of chivalry,
we were entitled to consider the enemy had defaulted and to leave
the field, but I knew in my bones—as did several others—that
the Earl of Surrey did not mean any longer to fight by the code
he had originally adopted (his flanking movement earlier might
have given us a hint). If we broke line, his men would fall upon
the lot of us to cut us down, on the principle that he who dies
first has least to say about it. To hold our position, and to hold
together, was imperative.

We mounted spears again, ready for the attack. The waiting
did not merely tire us, it made us restless and uneasy. We had to
stand another hour before we sighted the English curving in a
silent steel line below the foot of our hill. I do not say that Surrey
did this deliberately, but having sent his challenge in accordance
with the code of chivalry, he should have followed its customs
and not have made up a new set of rules of his own (there were
only two acceptable ways to engage an enemy: the fixed engage-

ment or the surprise attack). It may have been an accident on Surrey's part: I hope it was, for honour's sake. But it meant that we were past our best when his force eventually arrived. Having thought we were too short of time to select the best position, we had then been left standing for four hours, our spirits declining and then, uneasily, building up again. I was there, with a spear, and exhaustion had replaced my battle urge before the fighting started. I was but one of twelve thousand spearmen and two thousand cavalry, and I can tell you, my men had lost their vigour before the battle even started.

Our guns opened the attack. I could imagine Paniter, my wee goat man, lumbering across everybody's feet, full of eagerness, and I quailed at the thought of it. First they sighted too low, then too high. By this time, the English guns had learned from our mistakes and sent home a volley which must have wrought havoc upon the slope behind me.

Then the cavalry went in—Hume against Dacre. I had not had time to think of Dacre until now. Dear Christ: When we had tried so hard to make peace upon the Border together, to have to face each other as enemies upon the field! Oh, the damnable folly of it all was unbearable! But he was now my enemy; and my good Lord Hume, charging across the field, put Dacre's men to flight. It was a splendid opening.

Then clashed the Highlanders upon my left, and what happened there I cannot say. They had the worst ground and came upon the English at an angle. This should not have mattered, but the English were square-set, and their archers sent up a volley in magnificent conformity, which must have distressed our men considerably. Our archers had shot steadily throughout, but they had not yet put in an ordered volley.

Then, suddenly, everything began to happen at once. The trumpet blew for the phalanx on my left to advance. I turned to Alexander, tall in steel beside me, and ordered him to stay close to my sword arm if we broke and to use it as his line of vision. He lifted his vizor to answer me—with arrows flying all about us, the fool (although I suppose he may not have seen them). I roared at him to put his vizor down; he began to argue; and I said it for the last time—'Ah, aime yur *King*, Alexander!' So his vizor clanked down in a fury. They were the last words I addressed to my precious son, Alexander Stewart.

Then, suddenly, I felt behind me a heaving and realized, our phalanx too was on the move. We were not advancing—yet; but we were *on the move*. I remember swinging round to see—so far as I could see through my vizor grill—what was happening. I saw the great sea of helmets and of faces behind me, and upon all of them there rested a mantle of blue light. I looked up at the sky, to see whether a rainbow or a sudden shaft of sun had struck us, but there was nothing: only the grey cloud scudding by. There was no time to think more about it then. I realized that our inexperienced men, over-tense after their long wait, must have mistaken the trumpet sound and started to move forward in response.

The safest feature of the phalanx was the worst feature of the phalanx: what happened to one of us became the fate of all of us. Locked shoulder to shoulder sideways, locked shoulder forward and backward by the link of our great spears, we at the front had to move if the back moved, or else be trodden underfoot. There were horror-stricken glances along the front line, and for a moment all of us tried to stabilize with our backward-leaning strength the pressure from behind. But it was no use. The heavier pressure surged forward. We had to go with it. I remember shouting an order to advance—if we must—at least with cohesion; and I think I realized then why I had known it was a terrible mistake to leave Angus 'Bell-the-Cat' behind. If he had been upon that hill behind us, the man with the quick grasp of what was needed and sixty-eight years' service in the Kingdom, he would have roared out 'Yeh-heuw!' and brought the learners to their senses—as he had brought a sense of security to me across the melting snows of Linlithgow park, when I had been a learner and a rebel. But Angus we had left behind, and there was only myself, in the front line, to call those nearest to advance, there being no way out of it.

As it was, we began jaggedly. And then, thank God, we righted ourselves by our lines of pikes. We came down the hill in silence, all of Scotland on the march together. We must have been to the Englishmen a terrifying sight—a wall of steel blades, with grim, silent, giant men beneath them. My middle battle had chosen its men for their height and brawn, and after twenty-five years of peace and good Scots feeding, we had sprung up a generation—just one—so big and tall (like my Alexander) that they far outstripped all other men in Christendom. We came down the hill silently, below our spears, grimly intent to save the good land we had made of Scotland.

We went through the English front ranks of halberdiers as though they had been water, falling back from us to pour away at either side. The English arrows did small damage to us—at first—for a phalanx was protected by its spear-shafts, which deflected the arrows to fall harmlessly. Only the front ranks were vulnerable, and we had steel to protect us, both our armour and the blades held out at ten-foot distance. If we continued like this, we were invincible.

And then—oh God!—somebody must have slipped. Who slipped? Does it matter? The sliding mud was everybody's problem. And, in the phalanx, if one falls, we all tumble after. In no time at all the front lines had broken, and we were fighting hand to hand. My spear was broken and I threw it away, glad to be rid of its cumbersome length. Thereafter I fought with my Toledo blade of Damascus steel, using it two-handed as it was designed for, as a battle weapon. Halberd shafts and men split clean in two beneath it. And at last my patience, which I had held these thirty years, broke.

I can remember raising my great blade with all the ferocity I had concealed these many years. I was filled with a glorious, deadly exuberance, to slash and smash and kill what had defeated all my gentler efforts. That for my father! That for Margaret Drummond! That for the marriage treaty I had never wanted! Oh—and that, that, that! for your posturing, money-glutted, power-drunken, bawling-baby Henry Tudor! I had never seen Henry Tudor, but every man's face which loomed as I smashed it down was for me the face of King England, whom I had known and hated all my days.

And there my memory pauses. . . . I have yet before me, very clear—it cannot have been more than five yards away—the steeled figure of the Earl of Surrey upon his chestnut battle-charger; next to him his standard-bearer upon a white horse with mud spattering the creamy feathers of its great legs—and, as my sight-line altered, obscured by the vizor, it was the legs I saw, with the threshing staves and hooks and moving headpieces filling the ground between us. I may unconsciously have paused to look at Surrey, whom I meant to kill within our next few moments.

Then an explosion seemed to erupt in my face: I saw before my eyes a coloured star with four points, which my mind changed to the shape of a plummeting falcon. . . .

What hit me, I never knew, but I must have blacked out for a second. The next, I was helpless upon my back, looking upward through the vertical lines of my vizor grill at the shafts, and the hands, and steel points of all the world's hate coming in at me. I flung up my left arm to save myself—and felt my armour plates peal off it with a jerk; I realized in a mindless flash what an effective weapon was the new English brown-bill—it could strip a man of his armour as a crab is shelled. A crab . . . ! It seemed a long while I lay looking up at those massed points of steel outside my vizor, like a nut waiting for its shell to be cracked. Then all of them came driving in at me—and I shrieked for Alexander, although I think Alexander's tall presence had gone down from my side long ago.

There was no time to feel pain; only fury and terror because all the world's savagery had turned on me alone, and there came nobody to help. My long howl lacked all dignity.

I had learned my final lesson in kingship, which my father had known. A king may live like a man, and fight like a man; but when he dies he is butchered like an animal, by as many as can take part in it, so that every man who is a soldier (bless him) may bear home a soldier's tale of how he killed a King of Scots.

Also recently published in Arrow Books by Barbara Cartland

THE COIN OF LOVE

A sparkling tale of adventure and romance

Cleona Wickham was eighteen when her fortune changed so unexpectedly. Italy. She was to go to Italy, accompanying Lady Beryl and under the protection of the cynical Lord Raven. But the journey was only a prelude—a prelude to Cleona's search for love and happiness.

STARS IN MY HEART

by Barbara Cartland

Gisela's home life was unhappy. But a chance meeting was to change her life. The year was 1876, when, hunting in rural Northamptonshire, she met the beautiful Elizabeth, Empress of Austria.

Soon she was to escape into the sparkling, romantic world that revolved round the Empress — a fabulous world . . . at first! For Gisela gradually discovered that, however romantic, it was a world that was taut with menace, seething with intrigue. A world where every gesture, every conversation, however casual, was a move in a terrifyingly dangerous plot.

A HALO FOR THE DEVIL
by *Barbara Cartland*

In fact there are two devils in the story: two men, known to the bucks of White's Club as the 'Old Devil' and the 'Young Devil'—respectively, the Duke of Accrington, wicked and sinister, and the young Marquis of Thane, raffish and cynical.

Both were compulsive gamblers, and between them was hatred. A hatred that had its origins in the Duke's vicious deception of the Marquis' dying father.

Then, when Fortuna of the mysterious origins and distinctive beauty arrived unexpectedly at his house, the Marquis soon realised that he could use her as a weapon against his enemy.

But Fortuna's innocence, her charm, spirit and loveliness, seemed likely to dissolve the hard shell of worldly cynicism that surrounded his heart. Would he really be able to use her, coldly, ruthlessly, or would he have to acknowledge his love?